THE

GLOBAL ECONOMY IN TRANSITION

Debt and Resource Scarcities

THE

GLOBAL ECONOMY IN TRANSITION

Debt and Resource Scarcities

Jørgen Ørstrøm Møller

Institute of Southeast Asian Studies, Singapore,
Singapore Management University, Singapore
& Copenhagen Business School, Denmark

Foreword by
Professor Jagdish Bhagwati

 **World Scientific**

NEW JERSEY · LONDON · SINGAPORE · BEIJING · SHANGHAI · HONG KONG · TAIPEI · CHENNAI

Published by

World Scientific Publishing Co. Pte. Ltd.

5 Toh Tuck Link, Singapore 596224

USA office: 27 Warren Street, Suite 401-402, Hackensack, NJ 07601

UK office: 57 Shelton Street, Covent Garden, London WC2H 9HE

Library of Congress Cataloging-in-Publication Data
Møller, J. Ørstrøm.
  The global economy in transition : debt and resource scarcities / by Joergen Oerstroem Moeller.
  pages cm.
  ISBN 978-9814494861 (hardcover : alk. paper)
  1. Economics. 2. Economic development. 3. International trade. 4. Debt. 5. Scarcity. I. Title.
HB171.M558 2013
330.9--dc23
                                                    2013003814

British Library Cataloguing-in-Publication Data
A catalogue record for this book is available from the British Library.

In-house Editor: Monica Lesmana

Typeset by Stallion Press
E-mail: enquiries@stallionpress.com

Printed in Singapore.

Foreword

This collection of essays by former Ambassador Joergen Oerstrom Moeller on different aspects of what he aptly calls *The Global Economy in Transition* reminds me of the older tradition of diplomats in the colonial and earlier times when, on retirement from active careers, they wrote fascinating reflections on their variegated experiences. We see here a lively intelligence and an ability to transcend current events so as to take a broader view of the social and economic context in which these events are occurring.

The essays range over a mind-boggling variety of subjects, and the reader will find here Ambassador Moeller's insightful observations on almost any topic one is interested in. What stimulated me most however are two issues: has the current crisis affected adversely our view of Globalization for the worse; and has the rise of Asia, especially China, undermined our thinking about the role of government in the developing countries?

CURRENT CRISIS: HAS IT UNDERMINED THE CASE FOR GLOBALIZATION?

Let me first say that the current crisis was brought about by the collapse of Lehman Brothers in 2008. My MIT student Ken Rogoff and his co-author Carmen Reinhart claim that in the stretch of time over many centuries, observers have always said erroneously of their specific crisis that "this time it is different" but that this is not so. As Ambassador Moeller correctly says, this assertion by Rogoff and Reinhart is not true. In my view, just the contrast between the earlier East Asian crisis and the ongoing 2008 crisis is enough to demonstrate the fallacy of their assertion.

The East Asian crisis was caused by the sudden outflow of capital which was possible because capital account controls had been dismantled. The earlier inflow of massive foreign funds helped precipitate the crisis though domestic funds also left and, some argue, were the first to flee. Adjusting to this outflow was possible but surely disruptive. By contrast, capital outflows were *not* at the heart of the current crisis starting with the failure of Lehman Brothers in 2008.

The problem with the current crisis has been what I have called "destructive creation" of new financial instruments whose potential downside few understood. Equally, there was what I have called a Wall Street–Treasury Complex where CEOs from Wall Street went into the U.S. Treasury (or IMF) and then back again on Wall Street. The result was shared euphoria among this group, emanating primarily from Wall Street but overwhelming even smart economists like Larry Summers and Stanley Fischer who surely should have known better. In consequence, any dissent from this euphoria was discounted.

Mind you, I proposed the notion of the Wall Street–Treasury Complex in my 1998 article in *Foreign Affairs*, not as a conspiracy but as a sharing of euphoria by people wearing the same school ties and club memberships whereas later, the distinguished MIT economist Simon Johnson called it the Wall Street Treasury Corrridor, in *The Atlantic* but with a dose of conspiracy element which I do not buy into. Nonetheless, since President Eisenhower as President of Columbia University had talked about the Military–Industrial Complex, and Wright Mills, the Columbia sociologist had written about the Power Elite, the three of us have at times been called the Columbia Trio! Amusingly and ironically, my colleague Joe Stiglitz arrived at my views later and must take the back seat, if at all he can with our indulgence — we may take the view: better late than never — climb on to our bandwagon of political-economy analysis of what happened in the current crisis.

But let me turn to whether the current crisis means that Globalization must now be abandoned. Globalization, of course, means the integration of a national economy into the international economy. This can happen typically on five very different dimensions: trade, equity capital flows (or "multinationals"), short-term capital flows (or portfolio capital), international flows of humanity (legal and illegal immigration plus refugee flows), and diffusion of technology (or patents).

It is widely agreed that the Far Eastern economic miracle was a result of outward trade orientation while India's stagnation prior to the 1991 reforms was due to extremely autarkic policies. The outward orientation increased the inducement to invest by opening the huge foreign market to its sales whereas inward orientation constrained it as it depended on the growth of agriculture, which rarely exceeds 4% annually for sustained periods. Besides, the growth of export earnings meant that the Far Eastern economies could import for investment a lot of machines with embodied technology. In turn, a high rate of literacy ensured that the technology could be mastered and high productivity would follow. The shortage of skilled people was remedied in the short run by importation of professionals; in the long run by sending students abroad for high-level training in several fields. At the heart of this virtuous circle of policies, however, was outward orientation.

So was a welcoming attitude towards Direct Foreign Investment (DFI) by Taiwan, Hong Kong and Singapore, but not by South Korea which opted for the older Japanese Meiji era model.

This miracle was interrupted, not by diminishing returns to capital as Paul Krugman had predicted, but by the sudden and premature liberalization of capital flows, often sanctioned, even required, by IMF and the US Treasury. Freeing of capital flows was a mistake. But that is not what happened in 2008.

So, in terms of trade, DFI and capital flows, the crisis beginning 2008 could not be used as a critique of Globalization.[1] Yet, NGOs and even economists like Stiglitz advanced condemnations of Globalization, asserting that the post-2008 crisis was a nail in the coffin of Globalization. But these critics had no intellectual strength to drive the nails into the coffin! Indeed, their conclusions were more obvious than their arguments. Consider just two.

Morality: The one strand of argument that was leveled against the financial sector and became very popular, especially among the populists in the Democratic Party in the US and among the Occupy Movement, was that the sector corrupted morals, leading to "greed". Just look at Bernie Madoff, they asserted, though I must confess to cynicism that the liberal supporters among the CEOs, such as George Soros (who has been convicted of insider trading in Europe), were let off the hook: just as the demonstrators in Chile when President Allende was facing chaos in the streets in 1973 carried posters saying: "The Government is shit; but it is ours!".

The problem is that the relationship between greed and fraud may run from the players to the sector, rather than the other way around. The notion that where one works determines one's values is, at one level, a quasi-Marxist fallacy which assigns an undue weight to the mean of production. Surely, one's values are determined by one's family, the church, even by literature: who cannot have been influenced by reading Dostoevsky's *Crime and Punishment* where Sonia has the choice of being a prostitute or letting her family starve: a classic moral choice, or by reading Shuck Endo's remarkable novel *The Samurai* which could have been written by Tolstoy and surely deserved the Nobel Prize which went instead to an inferior Japanese novelist. So, while the financial sector has its Bernie Madoffs, it also has many virtuous players.

---

[1] I have no space to discuss cross-border flows of humanity or patents. But arguments that the post-2008 crisis made matters worse in these areas as well are hard to make.

But what is certainly true is that different sectors promise different payoffs to crookedness. In the United States, if you were crooked, you would hardly go into the agricultural sector: yes, you would get some subsidies after lobbying with Congress but it would hardly be worth opening a bottle of champagne. In the manufacturing sector, you may get away with $150 to $200 million if you were lucky. But in the financial sector, that is small change. You can really hit pay dirt there. So the crooks are going to be attracted to the financial sector where the returns to crookedness are the highest. [One qualification: high rewards to crookedness can also seduce some of the virtuous into being crooked. This may well be true of George Soros who was found guilty of insider trading in Europe and of Rajat Gupta who was convicted in New York of similar malfeasance: both were good men turned bad because of their life in high finance, it seems).

Impact on Governmental Intervention: The effect of the crisis may also have raised a different, equally implausible concern: that the advocacy of markets is now shown up to be wrong-headed. In particular, the critics such as my colleague Joe Stiglitz and George Soros have been claiming that we had gone over to "market funda-mentalism", thanks to the so-called "Washington Consensus" and the imposition of such conditionalities from Washington (i.e. Bretton Woods institutions) and were shown up to be wrong.

They are wrong themselves. First, three important countries, the Soviet Union, India and China went over to the liberal, market-exploiting reforms, not because Washington institutions or the U.S. Treasury asked them to, but because their leaders had endogenously convinced themselves that their previous illiberal policies had been disastrous, not merely in terms of growth but also (for India and China) in regard to reducing poverty. Second, these gentlemen were wrong because these countries had moved from policies that could be described as "anti-market fundamentalism" to the pragmatic center whereas these critics assumed that they were moving from a non-existent pragmatism to "market fundamentalism"! Finally, the debate in India, for sure, has been on the nature of the market intervention and not whether there should be any. Intervention everywhere was the order of the day, leading me to remark once that the problem in India and other developing countries like Egypt and Indonesia was that Adam Smith's Invisible Hand was nowhere to be seen!

Meanwhile, China is held up as a model of appropriate intervention that has pushed China into stratospheric growth rates. Yet, we know that high growth rates can follow when there is a reserve army of labour at a given real wage and growth of demand leads to more jobs rather than higher wages. Equally, the kleptomania that characterizes the Chinese bureaucrats and politicians, amply and beautifully documented by the *Financial Times* reporter Richard McGregor in his book, *The Party* (Harper 2010) also meant that this corruption was what I have called the "profit-sharing" corruption where the returns to corruption increased with growth. These functionaries had their straw in the glass and their intake depended on how much the glass contained. By contrast, countries like India and Indonesia had "rent-seeking" corruption where monopolies were created and handed over to the families of the corrupt politicians: as Prime Minister Indira Gandhi did with the Maruti car which was sheltered from competition and handed over to her corrupt son Sanjay, and similar actions by President Suharto in Indonesia.

The Chinese model is not sustainable as the populace is unlikely to put up for long with even profit-sharing corruption; and an authoritarian political system is bound to run into conflict with the demands of political rights by the citizens, as we now are beginning to see in China. Besides, few nations or intellectuals are likely to renounce democracy, a good in itself, to get growth whose fruits they are unlikely to get to share with the kleptomaniac bureaucrats and politicians. So, it is a mistake to think that Chinese developmental model offers an enticing alternative to the democratic alternatives such as India's.

Jagdish Bhagwati
University Professor (Economics, Law and
International Affairs) Columbia University and
Senior Fellow, Council on Foreign Relations, New York

About the Book

This book is a collection of essays written by Ambassador, Professor Jørgen Ørstrøm Møller from the middle of 2009 to end of 2012, commenting on global economic and political events, which reflect Møller's judgment and evaluation on these issues.

Readers get an overview to the collection of essays and the worldview they represent in an introductory chapter weaving together strands of economics, politics, and societal issues. Møller goes a step further by sketching up a picture of how a future economic model and political system may look — forged by debt, scarcities, economic integration, and the rise of Asia.

Part I deals with global systems and possible long trends shaping the future over the coming decades, as the current political system and economic model, having run their course, come to an end.

Part II discusses how the era of scarcities will change economic behaviour in terms of economic models.

Part III looks into the global debt problem, which confines the world to low growth over one or two decades as the world tries to get rid of the debt burden.

Part IV forms an analysis of what has happened in the Euro-zone and how the global debt crisis has compelled the Europeans to take the next steps in integration and address the shortcomings and flaws in the original treaty from 1992.

Part V turns to Asia and its future in the global economy. It concentrates on Asian integration and how the Asian countries will fare in the future under much changed circumstances compared to how things looked when the Asian adventure started some 30–40 years ago.

At the end, readers will find a short post-scriptum with some of Møller's afterthoughts on the important issues discussed throughout the book.

About the Author

Jørgen Ørstrøm Møller received a Master of Science in Economics from the University of Copenhagen, and served from 1968 to 2005 in the Royal Danish Foreign Ministry at a variety of posts, including State Secretary (1989–1997) and Ambassador in Asia (1997–2005). Since his retirement in 2005, he has been a Visiting Senior Research Fellow at the Institute of Southeast Asian Studies, Singapore, and an Adjunct Professor at Singapore Management University & Copenhagen Business School. He is a member of the Global Advisory Council, World Future Society. Former books include *How Asia can Shape the World: From the Era of Plenty to the Era of Scarcity* (2011) and *Political Economy in a Globalized World* (2009).

Preface and Acknowledgements

The present book is a sequel to *Political Economy in a Globalized World* published in 2009.

Both books grew out of my interest in political economy as the classical economists saw it — combination of politics and economics.

Over the last 3–4 years, evidence has been strong — almost irrevocable — that economics as it has developed over the last decades does not deliver. It runs the risk of becoming *'l'art pour l'art'*, which means a kind of science enmeshed in its own paradigms irrespective of the realities. I once heard the phrase 'do not let realities stand in the way of a good regression analysis' and it aptly describe where economics is today. Another resemblance is the highly interesting debate in the middle ages whether angels had wings or not. Intellectually stimulating, but not really relating to earthly life.

Confronted with the discrepancy between economic models and the realities, we must change the models and not explain what is wrong with realities!

Over the years I have been in the fortunate position meeting many people coming to take the same view. They may still be in a minority, but their influence and indeed their frustration hopefully forces economics to change track. Otherwise policy makers will not be well served by their economic models.

Professor Jagdish Bhagwati, whom I first encountered as author to the essay *The Pure Theory of International Trade* published in Surveys of Economic Theory from 1966 — as an eager student of International Economics I came to love it — graciously agreed to write the foreword. I am truly grateful for that. Professor Bhagwati has had a remarkable influence on the theory of trade as a strong voice not only on theory, but also on policy making. Never deviating from the course, he found the correct one and often castigated those who took the easy way. In the foreword, he puts forward his view on crucial issues in a clear and uncompromising way, giving the reader food for thought on what is happening in the world. A strong voice with strong views and ready to argue for them.

Let me thank Derek Shearer and Indermit Gill for writing blurbs and sharing many of their thoughts with me.

My gratitude goes to colleagues and friends at the Institute of Southeast Asian Studies (ISEAS), Singapore Management University, National University of Singapore, Nanyang Technical University, Ministry of Foreign Affairs Diplomatic Academy, and Copenhagen Business School who took time to enter into discussions and thereby contributed to the essays presented in the book. Special thanks go to the Director of ISEAS, Mr Tan Chin Tiong, who opened the door for publication and Professor Euston Quah for his encouragement and interest in my work.

As for *Political Economy in a Globalized World*, I have enjoyed working with the people at World Scientific Publishing Company.

My wife Thanh Kieu Møller has fully supported me and often listened to my views with great patience. Without her support this book and the essays collected here could not have been written.

Contents

Overview of *The Global Economy in Transition: Debt and Resource Scarcities*

The global economy is in deep crisis. Trend growth looks to have fallen by a full percentage point over the last five years and there is no real prospect of getting back to the previous level of around 4.5 percent per year.

This is not a cyclical phenomenon where we expect to get back to normal — a blip on the curve.

It is due to two gigantic transformations which cannot be compared to anything the world has seen — ever.

The first one is the transfer of economic power measured in purchasing power, savings, growth and investment from the Western world, primarily the U.S., to Asia with China in the forefront, but also including Korea, India and Southeast Asia with Bangladesh catching up. The figures are so staggering due to population size that many observers forget that Asia also has its problems and even if the picture looks rosy the way ahead is not without obstacles and challenges that can derail growth if wrong policies are adopted.

The second one is the phasing out of the established economic model around mass consumption, industrialization, and American style capitalism to a model with mass communication and resource scarcities as its flywheel. This obviously calls for a new set of parameters to steer the development realizing that conventional economic thinking is not only obsolete, but in many ways counterproductive.

These two transformations and transitions interact with each other. The picture becomes blurred, making it difficult for politicians to find the way ahead overloaded with advice rooted in exactly the economic philosophy that has no answer because it was forged over 200 years ago. It was designed in an era of growth and distribution of more when we now face scarcities, less, and burden-sharing. Indeed the substitution of distribution theory, consumption theory, and growth theories with mass communication, less materialistic consumption, and burden-sharing has shown that we need a more comprehensive theoretical framework, interdisciplinary, and intersectoral drawing in other social sciences than economics. People do not only act according to economic incentives. The cornerstone of most economics, the utility theory does not provide adequate guidance — sometimes it is plain wrong. Research in neuroscience, psychology, sociology, and anthropology shows how sophisticated human behavioural pattern is. Indeed it tells us that human beings are much more likely to help others and work in groups than we are led to believe by economics. The economists have over the years monopolized the role of advisers to politicians and find it hard to swallow this, explaining why they fight a desperate rear-guard action despite being proven wrong in almost all their forecasts, prognoses, and policy prescriptions.

They maintain that through "correct" application of existing economic theory and economic policy, all will be well again. This is a dubious platform for a variety of reasons of which the first one is that economists do not agree on what the "correct" policy is!

Asia's economic strengths are obvious to spot even if observers sometimes forget that the G-3 countries (the U.S., the Euro-zone, and Japan) still account for close to 60 percent of global Gross Domestic Product (GDP). The difference is that the growth overwhelmingly come from the emerging countries, most of whom are found in Asia. China, India, and Southeast Asia still account for only around 16 percent of global GDP, but over the last decade, their contribution to growth was more than 35 percent. An X-ray tells that the world economy is dominated by G-3. Trend spotting tells that China, India, and Southeast Asia matter more. The notion of BRICs (Brazil, Russia, India, and China) is often brought forward and sometimes with the addition of South Africa and Indonesia, but there is very little congruity among these countries. Russia is a resource economy and Brazil, although prospects look good, is not in the same league as China and India.

Demographics are the starting point predicting future trends. The long term shift is visible with population starting to fall in most of Northeast Asia while continuing to rise in South Asia, Vietnam, Indonesia, The Philippines and Myanmar. By 2050, Africa will be the only continent with rising population.

The pivotal year is 2015, when the labour force starts to fall in China while still going up in South Asia and the countries enumerated above. This augurs a transfer of labour-intensive, low-cost manufacturing from China to other Asian countries of which India stands as the main recipient. China must improve its competitiveness by moving into higher value-added manufacturing and focusing on competitive parameters such as skills, technology, quality, accompanying services, and design. Only massive investment in these sectors can maintain China's role in the global economy. India needs to go in the opposite direction, investing in basic skills and infrastructure such as ports, roads, railroads, and airports. It is fascinating to watch the two Asian giants moving in opposite directions — indeed away from the foundation of economic growth so far. The future of economic globalization depends on whether they manage to do that and possibly to help each other.

The education system will be decisive. Supply of skills must match demand for skills, but how to guess which skills will be in demand 10 or 20 years from now? If the education system gets it right, the economy will run close to its capacity (in economic terms the supply gap will be small) and social tensions will ease as few people can ask for and get a premium for their skill. If it goes wrong, growth will fall below its capacity and on top of that, social tensions will deepen as people in possession of skills in demand without corresponding supply will ask for and get a premium leading to high and rising economic inequality as seen in the U.S. over the last 30 years.

In Asia as a whole, the "right" distribution of skilled people may be there, but not in the "right" countries. China's development may bring about a shortage of highly qualified people with adequate skills for more value-added production; these workers may be found in India. India itself may suffer from a shortage of workers with basic and medium skills suitable to low cost manufacturing with China still having ample labour force in this category. One way out of this dilemma is to open up for immigration among Asian countries, but the political obstacles for doing so between China and India is obvious. The economic and social costs of not doing so are similarly obvious, and this may pave the way for opening the door in the context of Asian integration.

The age distribution with more people above 65 year needing health services poses an enormous problem for China which may have the money to deliver, but not the social infrastructure in the form of homes, trained staff etc. This augurs a social challenge and will have consequences for the savings rate in the Chinese economy. As long as this problem remains unsolved, it is unlikely that the Chinese savings rate will start to fall. The economic result is that the hope for a falling savings rate may not be fulfilled, keeping the Chinese economy in a permanent surplus on its balance of payments.

If China looks to solve the need for health services and care by buying from abroad, it unavoidably puts the question of immigration on the political agenda. Who is going to provide these services to the Chinese population? Where do we find the trained people willing to do so? Not in China, but maybe abroad.

The world's savings may thus still predominantly come from China and a few other parts of East Asia. The expectation of a *grosso modo* unhanged Chinese savings-investment balance has a number of repercussions for not only China and Asia, but also the global economy.

Private consumption in China will rise as it has over a number of years, but in absolute terms and not measured as share of GDP. Actually, over the past two decades, annual increase in consumption is below the growth rate. Compared with Korea and Japan, consumption has fallen more and steeper from around 50 percent of GDP in 1990 to a little bit above 30 percent in 2011. The hope of a consumer driven growth will not materialize. The lure for many Western companies that the Chinese consumer will emerge as King will not come true. Yes the market due to size and number of consumers will be attractive and in many ways, we can expect the patterns of consumption to be defined in China, but anything like the role the U.S. consumer occupied for the past decade or two is Illusory.

With a savings surplus (surplus on the balance of payments) and on top of that foreign direct investment that may fall, but not dramatically, China sits on a pile of cash not yet seen in the global economy.

How to invest it will be a major question. Currently China is the biggest holder of U.S. treasury bonds (end 2012) with about USD 1.2 trillion followed by Japan. The savings-investment balance in the U.S. is not likely to change very much. The savings rate may go up as deleveraging of debt takes place, but so will investment among having to compensate for a decade or two of underinvestment both in the private and public sector. Much is being talked about shale gas, but while diminishing the U.S. dependence on energy supply from abroad, there is no rationale that it will change the savings-investment balance. Indeed, it requires large investments to be put on the market.

U.S. treasury bonds offer remuneration below inflation, forcing the paying creditor in purchasing power to acquire them. That can go on for some time — maybe a long time — but not indefinitely, especially if the U.S. borrowing demand continues to be substantial, which is the most likely scenario.

China and other creditors will increasingly look at other opportunities for investing their savings. Over a number of years, it has become clear that China follows a road map for Overseas Direct Investment (ODI):

- Buying into financial institutions hitherto the prerogative of the Western world to control how its own savings are shuffled around. Until 2007/2008, China felt that the well-known and reputable Western financial institutions had the expertise to do so. The financial crisis changed that perception. Now China wants to have a hand on the tiller and in a longer term, take over some of these institutions or build their own, which takes time, so they find it better to buy existing ones.

- Buying into high technology and/or companies having the management know-how to learn from these companies — transfer their knowledge of what it takes to turn research into technology and how new technology is produced and marketed in a global economy.
- Buying commodity sources and raw materials plus agricultural land, realizing that the access to commodities may not necessarily continue to be open. Prudence leads to control over such sources, making sure that the Chinese economy can run without the risk of being cut off.

In many cases, these three reasons overlap. China has bought the Canadian oil company Nexen, which gives access to new technology extracting shale gas, and represents control over resources. The acquisition of IBM's computer division and Volvo cars provides access to technology and managerial know-how. Cubbie cotton station in Australia is an example of China's agricultural purchase in a broader sense of that word. China has invested in African farming albeit not to the same extent as in other resources, but leaving little doubt that the underlying motive is food security.

Many countries, especially among Western nations, feel worried and question the Chinese motives — referring to sovereign wealth funds or in state-owned enterprises, presumably hinting that more than commercial interest guide these investments.

But China is doing what Europe and at a later stage of the global economic development, the U.S. did. Compared to international rules and historical experience there is nothing new with this policy except that it is China that is doing it!

The potential problem is that this worry may spill over into outright animosity and/or barriers for Chinese investments — because they are Chinese. In the case of Nexen, the Canadian government gave its consent, but at the same time it was made known that no further acquisitions were welcome or could expect approval.

The global economy may in a couple of years face the problem that China has a large surplus of cash to invest abroad and prefers to buy foreign companies or commodities, yet global rules do not allow China to do so and it pushes China into buying more U.S. treasury bonds which the U.S. desperately wants to sell but the Chinese do not want to buy.

Multinational companies have long been dominated by Western companies. The largest number of enterprises outside the U.S. and Europe comes from Japan, a G-3 country. China is now number three on the list, but except for China, Asia is sparsely represented with a limited number of companies from Korea, Taiwan and India. Again, the trend is more revealing than an X-ray. Fortune's list of top 500 multinationals shows U.S. as the undisputed leader, but the list of top 50 has 15 companies from Asia and asking for their view on what matters for future development, the share of business leaders from China and India points to innovation and they are actually planning to hike their innovation budgets that far overshadows what is seen from the U.S. and Europe.

The Asian multinationals take-off from their domestic markets is a blessing and a curse. A blessing because of its size which promises increasing returns to scale; a curse because it limits their ability to think and act internationally even globally. China is primarily looking at beefing up investment (ODI) and multinational companies in developing countries and use state-owned enterprises as the battering ram to get a foothold. India is much more orientated towards richer countries and aim often at the consumer segment. The difference may be due to the background where Indian enterprises grew in an economy which despite the talk of socialism predominantly was a market economy as far as consumer goods are concerned while the Chinese companies are more investment orientated or in the energy sector groomed under non-market conditions — a centrally command economy.

Whatever the difference, it can be taken for granted that 10 or 20 years from now, the world will see multinationals originating from China and India as the pacesetters.

That augurs a shift in *corporate governance*, a concept largely born and forged in the U.S. — economy steered by the market and profitability.

It is unlikely that corporate governance as defined by the American style capitalism — growing profit each quarter despite all the talk about corporate social responsibility and corporate citizens — will survive. Almost all big Asian companies are state-owned, having the state as important stockholder (sometimes in form of a sovereign wealth fund) or family owned/controlled. Contrary to the Western enterprises, this eliminates or at least reduces the role of the stock market as provider of capital. They get the capital from the state or other non-market sources (state-owned banks or state-controlled funds), which may be less interested in free-market-defined profitability, which instead looks more on how and what the enterprise can do to contribute to society — a point of view shared by many Asian consumers as revealed by a recent poll asking 28,000 consumers about values and getting the answer that giving back to society was an important item in judging companies.

In China, this philosophy finds support in ancient Chinese thinking connoting the crucial role of society versus individualism, combining well with the political ideas of the ruling communist party — Chinese Communist Party (CCP).

If such new philosophies strike roots and redefines the concept of profitability in the context of the free market economy and individualism to how the enterprises contribute, to society looking at the profitability for society as a whole, the behaviour of multinational enterprises will undergo a seminal change.

Weighing up economic growth, demographics including population size, higher or lower population, age distribution, and the expected savings-investment ratio for the main Asian economies, in particular China and India, confirm that the size factor pushes future consumption in the Asian economic area above the level in the U.S. and Europe. Over the last decade Chinese consumption rose from 22.6 percent to 38.5 percent compared to American private consumption. Size is not unique for consumption. It casts its shadow over almost all economic figures when comparing Asia with the U.S. and Europe. How can it be otherwise with a total Asian population around 3.5 billion people with only 312 million Americans and a little more than 500 million Europeans.

The driving force for growth in the coming decade or two will be *urbanization in Asia* and primarily in China.

The figures are staggering. In 1975, 17.4 percent of China's population lived in cities. In 2013 it is about 43 percent and the prognosis is that in 2020 it will be 60 percent implying that 800 million Chinese will be urbanized. In India the corresponding figures are 21.3 percent in 1975 going up to 41.5 percent in 2020 with 640 million people urbanized. Both Asian giants go through a colossal movement of people from the countryside to urban areas with almost unimaginable economic, social, environmental, and transportation consequences. Most important of all will, simply speaking, be the search for an urban model making it possible how can such a number of megacities exist and operate as a coherent social framework.

As the incoming Chinese Premier, Li Keqiang stated this will be the main driving force for growth. Public investment will be kept at a high level sending the signal to the Chinese citizen that savings have to be maintained at a similar level — at least. This is however not new. Over the last decade public demand and investment has accounted for approximately 75 percent of China's growth and over the decade, export does not contribute more than between 15 and 20 percent.

More than half of the global population living in cities is found in Asia using 12 percent of total resources and accounting for 35 percent of carbon dioxide emission.

Just to maintain status quo there is a need for 20,000 new dwellings, 250 km new roads and provision for six million litres of water — every day.

It can be estimated that over the current decade, new infrastructure in Asia triggered off by the urbanization requires USD 8 billion of which two third can be used to introduce sustainability.

The emergence of megacities and megaregions turns the usual way of seeing things around. The world is not flat. It is spiky. The major part and especially the interesting part of economic and technological activities take place in megacities and megaregions. Therefore the *supply chain* changes from global to regional, yes, in some cases even local and outsourcing or off-shoring will lose much its flavour to be replaced by a more sophisticated distinction between local, regional, and global production.

East Asia has actually seen a deep and strong supply chain building up over the preceding decades with China as the manufacturing fulcrum and the other countries in the role of suppliers of semi-manufactured goods or other inputs. Much of this manufacturing has found its way as export out of China, but even if statistically registered as such, it is more correct to talk about export out of Asia. Analyses bear out that about 20% of Chinese exports to the United States reflect domestic Chinese content. Components and inputs from China's trading partners, predominantly other Asian countries, account for the lion's share — by far.

The writing on the wall predicts a more compact supply in the future. Rising oil prices make transport more expensive and while transport costs will continue to be a small even negligible part of total costs, it can no longer be ignored. Large multinationals discover that a more critical look at the supply chain delivers savings of a tangible size and competition forces them to go that way.

The emerging trend highlighting megacities and megaregions reinforces this development as this is where the market and the labour force is and if companies can find suppliers there, even more attractive if sources for raw materials (input) can be found nearby, the costs savings will be a sizeable figure. Megacities and megaregions start to move into the role of more economically sustainable economic entities. The falling global transport chain as reflected by the economic hardship for large global container transporters enhance the outlook for regional or local transport companies benefitting from the more compact supply chain.

There are also big advantages for the environment and the fight against global warming as less transport obviously reduces carbon dioxide emissions, putting megacities and megaregions forward as both economically and environmentally more sustainable operators.

A wild card in this, if it lives up to expectations, is three dimensional design or additive manufacturing. The plinth for this technology is that every individual can design, create, and produce items such as clothes, shoes and most things classified under materialistic/durable consumption goods. The technology is there, but it remains to be seen whether it actually delivers what it promises to do. If so the hard core of the international division of labour leading to outsourcing and a global supply chain will lose much of its attractiveness: increasing returns to scale will be gone.

Old fashioned manufacturing required a large market for standardized goods to open the door for mass production of the same item thereby depressing costs, reducing prices, and further augmenting the market.

But if the individual goes into a centre or shop to design his/her own item admittedly on the basis of available designs patterns, we will no longer see mass produced standard goods.

The consequence will be to further enhance the role of megacities and megaregions and maybe start a process where they interact with each other communication-wise and in several other economic brackets, but trade less with each other — why should they when the goods can and will be produced on the spot. The one item still needing to be transported around the world is commodities as they need to be available for production on the spot.

The obstacles for future growth in Asia is partly domestic, partly rooted in the global economy.

Asia's policy-makers need to get it right as they face a large number of *crucial domestic issues* and difficult choices in a time of turbulence. The education system must be geared to future needs. Social coherence must be ensured while being under pressure from a skewed development for the first time, locking some Asian countries into stagnating or even falling populations, with a smaller share of the population in the 15–64 age range to support the economy and the welfare of those not taking part in production. Inequality threatens to derail the process. Economists are divided about the impact of inequality on growth prospects. There may be near unanimous sentiment that some inequality is good for growth through savings for investments and rewarding entrepreneurs. The feeling is growing, however, that an inequality too high in the long run saps the economy for power and dynamism by concentrating wealth in too few hands. Several Asian counties in particular China is approaching a stage where the Gini-coefficient is closing in on 0.50 while the warning point is much lower, at 0.40. Despite growth and dynamism, most Asian countries suffer from distortions through regulations and corruption putting spanners in the wheel, making it difficult to channel capital to the most profitable investment projects. That may be a minor problem as long as savings are at a high level — capital is plentiful — but if the savings rate starts to level off, such distortions may pull the economy below its growth pattern. Social unrest may follow, undermining confidence in the political system and pushing it towards populist measures to avoid being toppled. Research and development is still largely confined to applied research. This casts doubt on Asia's capabilities to enter the high technology bracket.

There is much talk of an Asian model and in many respects, Asia and individual Asian countries have mapped out their own way to promote growth and social development, but a common denominator is that the game has been to catch up with the West. In so doing, Asia has been tremendously successful. The caveat is, however, that when having done so or closing in there is no longer a blueprint to follow. The game becomes completely different when entering uncharted waters and so far no Asian countries have opened this door, giving no clue of whether Asia or individual Asian countries will be able to find a way ahead — to lead.

There are other barriers, obstacles, and dangers among Asian countries underlining that. Yes, Asia has managed one of the biggest, maybe the biggest, turnaround from underdevelopment and the poverty trap in world history. Yet, continued progress depends largely on leadership, far sightedness and the grasp of what needs to be done combined with willingness to run risks and populations trusting their political systems. The omens are not bad in the sense that several Asian political systems speak about these deficiencies, bringing across to the population that unless they can be solved the jubilant times may come to an end. As we all know, spotting the difficulties, intercepting them, and starting to look for/ grope for solutions are the first steps to overcome them.

Had this been the case in a time of high global growth, the prospect for success would have been relatively high. This is not the case, however. The world is entering a long period of *lower — not necessarily low — global growth.*

The main culprit is the mountain of debt amassed by the G-3 countries and a few other countries around the globe, but good for Asia as no Asian country is found in this category. The debt issue confines the world to lower growth in a foreseeable future. Debt does not go away. It has to be repaid. It is not a monetary phenomenon; it is about spending and income — in the past and in the future. Repayment takes the form of lower future consumption as past consumption was higher — past and future measure against production capacity. There is no escape clause or emergency exit. The debate and political infighting is not about whether or not to repay, but who is going to shoulder the burden and over how long a period — who is going to reduce consumption?

If inflation is chosen, the purchasing power of debt is reduced, putting the burden (lower consumption) on the creditor. If austerity is followed, the burden will be borne by the debtor. A model playing both cards can also be chosen. The end result is that whatever policy is chosen, lower consumption means lower demand that pushes production below capacity bringing along unemployment. This equation cannot be solved by 'smart' or sophisticated economic policy getting us back to 'normal'. It takes time and is an acrimonious process with high risk of social tension as groups fight against each other to avoid as much as they can to shoulder the burden. The political and psychological tensions are aggravated if policies pursued to a large part put the burden onto those who were not among the "overconsumers" in the past — a phenomenon seen in the U.S. with "Wall Street versus Main Street" and the bailing out of property owners having taken on too high mortgage burdens.

Never before have rich countries been so heavily mired in debt as is the case now. Over a couple of decades with high growth they did not save, but borrowed to accelerate spending in particular private consumption in the U.S. The result is an almost dramatic debt picture aggravating the financial crisis that was mainly due to accumulation of debt. The U.S., the Euro-zone, Japan, and Britain all display total debt (households, corporations, financial sector, and the public sector) of between 400 and 500 percent of GDP. When the recession struck they should have resorted to full coffers to stimulate the economy, but instead discovered that empty coffers worsened the outlook, shutting the doors for traditional economic policies to turn recession into recovery.

As the recession hardened, policy disagreements grew between the two biggest global economies. The U.S. looked to traditional Keynesian policies, which means that money is pumped into the system to stimulate economic activity. The Euro-zone picked austerity reining in public deficits.

This was unfortunate to say the least in the sense that no common approach was at hand or mapped out. It was doubly unfortunate as it was confusing for the financial markets to hear one interpretation from the U.S. and another one from the Euro-zone about what should be done. The financial sector spotted prospects and opportunities to make money manoeuvring to exploit weaknesses or shortcomings of the government's policies. The crisis showed that the global financial markets were not disposed to "help" governments to sort out the problems and get out of the crisis, but instead were guided by profit motives. Aside from making policies even more difficult for governments, this casted doubts upon corporate governance pursued by the financial sector undermining one of the cornerstones of global economic policy over the preceding two decades namely the Washington consensus focusing on the virtues of free market economics. Not only did a policy vacuum emerge, but severe doubts about the existing and hitherto celebrated economic model entered the mindset.

The U.S. took stimulatory measures even if debt levels and deficits were already high, hoping that consumers and investors would react positively to such stimulus. They did, but not to the extent expected by policy-makers with the result that growth became stuck around 2 percent while debt was going up. The fact that the stimulus was made through borrowed money undermined confidence as both consumers and investors realized that the money spent would have to be paid back, which could only take place *via* higher taxes. Instead of spending they saved to be able to pay the future tax hikes. The household savings rate in the U.S. went up. In reality this policy landed the U.S. between two chairs. Household savings went up, kept growth low, but not sufficiently to rebalance the savings-investment ratio to bring about a genuine improvement of the large and persistent U.S. deficit on the balance of payments. Five year later the U.S. still has lower growth than before the financial crisis, high unemployment, growing public debt plus seemingly permanent deficit on public finances, and a savings level insufficient to finance investments keeping the balance of payments in deficit of the magnitude a little bit above 3 percent of GDP. None of the fundamental problems had been solved and worse — no prospect of this happening in a foreseeable future.

The Europeans hoped that a rigorous policy of austerity reigning in debt and public deficits would instil confidence in the economy so that eventually consumers and investors would start to spend even if in the short run the economy would contract — and it did contract, but not to the extent feared and expected by some economists. The confidence factor played its role in holding up private consumption limiting the contraction to 0.2–0.3 percent.

The Euro-zone took the pain now, hoping to be rewarded later by higher growth through higher consumption and investment when public finances were under control. In the course of 2012, the public debt/GDP ratio stabilized somewhere between 85 and 90 percent of GDP. Public deficit/GDP fell from 6–7 percent in 2008 and 2009 to 3.3 percent in 2012 with a forecast of further reduction for 2013 (2.7 percent). The Euro-zone has gone through a sharper and deeper contraction than the U.S., accepting higher unemployment while doing much better in stabilizing debt ratios and achieving a surplus on the balance of payments.

Both gradually move into the phase of the business cycle where there is a pent-up demand. Investments have been low for both currency areas telling that in a few years time it will start to go up. For the household sector, the U.S. still has a large part of deleveraging to do, putting a brake on consumption while the Euro-zone households have a smaller debt, making it much more likely that when the signs of an economic upturn become visible, private consumption will go up. The decisive factor is that public finances in the U.S. constitutes a brake on private demand calling for policies to bring them under control. The Euro-zone has that phase behind it and therefore more room for the manoeuvre of economic policies to sustain growth.

The financial press has focused on the Euro-zone and its difficulties, predicting that one or more member states would leave or even worse that it would break up. The facts are, however, that the Euro-zone policies work, putting all member states on the trajectory of "you spend what you earn" when at the same time imposing a heavy dose of necessary reforms on the Southern European countries. The crisis has brought about significant steps toward a fiscal union and a banking union taking the Euro-zone one step further toward integration of their economies. The flaws and shortcomings in the original treaties establishing an economic and monetary union (Treaty on European Union — TEU, or Maastricht Treaty) were addressed by these steps to be translated into new treaties in the course of 2013. This demonstrates the political dimension of the Single Currency — the Euro — not only established for economic reasons and therefore not exclusively a question of economic theory.

The U.S. may see growth in the immediate future, but not much above 2 percent and with debts and deficits (domestic and foreign), it is a big "if" whether the U.S. can keep its economy on an even course during the second half of this decade.

Figures point to a U.S. default on its sovereign debt. Many people do reject that out of hand saying "the U.S. cannot default", but it can. The main problem is not so much the size of the debt, as there is an adept monetary policy and a likely willing-ness of overseas creditors to hold U.S. dollar assets in view of even less attractive alternatives. The problem is the net interest burden.

The federal budget does not amount to much more than 20 percent of U.S. GDP, making a net interest burden in absolute numbers manageable for countries with a larger government budget — *inter alia* the member states of the Euro-zone — unmanageable for the U.S. Currently the net interest burden runs at around 1.5 percent of GDP, which corresponds to 8 percent of the federal budget. On the basis of a realistic forecast, taking policy changes in the pipeline or the like into account, what is doable and what is not, the net interest burden will rise to 3.4 percent of the federal budget, equal to about 20 percent of the federal budget in 2020. Such calculations were made by the Congressional Budget Office in 2010 under assumptions, which now seems over-optimistic with regard to growth rates over the decade. The monetary expansion programmes known under QE1, QE2, and QE3 (QE stands for quantitative easing, which is a euphemism for enlarg-ing the money supply) will in the short term keep interest rates low, but risks to embody higher rates in the future in particular if inflation starts to increase even moderately. The U.S. enjoys the privilege of negative real interest rates meaning that its creditors — mainly China, Japan, and some Middle East countries — lose purchasing power when they lend to the U.S. It is very unlikely that they will continue lending under such conditions; maybe for a year, maybe for two, but not for long. A genuine hike in interest rates would play havoc with the size of net interest payments on the federal budget depending partly on how much debt is short versus long term.

It is a reasonable assumption that the burden of net interest rates will at the very best be at 3.4 percent of GDP in 2020 and more likely higher mainly depending on outlook for growth and interest rates neither of which looks favourable for net interest burden.

The real problem is that two thirds of the federal budget is mandatory expenditure (spending enacted by law) leaving one thirds (discretionary spending requiring an annual appropriations bill) for funding the sharply rising sums for net interest payments. A simulation based on current figures show how awesome the task is. Eight percent of the expenditure side of the federal budget amounts to around USD 256 billion. Twenty percent amounts to USD 640 billion. The difference to be financed is USD384 billion to be found inside discretionary spending running at around USD 1.254 billion. Thirty percent of discretionary spending would have to be diverted to finance the growing net interest burden. Both financially and politically, this is simply not possible. Suffice to mention that defence is gobbling up more than 50 percent of discretionary spending. The other option is to raise taxes, but if that is done growth will fall, jeopardizing the future tax revenues casting doubts on where the U.S. economy is going.

A U.S. default will not take form of a formal declaration. Instead the U.S. will inform its main creditors that net interest burden has become unbearable so they can choose. Either they ask for their pound in flesh — every cent paid of net interest payments and every cent of debt paid back — and they will get it, but the U.S. will swing into lower growth maybe even contraction, semi-protectionist or outright protectionist pressures will grow, the U.S. Dollar will be allowed to fall on the currency market. All in all, this will make access to the U.S. market much more difficult and the U.S. a much more recalcitrant partner in the global economy. Or they can agree to some kind of restructuring of debt and/or paying back rescheduling and/or extended periods for interest payments or maybe even lowering of agreed interest rates. If so the U.S. economy will still grow, the U.S. market will still be easily accessible, semi-protectionist measures held back, and all in all the U.S. will continue to be a good and strong partner in the global economy. All this will not take place publicly as the debt is public, it will be government to government, but after agreeing the news will filter out to an astonished world.

The geopolitical consequences will be huge. China, the biggest holder of U.S. treasury bonds, will have seen it coming and can afford to accommodate the U.S., but will have a little list primarily about recognizing China's interest in a stable situation in East Asia allowing it to concentrate on domestic issues — reducing fears of efforts from abroad to destabilize its development process. China will use such a situation not to move its own chessmen forward, but to push the U.S. somewhat backward reducing the potential for American intervention in Asia. In a situation when the crunch is felt on American budgets, including defence, an understanding is likely. Japan will feel that after 60 years of a staunch U.S. ally this cannot be done to Japan. The Japanese have supported the U.S. and under pressures of various kinds adjusted its economy and now the reward is to wipe off a part of its savings invested in U.S. treasury bonds partly because the U.S. wanted it. Japan, contrary to China, has a debt problem of its own, with a public debt measured to GDP of around 240 percent. Fortunately the debt is domestic and as long as that is the case, it is a question of redistribution money among groups inside the country; a task Japanese politicians even if inept, facing other economic problems, have handled without much domestic quarrel.

This will be the moment — if not before — when Japan breaks away from the alliance with the U.S. to be a genuine Asian country instead of a Western country geographically placed in Asia.

It will be a demonstration of how economic power or in this case loss of economic power can and will change geopolitical status and room to manoeuvre. After this the U.S. may still, yes certainly will, continue to be the strongest power in the world, but its status and ability to support allies and pursue its own interests will not be the same.

An even larger challenge, which however in the longer run may turn out to be a blessing, is that the world is transiting from the established economic model to a new one.

For two hundred years we have lived in the era of industrialization where the manufacturing industry was calling the shots opening the door for mass consumption. Easy and cheap access to commodities supported this model and switched the terms of trade in favour of manufacturing countries.

Now the world enters a era where economics will be steered by mass communication instead of mass consumption and the era of plenty (easy and cheap access) to commodities will be replaced by the era of scarcities with higher commodity prices and growing physical shortages.

Mass communication among people is shown by the enormous numbers of devices in the hands of people all over the globe. At the end of 2012, China has about one billion cell phones and close to 600 million people has access to the Internet with mobile connection running at around 350 million. India is not lagging far behind, with about 900 million cell phones, and about 150 million people with access to the Internet.

The human mindset is changing through this communication network. Anybody can communicate with anybody about anything, anytime, and anywhere. Portable devices are the key to another lifestyle that is likely to be borne where the largest number of devices is found, and that is Asia and primarily China and India.

Productivity goes up, yes, but only if we share our knowledge with other people opening the door for another seminal change in our behavioural pattern: Group behaviour. Sharing knowledge rests on the expectation that other human beings will do the same; that is only likely if we work in groups with common and shared values making individuals trust each other.

The other side of the coin is mass communication among machines. IBM's Chairman stated in February 2012:

> "Let me give you some idea of its scope. We're all aware of the approximately two billion people now on the Internet. This number is growing rapidly in every part of the world, thanks to the explosion of mobile technology. But there are also upwards of a trillion interconnected and intelligent objects and organisms — what some call the Internet of Things.
>
> There are a billion transistors today for every human being on the planet. Intelligence is now embedded in the systems that enable services to be delivered... physical goods to be made and sold... everything from people and freight to oil, water and electrons to move... and billions of people to work and live.
>
> All of this is generating vast stores of information. It is estimated that there will be 44 times as much data generated over the next decade, reaching 35 zettabytes in 2020. A zettabyte is a 1 followed by 21 zeros. And thanks to advanced computation and analytics, we can now make sense of that data in something like real time. This enables very different kinds of insight, foresight and decision making."

Mass communication among people and among machines works together. They create an enormous flow of information that calls for a system (big data) to master all these data so that they can be used to enlarge possibilities for our daily functions.

The challenge for societies is how to do that. There is a good deal of evidence that the more open a society is for information to flow freely, the more likely it is that information eventually will flow to those who can and will use it to promote economic growth and pursue societal objectives. This again becomes a question of mutual trust in the sense that those in possession of information will be reluctant to open for access if they fear that such information will be used in a way counter to their own values. Social fabric, societal structures, confidence, and trust emerge as conditions for reaping the benefit of what mass communication and information & communication technology promises.

The world suffers from *scarcities/shortages* in five areas: food, commodities, energy/ oil, water, and clean environment.

The United Nation's Organization for Food and Agriculture (FAO) says that already now 40 countries face *food shortages*. A 40 percent increase in food pro-duction to 2030 and 70 percent to 2070 is required just to maintain *status quo*— unsatisfactory as it is. Various prognoses for food production in the com-ing decades are not optimistic. They point to falling food production in China, almost all of Southeast Asia, South Asia, the Middle East, almost all of Africa, the Southern part of the U.S. and almost all of South America. If we incorporate global warming (producing carbon dioxide is good for plants) the picture changes somewhat for the better with the following areas seeing falling food production: Southwestern part of China, most of Southeast Asia, South Asia, most of Africa, the Southern part of the U.S., and most of South America. The main difference between the two scenarios is that global warming will promote a strong increase in food production in the Eastern and Northern part of China, Central Asia, Russia, Europe, the Northern part of the U.S., and Canada alleviating somewhat the dark picture presented in the first scenario, but still leaving the world short of food.

The index for *commodity prices should reflect shortages* as a decline but this hasn't materialized in light of the global recession; the index is still close to a record high. Setting year 2000 at 100, the index was 50 in 1950 going up to 100 in 2001 and is around 300 in end 2012. It is above its level before the financial crisis and subse-quent economic downturn started in 2008. There may be many explanations, but it would not have happened without scarcities starting to influence the markets.

For commodities and food the world has seen a new phenomenon in the form of export restrictions and export taxes. Between 2007 and 2011, 33 countries have imposed export restrictions on food. News about export restrictions or export taxes on commodities are no longer "new", but quite common. In spring 2012, Indonesia announced an export tax on 14 commodities. China and some other countries have applied export restrictions for rare earth indispensable for a number of electronic products including cell phones.

Aside from the consequences for the international trade system geared to deal with import restrictions and import duties, this augurs a real, tangible, and visible shortage — otherwise it could not be done.

Energy and oil has for so long been the subject of shortage and rising prices that very little can be added — or so it seems. The world may not be running out of oil in a foreseeable future. And if it is happening there are ample substitutes in form of natural gas, shale gas, and coal. Sustainable energy and nuclear energy is accounting for an increasing share of total energy supply. Shale gas is looked upon as a game changer and maybe it is, but it is still the early days and opposition is growing, as there is fear of the negative environmental consequences. Particularly interesting is the need for special sands to extract it and even more is needed for water. China has large reserves of shale gas estimated to 50 percent more than the U.S., but extraction through hydraulic fracturing (fracking) requires 50 percent more water due to geological conditions. This is no light issue bearing in mind that two thirds of Chinese cities do not have adequate water supply. So the energy may be there for a long time, but extraction brings along a number of negative side-effects (external diseconomies).

Water is the next item on the list. Demand is estimated to rise with 40 percent to 2030, which is much more than sustainable supply. Currently agriculture accounts for 70 percent of global water demand with industry at 16 percent of which half is linked to energy. A prognosis to 2030 tells that industry will increase its share to 30 percent. Nowhere is the competition for water more visible than in China with rural districts (agriculture), cities, and industry all trying to get as much water as possible — all three of them cannot get what they want at the same time. Apparently the Chinese government has decided to prioritize cities and industry with the result that not sufficient water is available for agriculture leading to falling self-supply of food (China turned from net-exporter to net-importer in 2004). China is the world's biggest importer of soya beans, and is now entering the market as buyer in large scale of corn, wheat, barley and rice. From 2011 to 2012, China's purchase of grains almost tripled. There may be several explanations including changes in eating habits as people get richer, but the main ones is turning off water supply to agriculture to accommodate the demand from cities (China's urbanization) and industry. The decline of agriculture because of water shortage is one factor explaining why China buys into agricultural land overseas — in reality China buys water.

Time will show whether this policy is sustainable for political and economic reasons, but China is tackling the problem of water shortage with a clear idea of where it wants the water to go. Most other countries facing similar problems do not have such a plan.

Geopolitically this raises the spectre of potential conflicts about the right to water flowing in the great Asian river basins such as the Mekong River and Indus and Ganges. The most dangerous of all these sensitive issues is the water flowing from the Tibetan plateau into the river system in India. China can use this water. If the Chinese government decide to divert the water to flow into China instead of India a major conflict that threatens Asia's peace could rise. For India to maintain the water supply is simply a matter of survival — a vital interest.

Clean environment is on the list for the reason that more and more people insist on a better quality environment and is ready to pay the price in the form of lower economic growth or to be more precise lower material consumption. The balance between quality of life and mass consumption is shifting with more people reacting against seeing what they used to have — a clean environment — being taken away from them. In October 2012, China revised drastically its objective for the share of sustainable energy plus nuclear energy in total energy supply for the year 2015. The main explanation was pressure from below (unquestionable there also were strategic considerations *inter alia* higher self-supply). The Asian voter is getting more vocal and voice political preferences louder than before and governments are listening.

The World Bank has calculated that Chinese economic growth of 10 percent requires about half of that to be channelled into efforts to address distortions and other negative effects on the society/economy, leaving a question mark of what net growth in an environmental interpretation is — certainly not 10 percent. Another less environmental but nonetheless valid worry is the enormous waste this represents and whether any economy can sustain such losses in the longer run.

These five scarcities interact with each other. Efforts to solve one of them in isolation tend to aggravate the problem for some of the other ones. Extraction of shale gas requires more water, but water is already scarce. Grow more food to address food shortages yes, but that requires more water that can only be obtained through desalination, which ask for more energy producing higher carbon dioxide emissions and other negative environmental effects.

Therefore a solution of the scarcities leads to search for a completely new economic model.

The flywheel is the shift from the industrial age/mass consumption model with focus on the economic behaviour of the individual to *group behaviour*. The father of economics, Adam Smith, said in 1776 that wealth of society was equal to accumulation of individuals' wealth. The richer individuals became the richer society would be. This dictum worked miraculously well over the industrial age shaping our whole economic system, theories for production, consumption, distribution, and growth. Our political and economic infrastructure — the way we think — became tuned in to this wavelength. And it worked.

It no longer works. As seen over the preceding decades it is not a question of making people richer if this wealth is not used to increase societal wealth. Countries can actually get poorer, much poorer, if individuals keep their wealth and use it according to own narrow interests.

Much attention has been drawn to extracting systems (to gear society to channel wealth to a small group) versus inclusive systems (to gear society to spread wealth generated to society as a whole). Theories have focused on the political systems saying that preserving wealth for a limited number of persons — individuals belonging to the ruling "clan" — make society poorer than political systems distributing wealth to all individuals. This analysis is correct, but has to be broadened. As was seen with the financial crisis, precisely the same is the case if society tolerates a financial sector that increases its own wealth keeping it isolated instead of dispersing wealth to the rest of society. Half a century ago, the financial sector in the U.S. and Britain accounted for 2–3 percent of GDP; now it is close to 10 percent. The financial sector may by working better have contributed to a higher growth rate, but not to the extent justifying such an increase in share of the national income. In fact the sector has through invention of sophisticated financial instruments encroached on what the rest of society produced and by doing so may have reduced the growth rate.

Corporate governance has to a large degree been a question of profits and many of the financial institutions have gone far beyond what the rest of society approve with regard to salaries, golden hand-shakes, and bonuses to management. For the U.S., statistics discloses that in 1990 the ratio of average chief executive pay to average production worker pay was 100; in year 2000 it had risen to more than 500 to fall somewhat to the current figure of about 350. A think tank has revealed that in 2011, the group of 25 highest paid U.S. chief executives earned more than their companies paid in federal income tax. In 2007 the chief executive and Chairman of the Board, Home Depot, retired with a golden handshake of USD 210 million. He was chief executive for seven years and garnered a salary of USD 650 million while the stock price fell from USD 70 to USD 40.

These illustration shows that the focus on individual wealth has derailed the well-functioning of the economy. Apparently these individuals do not feel any commonality with the rest of society. They see themselves as entitled to such huge remunerations irrespective of the obvious damage for society as a whole. They behave extractive. They do not feel that they form part of a group. In an era framed by distribution of more, they may have gotten away with it, but as our societies enter an era of burden-sharing they are not doing what the rising interest shows.

A shift from the individual to group-thinking highlighting consequences of economic decisions not only for the person in question or the company, but for the rest of society is underway undercutting such behaviour. Group behaviour is the plinth for his development exposing that companies owe something to society and society owes something to companies. They live in a state of symbiosis. The way to acknowledge this is group behaviour based on common and shared values for society or groups inside society able to link up with other groups. Unless this gains ground, it is likely that the economic edifice built over 250 years will come crashing down.

Group behaviour is instrumental in facilitating mass communication (sharing knowledge), tackling the era of scarcities (burden-sharing), and introducing a new kind of corporate governance (giving something back to society, act as integrated in society in conformity with societal ethics). If individuals are allowed (even encouraged) to pursue own interests through pure market economy theory none of these challenges will find a solution; on the contrary they will lead to a breakdown of social fabric and social structures.

The production function has over 250 years been geared to relative factor prices setting manpower at a high level and commodities at a low level assuming, correctly, that manpower was scarce and commodities available for a low price. Waste was accepted to save manpower. Innovation was focused on reducing use of manpower regardless of the cost in the form of extensive use of commodities. Despite elaborated economic theory in many areas, economists have never been able to or interested in analysing the total use of resources for an end product — a new fridge is marketed by more energy efficiency, but nowhere is it disclosed what it has cost in resources to develop and produce the fridge. We do not take this into account when switching to a new fridge and do not know whether such an action reduces or augment total use of resources over its lifetime.

The lifetime itself is lower than some decades ago. A durable consumer good is today not durable at all, but can be expected to last for a limited number of years. In many cases the producer has openly or discreetly built-in a mechanism making its lifetime shorter than its hardware makes possible — planned obsolescence.

Established economic theory defines productivity as higher production per man-hour — note the words higher production and man-hour. Use of resources has no role. In the future under the direction of scarcities the definition will be how much more output we can squeeze out of one unit of input.

Waste will no longer be tolerated because commodities will be so expensive that it will undercut its competitive position if a company is not aiming at zero waste and optimized use of resources. Today we speak of no/less pollution; tomorrow we will generalize this notion by seeing anti-pollution and environment measures as one element in a process to produce with a minimum of resources.

Repairing, recycling, regenerating will be in focus. Re-manufacturing is on its way in as a way to use the platform of a product again and again while substituting the software — its capability.

Three dimensional design or additive manufacturing is on its way, introducing monumental changes in the concept of manufacturing. Some observers call it the third industrial revolution after the first one more than 200 years and the assembly line 100 years ago. The real news is the next step: three dimensional assembling accompanied by three dimensional disassembling means that all resources used to produce a good can be extracted for reuse when its useful life comes to an end. What this means is zero waste. Technology makes it possible. This tells us that the swing in innovation is underway. It is no longer how much manpower we can save, but how much use of resources can be reused aiming at no waste at all.

Consumption over the industrial age has been one way — up — and perceived as material consumption exclusively. In the future it will fall and be perceived as less materialistic and in many ways as non-materialistic consumption.

As Adam Smith has left us, so will John Maynard Keynes. His genuine contribution to economics was that focus on capital formation and interest theories dominating economics before him was wrong; what mattered was consumption for the individual. It should be the *raison d'etre* for economic activity — what else if not to make it possible for people to consume?

This fitted admirably in the manufacturing and mass consumption age, but is totally out of step with the era of scarcities.

The consumption function applied by economics is outdated for a variety of reasons. One of them is that future consumption of durable goods is uncertain. A consumer is rewarded if postponing consumption (buying a car) by interest rate making it possible to buy the car later. But today the consumer cannot can be sure that the car can be used in the same way as now five years down the road. A recent example is plans in Jakarta to restrict use of cars based upon license plates' numbers in areas of the business district — maybe in the form that cars with even numbers are allowed on even dates and cars with uneven numbers on uneven dates. The point is that this brings in uncertainty about the future use that unavoidably changes the consumer behaviour dramatically.

Durability takes on a new dimension as was the case for production, with much higher prices for durable goods not realizing the full lifetime potential and gradually higher prices for lavish use of resources as scarcities work their way through the system.

The next step is the concept of less materialistic consumption which warrants us to look at what makes people happy or, to use a lower profile word feel what makes people, at ease.

Economists define and got away with it when saying that people react to economic incentives and nothing else. The basis for economic thinking is utility theory, setting a price on everything. But this can be proven wrong if we bring in other social sciences and research such as psychology, sociology, anthropology, and brain research. They all show the basic element that people want to act altruistically. They tend to cooperate with others, and show empathy if somebody else is facing difficulties. Apparently human beings are genetically engineered to act with societal considerations and less egoistically than economics suppose. The more people do something for others and the more they work for a common purpose, the more comfortable (happy) they feel. In Denmark, almost half of the population is active in voluntary non-paid works oriented toward doing "something" for a community.

Group behaviour enters the scene. Analyses point out that groups composed of individuals that support each other, work together, see and identify a common purpose, and act accordingly stand a much better chance of doing well (in some cases survive) than groups where individuals compete with each other. For those interested in soccer this is no surprise — it has long been known that the true virtue of a manager is to set the best team and not to find the best eleven players.

Mass communication opens the door. People feel happy when they communicate. The French philosopher Descartes said "I think, therefore I am". Today we can say "I communicate, therefore I am". The point in his context is that communication in some degree replaces material consumption. Human beings look for happiness having managed basic needs and now they get communication and people cannot communicate and consume at the same time. In short: mass communication crowds out mass consumption as happiness factor. Brain behaviour and behavioural patterns disclosed by other social sciences than economics push the individual in this direction. This is the non-economic element in this shift.

The economic element is prices. Due to scarcities, prices on many consumption goods go up, hollowing out real income and purchasing power motivating people to buy less and use less materialistically. Communication devices do not generally follow this price trend and the communication costs are falling exponentially and will probably continue to do so or at least continue to make it more and more economically attractive to communicate and create your own world through communication. Many people "go virtual" in their leisure, work, and relations with friends because it is cheap and because they achieve satisfaction of some kind in doing so. Group productivity is enhanced by sharing knowledge. The zero waste society enters the game with environmental quality as one of its elements to go hand in hand with less consumption in the traditional sense of that word. No country can afford to channel back some of its growth to address distortions and deterioration of the environment in the slipstream of growth — we move into a kind of net growth societies where only "production" directly aiming at "happiness" for the citizens is accepted.

Economic integration is the child of economic globalization. Its role will be pivotal in masterminding an orderly transition to burden-sharing, keeping the information flows open, and introducing a new edition of corporate governance. In short: economic integration is the vehicle for making nation-states, corporations, regions, and other non-national political structures plus and maybe even more important civic society work together.

Without economic integration, free market forces through international and global activities would side-line national political systems. They would use free trade and free international movements of capital to obtain maximum advantages without much concern for the nation-states and their populations. While some may herald free markets without control or framework, the political consensus and the general feeling among populations points to a wish for some control — a mix of market economics, political steer, and social welfare. Almost all nation-states find themselves placed somewhere inside this spectrum; some closer to free market, others tilting toward social welfare — but both inside the box.

There are a lot of misunderstandings and misinterpretations about economic integration, what it is, what it stands for, its advantages and disadvantages. It may therefore be useful to make some fundamental observations.

First of all, economic integration is the national political system's counterattack to maintain or regain some of the political control the population look for but has been lost because the objects — economic activities — have escaped national borders. A rising share of economic activities take place internationally or globally. National rules, regulations, and legislation become a torso because economic operators can and in most cases have evaded them by going international. The political systems have to catch up by doing the same: Move toward international decisions and international rules.

End 2012 saw a vigorous debate taking place inside many countries about multinational companies evading national taxes by book-keeping, transferring profit to nation-states with lower tax rates. Obviously the only way to solve such a problem is to introduce some kind of international rules.

Secondly, there is much confusion about sovereignty with many observers and politicians speaking about abandoning or giving up sovereignty *inter alia* in the European Union the prime illustration of economic integration. This is wrong, however. Sovereignty is not lost, but transferred or pooled to be exercised in common with adjacent nation-states pursuing analogous political goals.

Precisely because of economic globalization, sovereignty has stopped being an instrument to preserve the nation-state by protecting it from outside interferences. How can such an outlook work in an age where all domestic economic activity depends on participation in the global economy? Just think of the supply chain. Instead, sovereignty has become an instrument to take an active role in the work of international organisations to ensure that rules adopted there conform to national policy objectives, not standing in the way of implementing national policy without risk of violating international rules. Such an offensive policy gives a nation-state room to manoeuvre.

Thirdly, the words "adjacent nation-states pursuing analogous political goals" underlines that economic integration requires a high degree of commonality among the participating members. Pooling of sovereignty can only work if those who transfer sovereignty to exercise it in common know what they want to do with it and want to move in the same direction.

Fourthly, economic integration is not an end in itself, but an instrument to do things better than if the nation-states tried alone or even do things that no nation-state can do on its own. Only if these conditions are fulfilled will an economic integration be successful.

National politicians do not pool sovereignty unless they are convinced that the nation-state they lead will be better off inside than if they stood outside. Why should they do it if this is not the case?

It is only viable in the longer run if the advantages are visible through tangible results that can be spotted and understood by the general public. As the debate about Britain's future inside the European Union shows, if a sizeable share of the general public and a part of national politicians start to question whether that is the case — justified or not — the ground would start to slip beneath the feet of the consensus to seek answers inside and as a member.

Fifthly, economic integration is often difficult to explain, a lot of technical vocabulary is used, and the elite may see advantages in the longer term, which is not so easy to recognize for the general public. The elite may be tempted to go too fast too far. The public feels that they trade in part of national identity to achieve economic benefits so for the integration to be viable these benefits must clearly be seen as weighing more if the elite wants the general public to be "onboard" and feel that this is the right policy to adopt.

The Europeans have grappled with this dilemma over many years, seeing the integration go deeper and deeper penetrating more and more sectors of daily life while the public still feel that it lives with a national political system not really familiar with EU's institutional set-up frequently depicted as far away and fall prey to the trap of "them and us" contrary to the national political system seen and perceived as ours.

Sixthly, it is a movement toward some kind of global governance. This must start by nation-states sharing interests and policy objectives getting together for a basis serving to link up with other groups forming a gradual networking that can evolve into a genuine global decision-making machine. It is neither possible for individual nation-states to do that alone even if the U.S. for some decades since 1945 came close to fit that bill nor for "globalism" to emerge out of nothing bearing in mind the different interests among countries. The world has seen G-7, G-8, and now G-20; they have all been useful, but few will dispute the verdict that very little global governance has come out of these groups.

A sense of commonality is the key to a successful integration and the true virtue that cuts across any brand of integration is a sense of discipline and/or self-discipline. Integration forces any nation-state not to act unilaterally pursuing own interest solely, but take into account repercussions of its policy actions on other member states. Taken together, a sense of commonality and a dose of discipline forge integration — the incentives to get together and the glue that keeps members together.

Nowhere has this been more visible than for the EU after the outbreak in 2007/2008 of the global financial crisis.

What kept the European Union together and prevented introduction of semi-protectionist measures was the discipline and realization that resorting to such steps would destroy the single market and consequently lead to the breakup of the union.

What kept the Euro-zone together despite an enormous amount of pressure and advice from economists all over the globe — almost all of them from countries outside the Euro-zone — was solidarity, a sense of commonality and discipline/self-discipline telling member states that unless they managed to get it back into shape the consequences would be disastrous for all of them. The strong countries saw through the haze and acknowledged that yes on paper they might be able to manage on their own and better, but in reality the single currency as a political guarantor for access to the market of other member states benefitted them far more than leaving might offer them. Germany would see a nation currency — a reborn Deutschmark — go through the roof undermining competitiveness of German industry and pulling the carpet from under the feet of the pride of Germany: high quality manufacturing. The weak countries could fall back on depreciating their currencies, but that would only serve to preserve a structure too rigid, petrified, and non-competitive, postponing the inevitable reform and restructuring. So better to do it now even under strenuous conditions with the help of the other member states than alone risking that the financial markets would stop lending, throwing them into economic and social collapse.

There are many lessons for the rest of the world to learn from the pain and soul searching the EU has gone through over the preceding five years.

The two main ones may be:

First, economic integration is a process not an isolated event. Only if the political will is there — the resilience — to stay the course and keep together when circumstances become less benevolent can the integration can be expected to last. It is the will to survive and keep together realizing that despite odds and lures of all kind to break away, the long term interest is to go on and face the music. If this will is not there, it won't work. Many observers and commentators applied various aspects of economic theory to show that the single currency could not work or that this or that country would be better off by leaving. They missed the point. The single currency is not an exercise in economics subject to be approved as a Ph.D thesis. It is a political enterprise formed on agreement that the member states want to stay together and, are ready to pay the price because they have formed the opinion that this serves them best. No member country of the Euro-zone would like to face the global financial markets alone knowing well that if so they would be a plaything used according to global financial institutions calculation of what gives them the highest profit.

Second, the population must support the integration especially during crises. When everything goes well popular support is not in doubt, but when the sea turns rough integration may be an easy scapegoat and popular support becomes a priceless asset. In such cases, there is a need to explain why integration is still so much better and maybe even the only way ahead through the crisis. As seen in Europe with populism and nationalism, political movements blaming foreigners easily surfaces.

Many people have missed the main point in the Euro crisis overshadowed by economics, banking crises, non-competitive economies, and public plus private debt. The main point, realized by a large part of the Europeans and a political majority, is that the European welfare state needs to be trimmed — expenses got to be cut back — to preserve the core of the model. The efforts to do that in the middle of a financial crisis and the great recession constitutes the most important socio-engineering process undertaken by the Europeans since the introduction of the welfare state and the beginning of integration both going back more than half a century. It — again — underlines the political aspects of integration. Individual European nation-states would find it difficult to manage on such an enterprise alone. Through mutual support it may prove possible even if the jury is still out as the process has far from coming to a stop.

For Asia and other areas around the world the EU is worthwhile to watch and follow as the economic integration, having gone furthest and tested the limits for what can be done and how national politicians and populations react.

But it is not the same as saying that they should design their own integration copying the European blueprint. Circumstances, experience, history, tradition, and challenges in other parts of the globe are different from those confronting the Europeans. Any other economic integration must be tailor-made to circumstances where they take place. Asia can learn from the European experience — what works, what does not work, how to do it, how not to do it. In a way the EU is a toolbox for other integrations from where they can loan to adapt and adjust to find out what is right or best for them to do.

The key words to recall are "to pursue analogous political goals with adjacent nation-states". In Europe the goal was "an ever closer union among the peoples of Europe". That was — and still is — good for the Europeans even though that may not be what is on the wish list in other parts of the globe.

Part I
The Global System

Introduction to Part I

People today may take the economic model and political system for granted — something that has always been and will always be there.

History tells us, however, that every age of civilization shapes its own way of producing wealth, its own economic model to do it, and its own political system to distribute the wealth. So it is with industrialization, manufacturing, mass consumption, or whatever label we prefer for the phase of civilization we have seen over the last 250 years, that brought us to where we are today.

Therefore it is not only likely, but almost certain that the economic model, which is primarily a market economy focusing on the individual's possibilities for creating wealth, and political system — which is primarily represented by democracy — have run their course, as has the industrial age itself.

Over the last decades, the flaws, failures, and shortcomings have been all too apparent. It is both a question of ethics — how do we behave and what is permissible — and distribution plus allocation of wealth and income.

Inequality is one of the best illustrations. Figures are available showing that income and wealth are increasingly concentrated in the hands of relatively few people. One percent of richest people worldwide owns 43 percent of wealth. Fifty percent of the poorest own 2 percent. Not only that, these people through their wealth and their economic power command influence far beyond pure economics and business life. A total of 1318 of the largest transnational enterprises control 80 percent of global business life. Ten percent of those control 40 percent. The world has never seen anything like that.

The negligence of negative side effects on nature and depletion of resources — external diseconomies in the jargon of economics — has started to threaten not only continuation of growth, but the well-being and health of large masses of people.

It may still be so that the market economy (in whatever edition we meet it) is the "best" to produce economic growth, but the flaws in the concentration of wealth in the hands of few and to undermine the future of economic growth through extensive use of resources are obvious.

Corporate governance has been developed to focus almost exclusively on profitability. In many reports, good corporate governance is depicted as augmenting profits by retrenching large number of workers. While that may make sense in business, outside the realm of business, people ask: if employment and the well-being of fellow citizens are not the goals for corporations, then what is their objective? To make as much money as possible for a limited group of persons — the stockholders — seems a strange goal if the only one? If it is so, why should society support these corporations, which do not give back to society? Two banks — Barclay's and UBS — have agreed to settle accusations that they tried to rig benchmark interest rate by paying US$ 1.9 billion (more than one pro mille of U.S. GDP). The U.S. government has taken Bank of America to court seeking at least $1 billion in damages alleging the bank saddled taxpayers with losses by misrepresenting the quality of home loans sold to mortgage-finance firms Fannie Mae and Freddie Mac.

The link between workers and owners that is so vital for the first phases of industrialization has been broken with ownership slipping into the hand of institutional investors, many of whom do not take the slightest interest in how the corporation is run. Instead, they are on the lookout for opportunities to split it up and sell parts of it separately or seek a fast financial profit through other ways.

The combination of the concentration of wealth and income, and the control over half of global businesses to less than 200 transnational enterprises, has turned the global economic system into some kind of institutionalized corporative capitalism — not state capitalism, socialism or genuine private ownership capitalism, but structured and organized capitalism , exercising power through enormous funds, many of which are outside political control and can evade being on the radar screen.

This kind of corporate governance is linked to the need for capital via the stock market. It is therefore a Western — an American — model with corporations not only listed on the stock market, but in reality owned by stockholders, from which much of their capital is obtained from. In Asia, it is different. Most of the large corporations are owned both by the state or families, and in some cases both. They may be listed on the stock market, but they do not get their capital from there. It is therefore a different and less profit-oriented form of corporate governance.

The public feels that there is something "wrong" with the way the system works, more than many decision-makers do; that is so maybe because decision-makers are part of the system while the general public tend to see it more from the outside, where they experience the inequality and abuses of powers that divides "them and us" or "Main Street versus Wall Street".

This introduces an ugly phenomenon in the form of *nationalism* and *populism*. The general public finds it difficult to understand what is going on. They thought we were living in a society where burdens and benefits were shared, albeit with a degree of inequality within limits and under control, because they believed that to run a society, talent and exceptionalism must be rewarded. Yet, events proved them wrong. They look for whom to blame; they fall back on foreigners and the outside world. The easy answers and explanations are what they seek and accept.

They do so because the authorities used to have a near-monopoly on news and could in many ways control the access to information, although not completely so. This is however no longer the case. Information and communication technology combined with the negative feelings that the authorities have failed, make every bit of information — wherever it comes from, whatever it says, and whoever is behind it — on an even footing. The playing field is leveled. The authorities face an uphill battle, which they are losing, because they are held accountable to every bit of information and news while many — maybe most — other sources are not scrutinized in the same way. This game puts the authorities on the defensive because they are forced to respond. Seen from the outside, it looks like they are being pushed around in the arena, unable to set the agenda and if that is so, there must be something wrong with what they are doing and saying. They lose credibility and in a world overloaded with information, people tend to believe those who have precisely that: credibility. The authorities — the establishment — have not learned how to handle information under new circumstances.

Measured by any yardstick, the progress of humanity over the last 100 years has been monumental. Nonetheless, many people are gripped by angst and uneasiness over what the future will bring. Polls show that this angst is deeper in the Western world than in many of the emerging economies where the population is convinced that their children will have far better lives than they had themselves.

Economic globalization may be the biggest and most overwhelming peace-making and peace-keeping machine the world has ever seen. It is however firmly anchored in the economic model of market economy, giving little attention to factors outside the spectrum of economics. It sounds like a normative — negative — statement to call it American capitalism, but that is the truth. Since 1945, the world has lived under the spell of American values and that has served the world well. Many of the virtues of American society could and was adopted by other countries around the world. The Americans believed in their own model and felt that it was worthwhile to "fight for" and put forward as a suitable model for others.

Over the last decades or so, these sentiments have changed and the change has accelerated since the financial crisis.

The American style capitalism and what is embedded in it may no longer resonate so strongly with what people in other parts of the globe wants. And the Americans themselves may have come in doubt.

That puts the problem squarely before our eyes — where to go from here, where to find leadership, and from where to expect thinking to frame our future.

The American dominance not only is economically and militarily coming to an end, but the first element running out of steam is the American right to lead via "superior" ethics, morale, and values, in short: a civilization model that discloses what is right and what is wrong, gathering a majority of people all over the globe behind it.

China's Effort to Redefine Corporate Governance*

Corporate governance as it exists today was practically invented in the United States. Current questions about the values embedded in the U.S. economy, the uncertain future of the American enterprise system, and — crucially important — the fragile status of morals and ethics in business management appear like writings on the wall, warning that the present form of corporate governance may have run its course.

Looking at what happens in the real world, good corporate governance as practiced by a number of large enterprises actually means bad — and in some cases, very bad — corporate behavior in the eyes of everyone but a select circle of people who live inside a world of their own.

J. P. Morgan can lose $9 billion on speculative trading in financial derivatives. Bank of America has lost $40 billion over the last four years on their failed acquisition of the mortgage lender Countrywide. A large number of big U.S. corporations pay no taxes to the federal government; instead, many of them receive tax benefits *from* the government. The Greek government can be forced to pay €436 million to secretive investment funds known as vulture funds who speculate against the established network of governments, central banks, and international financial institutions.

People watch all this with disbelief. It is not a question of whether the law makes such behavior permissible. It concerns the ethics of the very system that supports national economies and underpins the global economic structure.

History books are full of pages describing how originally successful systems have dug their own graves by allowing distortions, aberrations, exploitation, and abuses — in short, forgetting why they were established. Any political system or economic model finds its legitimacy in delivering human security, wealth, and welfare to the people. But what we see now is that a growing share of the enterprise system, particularly in the area of financial institutions, is violating this golden rule.

Do not forget, however: ordinary people are the voters, so they decide who is in government. Their patience may be long, and their willingness to suffer may be

---

* First appeared in *World Future Review*, Fall 2012.

taken for granted, but is limited — especially when the aberrations are played up by mass media and come to dominate discussion in social networks.

Many of those who exploit the system are not entrepreneurs. They have not launched new products, and they feel no responsibility to safeguard the livings of their thousands of employees. They merely shuffle financial assets around, they invent new and sophisticated financial instruments, and they display this ingenuity simply to enrich themselves by grabbing money from elsewhere.

As the profits they earn do not stem from production, they must come from other parts of the economy. Consequently, the part of the economy providing goods and services is forced to subsidize the nonproductive part.

The high and growing share of Gross Domestic Product (GDP) in the United States and Great Britain (close to 10 percent in each) now ascribed to the financial sector is an affront to the rest of the population. People normally do not mind when entrepreneurs, who have invented something or stand behind the growth of successful enterprises, get rich. They deserve it, more or less. They have contributed to the development of society and created jobs for thousands of people. But when people in the financial sector shuffle financial instruments around, what do they deserve? This has become a crucial question for the capitalistic system and corporate governance.

The system, though apparently blind to its own shortcomings and failures, is still not beyond repair — if only the will were there. Conditions in the financial industry today are reminiscent of the run up to the French Revolution.

The overwhelming majority of American and European corporations are shareholder-owned enterprises listed on the stock market. As long as the majority of shares were held by individual investors, the population was at least more or less linked to the enterprise system. The American population owned the corporations that provided the goods and services they needed. They worked in corporations owned by their fellow Americans.

The savings of ordinary people were channeled into corporations, and the profits were sent back to these same people. There was an intrinsic link between the owners, the corporations, and the workers in that all shared the same fundamental interest: Higher production produced benefits for all to share. We may call this an unwritten social contract among the various stakeholders all looking to balance profits, jobs, and contributions to society and all directly involved in running of the corporation. It was not perfect, but it worked, at some level.

This social contract does not exist any longer. Now, the individual investor has been replaced by the institutional investor. In 1965, more than 80 percent of all stocks in the United States were held by individual investors. In 2007 it was barely above 20 percent. At the same time, the financial industry has more than doubled its share of the GDP.

The point can be made that institutional investors are no more than individual investors who act together through pension funds, etc. But it does not work out that way. These investors no longer feel themselves to be part of the system. The workers no longer know for whom they actually work for, since ownership through funds is frequently obscure. The management and board of directors tend to be a tightly knit group.

The financial industry's move into the role of ownership through funds has greatly increased the pressure to produce short term profits. The aim is to maximize return on money invested and to run all corporations with this as their overriding goal. Many investors have little or no interest in the corporations they invest in; they merely seek to turn a quick profit — even if this means splitting corporations up to sell their individual units separately.

This creates a thoroughly unsound market situation in which capital chases profits instead of being channeled toward sustainably productive investments. In this merry-go-round system, the basic idea of enterprise and what ought to be the plinth of corporate governance — namely, how corporations contribute to the society in which they produce and sell — tends to be completely forgotten, with long-term disastrous effects.

Chinese/Asian ownership structure differs from that in American and to a certain extent from corporate structure in Europe, as well. Western companies primarily depend on the stock market to raise capital; Asian companies do not. It is, in fact, difficult — almost impossible — to cite more than a handful of large Asian corporations that are true multinational companies (MNCs) or even in the process of entering this category, and which are owned by a large number of shareholders.

Asian companies may often be listed on national stock exchanges, but the majority of their shares are owned by either the state in one form or another, or by families (and frequently these families have tight bonds to the state). Therefore, Asian companies are not so dependent upon share markets to raise capital and neither need nor want to pursue profit simply in order to lure investor money into their coffers.

Western journals analyze and discuss Chinese banks and the nation's banking system in the same context as Western banks. There is, however, no congruity. Chinese banks do not operate like Western banks, nor do they apply the same methods and analytical tools used by Western banks when deciding where to allocate their investment funds. Western banks fulfil two roles. They absorb savings and make sure these go into investment projects instead of lying idle — if necessary, by buying gold or foreign assets.

They serve as clutch pedals between savings and investment, encouraging savings by offering an interest rate high enough to make saving worthwhile, and at the same time screening investment projects so that available capital goes into the most profitable investment. But their goal is strictly profit as defined in the free-enterprise system — profit for their enterprise exclusively.

A Chinese bank is an instrument for channeling funds from the government to primarily state-owned enterprises on terms and conditions that promote goals set by the state, or rather, by the Chinese Communist Party (CCP). Their investment yardstick has nothing to do with what we see in the West. If a project is contributing to societal development on the wish list of CCP, it receives funds irrespective of its market economy credentials. If it is market economy profitable, but does not contribute to CCP societal development goals, funds will be withheld.

Foreign direct investment (FDI) is welcome precisely because the domestic system makes it difficult to gauge profitability. FDI investment works as a benchmark for providing China with an idea of which sectors are market economy profitable and which ones are not. Hence it serves as a kind of weathervane. FDI is a barrier against too much "misallocation" of investment and, as such, is welcome — so long as it does not undermine the preferred economic domestic model. This same function is performed by a limited number of private banks and special economic zones.

From the Western perspective, the wealth of a nation is the accumulation of individual wealth including the profitability of privately-held enterprises. As the Chinese see it, the wealth of the nation depends on societal wealth, or in other words how well society develops according to the goals and priorities set by the CCP. A large Chinese corporation may be unprofitable when judged by Western standards, but profitable in Chinese eyes if it contributes to societal development. In the West it would be starved of capital; the stock market would shun it. But in China there will be no shortage of funds.

It is difficult to analyze and assess the state of the Chinese economy exactly because the yardstick by which it measures itself is so different from that used in the West. Most Western analyses apply traditional economic theory, but in view of the acts noted above these tools rarely provide a satisfactory answer. If a Western government wants to cool the property market, changes in monetary policy will be introduced. In China, the government and the CCP step in with guidelines and declarations telling what they want, and the economic operators, in particular the banks, adjust themselves accordingly. In the West, a higher interest rate (the so-called price mechanism) will effectively block less-profitable investment. In China, the least interesting investment project as determined by CCP guidelines will be weeded out — what might be called "quantitative restriction."

Over the last 20 years, the Chinese savings rate has grown steadily from around 40 percent of GDP to almost half of GDP. With a comparatively small surplus on the balance of payments running at about 3 percent of GDP, the overwhelming majority of this saving is available for use in the domestic economy. The abundance of savings makes it superfluous to scrutinize investment projects so as to bring demand for capital into line with supply. The government finances show a very modest deficit of around 2 percent of GDP. And even if the statistics are opaque and results vary according to whether local government is included or not, no doubt exists that the state is sitting on a large pile of cash.

By about the year 2015 the Chinese labor force will begin to shrink. This, judged by experience, may lead to a lower savings rate. If so, the system faces an existentialist crisis as capital turns from abundance to scarcity putting the onus on the authorities to retool their economic model.

With its annual growth running in the vicinity of 10 percent over recent decades, China could have its cake and eat it, too. The CCP's objectives could and were pursued without harming endeavours to augment the living standard of the ordinary Chinese citizen. Societal policies and market economy policies, which in principle should clash, did not do so because of high growth feeding both.

Two factors make it unlikely that this rosy state of affairs can continue. First, the inequality is growing with a Gini-coefficient measuring inequality at 0.47 (very high). A large and rising share of private wealth is going to an increasingly smaller part of the population, and this casts doubt on prospects for a continued rise in living standards for a growing number of Chinese citizens. Second, lower growth will force a choice between policy objectives — societal policies versus market economy policies.

In April 2012, Premier Wen Jiabao reiterated that corruption was the greatest threat to the ruling party and its legitimacy. Corruption boosts inequality and even more worrying, adds to unseen inequality through kickbacks. Such distortion of the economy in the long run must have harmful consequences for economic growth. The dishonesty finding its way into the political and administrative processes undermines the CCP's claim of being a legitimate ruler in the manner of ancient Chinese tradition where the Emperor was considered as the son of heaven.

The phenomenon of increasing numbers of individual entrepreneurs linked to the party leadership by kinship who are profiting hugely from such connections and displaying their wealth without societal concerns could also be mentioned. Failure to embody the virtues expected of the Emperor could — and sometimes did — lead to being replaced in the role as son of heaven. To be emperor is wonderful as long as one's performance lives up to expectation, but it can become a fetal trap in case of mismanagement.

State-owned enterprises (SOEs) are still the dominating force in the Chinese economy. Until a couple of years ago, two trends were visible: a decreasing share of SOEs in GDP and higher productivity in privately owned companies. This gave rise to the expectation that a further tilt toward privately owned companies would bring with it a windfall gain in form of higher overall productivity.

It has not worked out that way, though. The share of SOEs in GDP has stopped falling. On the contrary, it is now rising. This rules out solving the problem of falling marginal capital productivity by switching resources from the SOE sector to the privately owned companies.

In 2007 the International Monetary Fund published a study revealing that 41 percent of China's manufacturing assets were held by domestic non-state-owned companies, 32 percent by state owned, and 27 percent by foreign-owned companies. A given amount of investment by state-owned companies generated much less value added than the same investment in other types of companies. Compared to domestic private companies, the figures said 32 percent less for wholly state-owned, 14 percent less for majority state-owned, slightly less for wholly owned foreign-owned companies and 10 percent more for majority foreign-owned companies.

It was not difficult to conclude that if state-owned companies lost ground to non-state-owned companies but subsequently caught up in productivity with the non-state-owned sector, capital productivity in China would surely rise overall. This, in turn, would open the door for sustained growth even in the face of a falling savings rate.

A study in 2011 by U.S.–China Economic and Security Review Commission came to the conclusion that 40 percent of China's non-agricultural GDP was directly controlled by SOEs and that, if indirect ownership were included, the share rose to 50 percent. Even with uncertainty about statistics and questions about the comparability of figures, this is considerably higher than the 2007 study. Provided the figures are correct, they disclose a lack of interest by the CCP in developing a full market economy and a preference instead for "socialism with Chinese characteristics." Clearly, the CCP wants to keep the Chinese economy dominated by societal interests.

The evolution revealed by these figures has been brought about by deliberate policies and does not come out of the blue. The market economy serves as a benchmark, a scoreboard, or guideline to prevent "socialism with Chinese characteristics" from falling too far behind with regard to productivity. The Chinese probably learned how disastrous a socialist policy without benchmarking can be by watching the Soviet Union.

The "new 36 clauses" first launched in 2005 constitute a framework for privatization in China perceived in a broad context to develop, manage, and regulate private investment. They aim at lower entrance limits and reducing barriers, thus making to undertake private investment *inter alia* in service industries. Yet despite this text and policy declaration, the plain truth is that they have gained little traction so far.

China's response to the global recession of 2008–2009 underpins these observations. A stimulus package of $586 billion was launched, with 90 percent going to SOEs and channeled through the banking system.

The Chinese authorities make clear that they do not aspire to genuine market economy emerging in China. The 17th People's Congress stated that China sticks to a multi-ownership-oriented basic market economic system, with public ownership predominating. The CCP does not envisage a growing equity market with private owners including a large part of the Chinese population as stockholders. In the wealthier Chinese cities, equities may attract attention, but except for Shanghai, the share of households investing in equities does not go above 20 percent, according to McKinsey.

The CCP sees SOEs as the drivers of economic and societal development in China. This gives rise to reflections in China about corporate governance that obviously cannot be cast in the mould of the market economy. Instead, they seek an alternative perception that can allow business leaders and managers room to maneuver yet allow party officials power to steer.

In an article published in the *Journal of Management Development* in 2011, Mike Thompson from the China Europe International Business School (CEIBS) explained how ancient Chinese values provide an instrument for turning Chinese business thinkers and managers away from pure consumerism and toward using the market economy to promote societal values.

The Chinese term 关系 *Guanxi* describes an extensive network of persons who through their connections gain benefits. A central idea is trustworthiness among individuals, which rests on the assumption of shared common values. In this context there is little need for law, litigations, or written texts. People understand each other and act in conformity with expectations, and this eliminates disagreements, misunderstandings, or surprises and facilitates management while at the same time minimizing transaction costs. Management by shared values is much more cost-effective than management through control or command.

Through the 仁义 *ren-yi* concept, profit is accepted provided that high degrees of morality, societal values, and righteousness are respected, and that making profit remains secondary to moral values. Deng Xiaoping said "to be rich is glorious," but that it was not the sole purpose, nor should it rule out other purposes. We do not know exactly what he meant, but looking at his policies the interpretation is permissible that he saw it as a prerequisite for developing China inside the CCP framework, neither as a goal in itself nor as a substitute for Chinese socialism.

Mike Thompson refers to the 君子 *Junzi*, a person whose humane conduct 仁 (ren) makes him a moral exemplar. A Junzi, in the words of E. J. Romar, "conceives an organisation to be what it truly is: a community with multiple goals including profit, survival, ethics, and meaning for all workers."

The Chinese Communist Party unquestionably sees corporate governance as being answerable to the Party and not to shareholders as in the Western philosophy. Huawei, the Chinese telecommunication corporation, sees itself as being part of endeavours to develop China in conformity with CCP goals. Like many other Chinese corporations, it may be listed on the stock market, but catering to shareholders' wishes comes far down the list of its priorities.

CONCLUSION

Chinese perceptions of corporate governance have very little to do with the Western definition of this term. Instead, they are anchored in the idea that corporations serve society by delivering goods and services, and that their purpose is not to reward shareholders through profits gained by marketing and price policies defined by the market economy system.

The cornerstone of this philosophy is the preponderance of state-owned enterprises. Despite much talk, the share of China's GDP coming from this sector is going up and not down. The private sector and foreign direct investment are not seen as heralds of a new epoch or a different enterprise system, but as benchmarks for how enterprises in a market economy system are managed. SOEs can, and probably should, measure their performance against this yardstick, but it is a mistake to believe that the next step will be for SOEs to behave just like corporations in the West.

There is no prospect that this situation will change. It is highly unlikely that the share of SOEs in the Chinese economy will fall significantly. It is equally unlikely that, more than serving as a benchmark, the market economy model will be embraced. It is definitely not seen as the future model for China's enterprise system.

The interesting question for the rest of the world is whether the tilt toward societal purposes instead of market economy profits will continue to serve as a platform for developing the Chinese economy — in other words, whether the focus will remain on how much enterprises contribute to societal development and thereby growth for society as a whole irrespective of profitability measured by the market economy. A telecommunications corporation may be non-profitable, but if its activities stimulate growth in other sectors and areas, the end result — total growth for society/nationwide — might still be higher than if each of these enterprises exclusively pursued the goal of profit.

It is too early to judge, but if the Chinese model continues to be successful, the likely outcome could be that the whole edifice of the Western economic systems shaped by Adam Smith's dictum that the wealth of a nation is the accumulation of individual wealth and the enterprise model forged by this dictum may ultimately come crashing down.

Many people speak about the twenty-first century as the Asian or Chinese century. Whether that will prove to be the case or not may to a large degree depend upon China's ability to invent and offer an alternative economic model better able to respond to today's global challenges than Western capitalism, which appears to be struggling and out of breath just now.

Welcome to the Age of Angst*

The world is gripped by angst. Angst for what the future will bring. Nothing is certain anymore. The edifices of a world view spanning over 200 years come tumbling down.

Omens point to a harsh or, even worse, a bitter future ushered in by a lack of new scientific horizons, subjectivity crowds out objectivity — the child of the Age of Reason — blurring the distinction between logic/rationality and superficiality, and a political system having lost confidence in itself and its ability to master the problems thus losing whatever credibility was left among the people it is supposed to govern.

Looking at the twentieth century, optimism and belief prevailed. People trusted the future to be better than the present. With hindsight we can see it was misguided and the world lived through some of the worst spells in history, but it was there. And despite excesses and extremisms the world moved on.

THE GOOD OLD DAYS

Before World War I, politicians broadly speaking enjoyed the trust of the people, the gold standard reigned supremely, and although the business cycle fluctuated the economy delivered wealth for all groups in society.

In the inter-war period, France and Britain seemed to have shaped a workable system for "peace in our time", an illusion holding till 1938.

After World War II, the United States rose to the occasion in the spirit of magnanimity and statesmanship. The Americans believed in their own system, they wanted to offer it to other countries out of idealism, and many other countries found it worthwhile to adopt its basic principles.

The U.S. global system using the United Nations, the International Monetary Fund (IMF), the World Bank and the World Trade Organisation (WTO) lasted 60 years. It survived not through projection of power, but because it worked.

*First appeared in *Today*, 14 August 2012.

After the fall in 1990/91 of its challenger, the Soviet empire, an era of progress and peace seemed at hand.

A STAGNATING WORLD

But now? Who really believes in the future? At best the world has come to a standstill; at worst it is going into reverse.

One hundred years ago, Einstein and Bohr opened the door to a new scientific age not seen since the age of Newton.

Today's scientific picture, our understanding of the world and the universe, is still anchored in the revelations flowing from the brains of Einstein and Bohr.

Implicitly, this tunes our mindset into an image of a stagnating or stationary world. What is today's equivalent of the theory of relativity and the model of the atom?

We are proud of technology such as the Internet, portable communication and biotechnology, but will it really change our daily life as the car and the aeroplane did? And new technology though useful is no substitute for new scientific understanding.

The economic model serving industrialisation and providing enormous increase in living standard has run out of steam. What is worse, the icons of the model, business leaders, appear to be either incompetent or morally flawed to a degree unheard of just a few years ago.

FAILURE TO DELIVER

The great entrepreneur creating jobs for thousands of people and being proud of it does not exist anymore. Today's rich people earn their money by speculating in financial derivatives diverting funds out of the productive part of the economy or they gain their riches by selling/buying property not augmenting the capacity of the economy to deliver goods and services to the people.

The political system delivered human security, prosperity and gradually also welfare to the people.

The Great Depression in the 1930s disrupted this picture, but did not really uproot its foundation as the world worked its way out of the crisis.

Today's political system has lost its connection to the people, failing to come up with solutions to problems high on the citizen's agenda. Legitimacy for any political system, irrespective of how leaders are selected, rests on its ability to deliver.

The political system in the U.S., Europe and Japan — the mighty economic powers called the G-3 — has not delivered.

Consequently, people start to ask the simple question, why the politicians are there, raising the spectre of flirting with other and less palatable and attractive systems.

So far we have been spared of a rerun of "isms", as we saw in the 1930s, but the sinister response to current fumbling is there, lurking just around the corner. Prick up your ears and you can hear the rumbling!

Who would like to live in a world governed by nationalism, xenophobia, populism and bigotry? Not very many, is the standard answer and yet their oversimplified recipes fundamentally blaming others, especially foreigners, are gaining traction around the world.

Wikileaks and Consequences for Modern Diplomacy*
Observations by a Foreign Policy Practitioner

Wikileaks did not reveal much, we did not know about U.S. foreign policy already. The true revelations were — as many had suspected — that some foreign leaders pursue a different foreign policy agenda than the official one. Sources providing information to foreign diplomats will be more prudent from now on. The main impact is a new type of diplomacy bypassing leaders to communicate directly with the people — increasing people's power and highlighting the growing importance of civic society and the social media.

WIKILEAKS AND *RAISON D'ÉTAT*

At the Peace Conference in 1918 after World War I, U.S. President Woodrow Wilson, often seen as the founding father of the idealist streak in American diplomacy, stated his fourteen points to secure a lasting world peace. He set out by stating the following:

> "We entered this war because violations of right had occurred which touched us to the quick and made the life of our own people impossible unless they were corrected and the world secure once for all against their recurrence. What we demand in this war, therefore, is nothing peculiar to ourselves. It is that the world be made fit and safe to live in; and particularly that it be made safe for every peace-loving nation which, like our own, wishes to live its own life, determine its own institutions, be assured of justice and fair dealing by the other peoples of the world as against force and selfish aggression. All the peoples of the world are in effect partners in this interest, and for our own part we see very clearly that unless justice be done to others it will not be done to us. The program of the world's peace, therefore, is our program; and that program, the only possible program, as we see it, is this."

---

* First appeared in *Politik*, 15 årgang, nummer 1.

Wilson then continues to present his fourteen points of which the banishment of "secret diplomacy" is the most well known and undeniably the most important to his own mind. This can be concluded from the simple observation that it was the first one on his list:

> "Open covenants of peace, openly arrived at, after which there shall be no private international understandings of any kind but diplomacy shall proceed always frankly and in the public view."[1]

The underlying principle here is the conviction that World War I was caused by secret undertakings and covert agreements among the Great Powers of Europe, guaranteeing to support each other in case of war. So when Russia felt it was necessary to counteract the Austrian-Hungarian aggression against Serbia, Germany had to support Austria-Hungary, which in turn forced France to become involved as well. Such a network of alliances made negotiations impossible and dragged peoples into war without giving them any opportunity to voice their opinion.

What is often overlooked, however, is that Great Britain — the most crucial Great Power — went to war to support France, not as a result of any treaties or secret undertaking, but rather because of informal consultations and coordination on a lower level — albeit tying the hands of the government in no less stringent a manner. It underlines, however, that despite all kind of commitments, it is extremely difficult — if not impossible — to box nation-states and their diplomacy into a strait jacket of rules that may force them to act against their interests.

As the French Foreign Minister retorted in those first days of August 1914 when asked by the German Ambassador, how France would act if Germany went to war with Russia, he replied: "*La France agira selon ses interest*".[2] Diplomacy is an instrument for nation-states to pursue their interests. No treaty, no agreement, no undertaking, nor anything else that can be put on the table will compel a nation-state to act against its interests. Formalities cannot bend realities.

When trying to distil the effects of Wikileaks for future diplomacy, *raison d'état* stands out as the first observation, but ultimately also the conclusion. The awareness that information may be made public — in despite the government's wishes — may change the working methods and instruments chosen by diplomacy, but not its *raison d'etre* — to pursue and safeguard interests.

---

[1] Wilson, Woodrow (8 January 1918). President Wilson's Fourteen Points. Retrieved on 12 March 2012 at http://wwi.lib.byu.edu/index.php/President_Wilson%27s_Fourteen_Points.
[2] France will act in accordance with its interests.

In the following we will first discuss secret diplomacy versus non-secret (open) diplomacy. Then the essay will examine what we learned from Wikileaks and how Information and Communication Technology (ICT) changes diplomacy. Finally the essay will conclude with expectations for the future of modern diplomacy.

SECRET VERSUS NON-SECRET DIPLOMACY

It should not be overlooked that there are indeed good reasons for secret diplomacy, even if abuses unveiled by history has discredited such undertakings.

One explanation — not necessarily a good one, but nonetheless one often used — is that foreign policy is a topic best dealt with outside the normal sphere of domestic policy processes. The reasoning goes that the majority of parliamentarians and especially the majority of voters do not have sufficient foreign policy insight to adopt a sensible attitude towards complex foreign policy issues. In Denmark this reasoning is institutionalized in the foreign policy committee, which is anchored in the Danish Constitution, § 19.3. This is the only example of a Parliamentary Committee being mentioned in the Constitution — clearly an indication that foreign policy is "special".

There may, however, be some truth to this view, primarily because diplomats are supposed to — and fortunately in most cases do — know more about the circumstances and dispositions of foreign nation-states. The fact, which is difficult to overlook, is that people who have lived their entire life inside a nation-state are likely to expect other nation-states to act analogously, while people having lived outside the borders (i.e. diplomats) know that this is not necessarily the case.

A good illustration of this can be found in the U.S. policy towards the People's Republic of China in the beginning of the 1970's when President Nixon and his National Security Adviser Henry Kissinger fundamentally revised U.S. policy towards China through secret negotiations. Nixon and Kissinger would probably never have been able to perform this diplomatic act, had they been forced into an open debate. The perception of China among the large majority of Americans and indeed the majority of members of the U.S. Congress would have blocked such an initiative. Admittedly this perception was fuelled by decades of American propaganda depicting China as an evil communist power. Nixon and Kissinger knew, however, that to counteract the Soviet Union and force it into agreements on weapons control, China was an indispensable card to be played in the dawning Triangular Diplomacy.

In Denmark we have also had our share of secret diplomacy. In 1957 there was secret acknowledgement by senior officials in the Danish government of "ammunition of a distinctive character" to be stored by the U.S. military in Greenland, despite the fact that Denmark's official policy was to reject nuclear weapons on Danish territory during peacetime. Apparently only two people knew about this — the Foreign Minister (who was also Prime Minister at that time) and his Permanent Secretary. They undoubtedly acted out of the belief that this was in the national interest, and that it was not a policy the public would endorse. It therefore had to be kept a secret.

To my mind — partly coloured by personal experience in the Danish Diplomatic Service — there are two motivations for secret diplomacy that stand even if scrutinized by a high moral standard.[3]

The first one is that in the age of multilateral diplomacy, the game has become much more complicated. Countries negotiate only not with one other country, but with many other countries simultaneously. And the result is not confined to one single issue, but covers a large number of issues as is seen e.g. in the European Union (EU), in the World Trade Organization (WTO), and in the United Nations (UN) and in many other international or multilateral organizations.

This demands the ability to weigh a concession now, given to one state in one issue-area, against potential future concessions offered in another area by other nation-states. A result may be seen as negative here and now with one nation-state seen as the loser, but concessions in the pipeline from other nation-states may alter the equation and ultimately produce a win-win situation for nation states.

The crucial point is that if the country offering a concession now cannot be sure of getting something in return at a later stage and in another context, it will not make the offer of a concession in the first place. In other words: leaks of secret diplomatic deals may force partners in the negotiation to abandon pledges given in good faith during earlier negotiations, jeopardizing much of the structure of multilateral diplomacy. Multilateral diplomacy rests on the assumption that in a longer run and seen as a whole, all countries benefit from international cooperation — but benefits and burdens from a specific negotiation do not necessarily accrue to the same groups inside a given nation-state e.g. a country may gain during the negotiations of agricultural prices in the EU and then at a later stage be asked to "pay" when fisheries quotas are negotiated. The negotiators may see the deal as beneficial to the nation-state as a whole, but the fishermen may not. Given the opportunity presented by

---

[3] Others may also stand scrutiny in a logical and/or intellectual analysis, if we accept the premise that those in power know best. But as history has shown this is not always the case.

leaks of such diplomatic understandings, special domestic interest groups may try to prevent the concession in the pipeline.

The second motivation is strategic ambiguity. Most observers would agree that strategic ambiguity has served the world very well *inter alia* in the triangle China-Taiwan-the U.S.

To prevent other nation-states from taking certain steps, a sensible policy may be to keep them guessing what would happen, if they actually did take these steps. But such a policy cannot be enacted if open diplomacy forces full disclosure about the foreign policy dispositions of countries in any eventuality. The guessing game is an important part of diplomacy and in most cases it works as a barrier to conflicts. The majority of nation-states adopt a prudent posture when they do not know what will happen if they do something other nation-states have signalled will be met with opposition. My professional experience is that the overwhelming majority of governments are risk aversive in foreign policy.

In a way we can say that open diplomacy in certain circumstances can tie the hands of governments in exactly the same way as secret diplomacy did before World War I. If nation-states and their governments publicly have committed themselves, the situation is not much different. They have to act according to their statements and resolutions adopted in parliaments and pledges during electoral campaigns.

In sum room of manoeuvre combined with wilful ambiguity are some of diplomacy's finest instruments — and it is hard to reconcile such instruments with openness.

WHAT DID WIKILEAKS TELL US?

The amount of diplomatic cables made public is enormous to be frank: 251,287 according to a figure mentioned in September 2011.[4] And yet the multitude of cables tell us very little we did not know or suspected about U.S. foreign policy already. In my opinion the following conclusions can be drawn from the Wikileaks.

The first one is that U.S. diplomacy is a gigantic machine, reaching far beyond classic diplomacy concentrated on foreign- and security policy items. U.S. diplomats looked for evidence of a wide range of policies of nation-states, covering even societal policies e.g. What does the country intend to do, what is its social fabric and how can it be expected to act in the future.

---

[4]BBC (2 September 2011). Anger as Wikileaks releases all U.S. cables. Retrieved on 12 March 2012 at http://www.bbc.co.uk/news/world-us-canada-14765837

Recently, collection of what is called "big data" — or "mega data" — has attracted attention as an instrument for predicting future trends (Weinberger, 2011, 32–37). The basic idea behind the "big data" idea is to simulate not specific topics but everything all at once thus getting answers or probabilities out of the data input. The U.S. diplomatic machine does not collect "big data" as such, but bears a certain resemblance in its seemingly unwritten drive to collect data from all sources and areas in order to shape a coherent picture of what other countries intend to do. Reviewing the magnitude of data published by Wikileaks, it is amazing what we have here.

The missing point — which the theory about "big data" tries to plug — is how to put all these pieces of data together — a model or theory so to speak. Comparing the diplomatic cables released by Wikileaks with the actual U.S. diplomacy, it is evident that this is exactly where the U.S. failed. All the information is evidently there, but the method to combine the data to form a holistic picture is absent. It is a kind of fast stream river rushing downstream without any kind of control.

There is one more conclusion to draw from the discussion about "big data", which is the changing perception of knowledge or the shift of borderlines between objectivity and subjectivity (Møller, 2011: 12).[5] Over the last couple of centuries we have grown used to see knowledge as something objective — something that could be verified. We relied on scientific methods refined over many decades to get to the truth, which subsequently was labelled knowledge. But Wikileaks shows how "big data" transforms knowledge from objectivity to subjectivity. The large stream of data being cabled in from capitals around the world is clearly not undisputed truths. In fact it gives rise to many arguments *pro et contra*, with different sources in the cables taking different views. Gradually, almost without really noticing, we see that data is something we can influence.

Science itself has since the Heisenberg uncertainty principle in quantum mechanics from 1925 moved away from pure objectivity towards as the words indicate uncertainty and more inaccuracy. In scientific terms this is obviously a watershed, but it may be even more important in implanting the fundamental philosophy that things are not so certain and accurate as science over several hundred of years had taught. In 1958, Norwood Russell Hanson put forward his theory that what we see is not objective, but that the result of observing something depends to a certain degree on the observer; what our senses receive is actually filtered sensory information.

---

[5] Objectivity versus subjectivity is discussed in my book *How Asia Can Shape the World — From the Era of Plenty to the Era of Scarcities*.

Most non-scientists have not really bothered about this change of direction in science, but with the data-stream, it becomes something relevant for the future direction of our societies.

The second conclusion is the confirmation of how much the U.S. relies on computerized input. Indeed one of the explanations for Wikileaks is that the data were there, available, having been collected by the U.S. foreign policy machine.

Old-fashioned diplomacy was much more dependent on human contacts supplying qualified information. The people who collected the information had used most of their lives to build up an understanding of the background and implications of the events they observed. Wikileaks reveals a trend towards raw quantitative data — information yes, but to a large degree unqualified and non-evaluated information.

What strikes a diplomat when reading through the Wikileaks cables is the raw nature of data coming into the U.S. State Department. There is nothing per se wrong with raw data, provided that somewhere in the pipeline some kind of examination or systematization of the data takes place. With Wikileaks this seems not to have been the case. As has been illustrated by subsequent analysis of the information available prior to the terrorist attacks on September 11, 2001, all the information predicting the attack was there, but the ability to put the pieces together was not.[6]

For a diplomat with 38 years of foreign policy experience, it seems evident that information is useless, if a machinery to analyse it to form a broader picture has not been established. What is the use of knowing the thinking of a large number of people, if that does not lead us to know or be able to predict what the country's policies are going to be?

There has been much talk about a coming new age of diplomacy after Wikileaks, where anybody may potentially get access to anything. An equally important conclusion to draw — and question — is how much personal diplomacy, personal relations, and qualified, individual judgment has been pushed into the background.

The third conclusion is — for many somewhat surprising but in a way rather ironic — the U.S. actually means what it says! Even close scrutiny of the vast amount of documents does not really point to discrepancies between public statements and official policy on the one hand and what U.S. diplomats around the world actually do on the other hand. There is a high degree of congruity, which creates credibility about U.S. diplomacy. Many observers and critics of the U.S. will certainly be disappointed about such a disclosure. Some of them may

---

[6]The same was the case prior to the attack on Pearl Harbor 7 December 1941.

retort that the discrepancy, which they want to see, is found if we knew equally well what the CIA or similar agencies were doing. Very little harm — if any harm at all — is being done to U.S. foreign policy room of manoeuvre at home.

The fourth conclusion may also come as a surprise at least for those acquainted with old-fashioned diplomacy. Much of the data is about what the U.S. is saying to other nation-states and how American diplomats are trying to persuade other nation-states what their policies should be. Genuine and old-fashioned diplomacy was primarily about finding out the intentions of what the host country intends. The golden rule was not to interfere in the domestic politics of other nation-states — if not for other reasons, then because interference would potentially reduce the amount of incoming information. Usually, people do not want to be told by foreign diplomats what their country should do or mean.

This is, however, how diplomacy carried out by large and more powerful nation-states has developed over the recent decades. My own personal experience bears witness to this. Ambassadors from larger countries often came to see me — not to hear about the Danish position, but rather to tell me what it should be or explain why Denmark should try to convince some other countries that their positions were wrong. I recall an ambassador coming to see me about an American initiative for US-EU cooperation. We agreed that it was not clear what the U.S. actually wanted, and subsequently he went on to say "as it is not clear what they mean, why don't we explain to them what they mean".

The U.S. as a global superpower is pursuing certain goals in its diplomacy through diplomats stationed in foreign countries. Wikileaks discloses how this big machine is used not only to safeguard American interests, but also to try to alter the policies of other nation-states in a direction conducive to American interests. There are serious doubts about the soundness of such an approach in the long run. American diplomacy has been extremely effective in what could be termed grand strategy i.e. overarching policies *vis-à-vis* the Soviet Union or *vis-a-vis* China. But the subtlety of U.S. foreign policy when dealing with medium sized powers and small nation-states has never won much praise. When you carry a big stick, it is apparently difficult not to let the person on the other side of table know that this is indeed the case.

The fifth conclusion is that a large number of political leaders in other countries have adopted a different — sometimes the completely opposite — attitude than the country's well-known and publicly stated policy, when dealing with the U.S.

Wikileaks reveals that most — if not all — of the countries in the Middle East favour action against Iran to prevent it from developing nuclear weapons. This does not come as a surprise to people following foreign- and security policy. We know it as the *raison d'étre* of nation-states. Politics is dictated by national interests and the countries of the Middle East know that a nuclear Iran will destabilise the balance of power in the region — with ramifications far beyond Israel (The fear of a nuclear Iran may be more manifest in some of Iran's immediate neighbours).

But over the years Iran has played its hand cunningly, by publicly stating again and again that development of an Iranian nuclear bomb should be seen in the context of hostility towards Israel, making it difficult, if not to say impossible, for leaders in Arab countries to speak out against it.

Wikileaks brought into the open, that Arab leaders in private conversations — not with standing that no such thing as private conversation exists between a political leader and an emissary from a foreign power[7] — strongly opposed Iranian nuclear weapons and even encouraged the U.S. to take action. The private exhortations by Saudi Arabia's King Abdullah for Washington to "cut off the head of the [Iranian] snake"[8] may again not be revelation for Western observers, but it may be for a large number of Arabs, having lived in the belief that Saudi-Arabia supported policies aimed against Israel. King Abdullah may thus face a problem vis-à-vis many of his own citizens and many citizens in other Arab countries, not only for stating this policy goal, but also for his choice of vocabulary. In the same way expressions detailing critical comments of Pakistan's political leaders by the King of Saudi-Arabia and Abu Dhabi Crown Prince Muhammad Bin Zayed will likewise give rise to lifted eyebrows in the Arab and/or Muslim world.

THE FUTURE OF DIPLOMACY

Much of the debate in the aftermath of Wikileaks has focused on whether sources will be as ready to talk as hitherto and whether they will weigh their words more carefully — even cautiously — in the future.

---

[7] During the Cuban Missile Crisis the U.S. at the eleventh hour offered the Soviet Union what Attorney General Robert Kennedy and Ambassador Dobrynin understood as a "private" deal about U.S. missiles in Turkey. The words "private" covered that it was never to be made public and if mentioned publicly would be denied by the U.S. This case offers an example of the virtues of secret diplomacy under special circumstances.

[8] Council on Foreign Relations (1 December 2010): Will Wikileaks Hobble U.S. Diplomacy? Retrieved on 12 March 2012 at http://www.cfr.org/diplomacy/wikileaks-hobble-us-diplomacy/p23526

The immediate observation is that interaction between a diplomat and a source is not one sided, but a *quid pro quo*. Sources willingly enter into conversation with diplomats either because it is their job to communicate with foreign diplomats or because the source may want to feed some input into the decision making process of the foreign country in question. The answer to the first question is therefore that there will not be much difference in the availability of sources in the future.

There may, however, be a difference when pondering about how open sources will be compared to the past and whether sources will use the same kind of vocabulary. This is a sensitive area. In my opinion sources — and I have often been a source for foreign diplomats working in Denmark — try to tune into their interlocutor for various reasons. It makes the conversation easier; it improves the chances of getting messages through; and it creates goodwill, which may come in handy at other occasions. Therefore not all they say can be taken at face value. A seasoned diplomat understands this and distils the information from the source, before submitting it back to capitals. I do not remember one single time in my capacity as an Ambassador to have transmitted *ad verbatim* as Wikileaks reveals has been the case on many occasions. When working at headquarters and receiving cables from Danish diplomats, I never took such wording at face value, but always tried to digest what the source really meant, trying to understand the deeper message.

Wikileaks disclose that many American diplomats did not understand this, conveying information from sources back to back to headquarters without reservation. This was a grave mistake. One does not need diplomats for doing that. No experienced and able diplomat would have conveyed expressions and exhortations as found on Wikileaks to headquarters. They should have known that this vocabulary was used in the context of a conversation and, although expressing a policy stance, did not reflect the full position of the host country. Headquarter has no need for specific phrases unless circumstances are special, headquarter needs input and judgment. Colourful language sounds good when spoken, but may lead to toe curling when put on paper.

Now when we know that American diplomacy and probably also the diplomatic services of many other countries have forgotten this or put that priceless dictum on the backburner, vocabulary may change, becoming flat, more obscure, more opaque and more ambiguous. Ambiguity is sometimes — maybe more often than not — a good thing in a policy stance, but it is extremely dangerous when collecting information and data to form a picture of foreign powers intentions. There is a place for ambiguity in policy stance, but not in the analytical phase.

History has many examples of how this kind of ambiguity has dangerous consequences. Two of them may have contributed to outbreak of war.

The first example took place in the aftermath of World War II and may have contributed to outbreak of the Korean War. In February 1950 Secretary of State Dean Acheson gave a speech at the Press Club in Washington D.C. and mentioned the American defence perimeter in Asia, pointing to a map indicating that it ran between Japan and Korea. In other words Acheson seemed to indicate that Korea was outside, rather than inside, the American defence perimeter. In June 1950 North Korea unleashed its army against South Korea. We do not know exactly what reasoning was behind the attack and what — if any — role Dean Acheson's speech may have played, but it is normally assumed that this speech was at least one of several indications that lead North Korea to believe that the U.S. might not defend South Korea (Matray 2002).

Another example is the still on-going debate about the meeting between Iraqi President Saddam Hussein and the American Ambassador April Glaspie in 1990, prior to Iraq's invasion of Kuwait. There is no clear conclusion whether her statements did or did not confirm Saddam Hussein in his belief that the U.S. would not step in to defend Kuwait. For this purpose it is sufficient to note that the American Ambassador when summoned without warning to the meeting did not make it abundantly clear that this would be the case. This is no criticism of her behaviour; there is no evidence to do that, but a statement of fact.

These two events point to the risk of unclear messaging. Wikileaks will push conversations between diplomats and their sources in the direction of boring and sometimes obscure vocabulary, making it harder for diplomats to get the sense of what the host country intends to do. A seasoned diplomat, a good diplomat, will not depend on the exact wording and will probe until he/she knows for sure what they have come to find out. But as history shows not all diplomats fall in this category, unfortunately. In short: Wikileaks enhances the risk of incomplete information gathering, because sources will be more cautious and ambiguous when talking to diplomats, thus making it more difficult for diplomats to get a final sense of what the host country intends to do.

A second risk stemming from Wikileaks is that sensitive information gathering takes place outside normal diplomatic circles, using non-diplomatic channels. Sensitive information may even be transmitted verbally to avoid archives and risks of subsequent leaks.

Obviously this increases the risk of misunderstandings and ambiguity. Sources outside normal diplomatic channels are associated with greater risk in the sense that they may not be used to talk with diplomats. They may not have the same access to government policies as "serious" sources, but unwilling to admit so. The quality of sources diminishes. It may also be unclear what they actually said if transmitting procedures outside established channels are used *inter alia* if it is done verbally through special emissaries.

As the Cuban missile crisis as well as Henry Kissinger's preliminary talks when establishing contact with China showed, channels outside diplomacy have been used successfully, but again this primarily took place in exceptional circumstances.

The real impact on diplomacy of Wikileaks is, however, to be found in an analysis of how Information and Communication Technology (ICT) i.e. Facebook, Twitter and other social media changes diplomacy. The U.S. government has set up a centre that follows up to five million tweets a day. The centre also pores over "Facebook, newspapers, TV news channels, local radio stations, and Internet chat rooms — anything overseas that anyone can access and contribute to openly".[9]

There are three major and fundamental changes in the pipeline. The first one is the ability of a given country to conduct a swift analysis of the public reaction in foreign countries of this particular country's own foreign- and security policy initiatives. The U.S. for example does that after major Presidential speeches or other policy steps (e.g. the killing of Osama bin Laden) to gauge the reaction of — not official sources or governments — but the public. This gives an immediate picture of the public sentiment. As phrased in the source referred to in the previous paragraph:

"From Arabic to Mandarin Chinese, from an angry tweet to a thoughtful blog, the analysts gather the information, often in native tongue. They cross-reference it with the local newspaper or a clandestinely intercepted phone conversation. From there, they build a picture sought by the highest levels at the White House, giving a real-time peek, for example, at the mood of a region after the Navy SEAL raid that killed Osama bin Laden or perhaps a prediction of which Mideast nation seems ripe for revolt".

The second change is the deeper understanding of what moves outside official circles in a country and which trends are emerging with the necessary public support to ultimately engineer changes. Most diplomats recall how unexpected the uprising in Iran in 1979 against the Shah was. Many people would think that the uprising in Egypt against President Mubarak also came as a surprise — albeit not in the same league. But for the CIA-unit monitoring facebook, twitter etc. it did not. The centre

---

[9] Associated Press (6 november 2011). CIA following Twitter, Facebook. Retrieved on 12 March 2012 at http://sg.news.yahoo.com/ap-exclusive-cia-following-twitter-facebook-081055316.html

knew of the discontent brewing in the Egyptian population and something like this would eventually come, even though the centre could not foresee exactly how and when. But it was enough to warn the U.S. government and may have been instrumental in the U.S. policy response, informing the U.S. government that the uprising enjoyed broad popular support and consequently that President Mubarak could not be kept in power irrespective of whether American interest pointed in that direction or not.

Compared to such analysis of ICT (with resemblances to "big data") traditional diplomacy falls short. Indeed traditional diplomacy may get it wrong, because it draws predominantly on established sources. It is well-known that the U.S. for many years relied — at least partly — on intelligence services in a number of Middle East countries (including Egypt), not so much to know about other countries, but to know about the country in question. The danger or risk is that if domestic intelligence services get it wrong, as they did in Iran prior to 1979 and may have done in Egypt when the Arab Spring erupted, the U.S. also gets it wrong. Intelligence services are not vaccinated against human errors and shortcomings in the sense that they are lured into seeing and thinking what they expect to see. They are also bureaucracies driving in the familiar side of the road and have evidently not in several cases been able to understand the implications of ICT for building popular support for or against the incumbent regime.

The third change may be the most intriguing one. It is the ability to manage foreign- and security policy over the heads of other governments, building coalitions or understandings with the people in other countries.

To a certain extent this was what President Obama tried to do with his speeches in Istanbul (April 2009) when he addressed the Middle East problems and a couple of months later when he addressed the Muslim world with a major speech in Cairo (June 2009). The aim may have been less to communicate with the political leaders in the region whom he knew quite well, but rather to reach out to the peoples in the region, trying to rally them behind alternative policies than the established line of thinking in these countries.

Technically, it may be possible to block or at least make such behaviour difficult and reduce its impact, but in the long run it is a lost battle as the message can and will be conveyed through ICT to the population. We do not know whether President Obama's two speeches played a role in what happened two years later in the Arab Spring, but it is possible that it fitted into one of many converging trends, pushing the populations of the Arab countries towards protests demanding regime changes.

Traditional diplomacy finds it difficult — maybe even impossible — to compete with this new and strong instrument for reaching out. A diplomat is constrained by a number of rules, which cannot be neglected. The host country expects diplomats to play by these rules and if they do not, they may be denied access to sources and in the worst cases be asked to leave the country as a *persona non grata*. No such inhibitions exist for using ICT to go beyond the governments and appeal directly to the people.

CONCLUSION

The following conclusions to draw from Wikileaks:

• Wikileaks had little impact on the U.S. itself as congruity between official policy and diplomacy abroad was demonstrated.

• Wikileaks had some impact on foreign countries, especially in the Middle East, where political leaders were caught supporting U.S. policies, which they had publicly denounced.

• More prudence and more ambiguous use of vocabulary in the future among sources, boding a deterioration of the quality of information gathered by diplomats abroad.

• A huge swing away from traditional diplomacy to the increasing use of ICT as both an instrument in intelligence gathering, but also as a new method of reaching out to the populations bypassing recalcitrant governments.

References

Hanson, NR. 1958, *Patterns of Discovery: An Inquiry into the Conceptual Foundations of Science*. Cambridge University Press, 1958.

Matray, Jl. 2002: 'Dean Acheson's Press Club Speech Reexamined', *Journal of Conflict Studies*, 22 (1).

Møller, Jørgen Ørstrøln. 2011, *How Asia Can Shape the World — From the Era of Plenty to the Era of Scarcities* 2011, ISEAS.

Weinberger, D 2011, 'The Machine That Would Predict the Future', *Scientific American Magazine*.

The Deadly Cocktail*

Nationalism, Populism, and Inequality

The current political system and economic model are both in deep crisis. The political system is rapidly losing its last shreds of public confidence, while the economic model continually demonstrates impotence in dealing with a crisis brought about by flaws in its design.

None of this should come as a surprise. Any political system and economic model respond to the challenge of the dominating worldview in the given era or age of civilization. Industrialization gave birth to liberal democracy and American-style capitalism. As industrialization now fades away, the accompanying political system and economic model do so, too.

We are now living amid the transition to a future system, one whose outline we may just discern in the distance. That transition could be a highly turbulent one, due to three strong and unpleasant dangers: nationalism, populism, and inequalities.

NATIONALISM

Nationalism is growing in most nation-states. The explanation is found in globalizations creation of uncertainties about jobs. Former British Minister and former Member of the European Commission Peter Mandelson puts it like this: "Opportunities for many, uncertainty for most." Fundamentally, people shy away from sharing jobs, income, and wealth with others outside the circle of common culture and shared values. Growing immigration in countries that used to be uni-cultural but now see several, sometimes non-congruent cultures inside their borders, accentuates what is fast becoming an identity problem. Under pressure from economic uncertainty and clashes between cultures, many people seek refuge in nationalism, blaming "foreigners" for the problems that they themselves encounter in their daily lives.

---

* This article is based upon a paper presented at the GAC/WFS Board meeting on July 10, 2011, in Vancouver, Canada. First appeared in *World Future Review,* Summer 2011.

This trend poses a danger to the future of globalization for two reasons. First, it lures politicians into pandering to nationalist-minded voters and gradually eroding the postwar gains made by free trade, international investment, and more flexible rules governing immigration. The international division of labor does not look so secure anymore. Second, the only way to solidify the ever-deepening international supply chain is through economic integration — which means transferring some political decision making from the national to the international level. But is this possible when people mistrust persons from other countries?

The dialogue between politicians and populations breaks down under the weight of mutual distrust. Gradually countries are becoming ungovernable and must rely more and more on international institutions, international communities, and other countries to bail them out. Such actions serve as proof in the eyes of a large part of a country's population that foreigners are indeed to blame for the nation's troubles.

Any attempt to shift the political decision-making process onto the same level as the economic and industrial phenomena that it is designed to control runs into nationalism as a barrier. Often, the result is an implacable dichotomy between global economy and national decision-making. The system thus remains impotent.

POPULISM

The long period of a steadily rising living standards has convinced many people that they have an absolute right to get more every year. Unfortunately, we are now moving into an era where there appears to be less to distribute, at least relatively.

Politicians know they depend upon a mandate given by the people — more clearly so in democracies than in other systems, but basically all political systems need the support of the people. They therefore shy away from presenting unwelcome truths, even though they know them, to the people. And so the merry-go-round starts.

Politicians attempt to circumvent the hard facts by doing two things. First, they encroach upon the future by running up deficits and debts, which we have seen over the last decades. This shifts to future generations the burden of paying for the present one's chronic overconsumption. It buys some time, but the birds let loose come home to roost very soon. Our built-up deficits and debts are now demanding painful adjustments. People react by accusing politicians of having reneged on their promises. Politicians, in their turn, attempt to make good on those promises by going ever further down the drain — using future income and hiking up deficits and debts.

Second, the nationalistic card is brought into play. The angry public is told that their problems are due to foreigners or the outside world or to globalization, thus adding petrol to the already burning fires of nationalism.

Whenever politicians fail to explain complicated problems, the whole idea of representative democracy is jeopardized. People have never been expected to fully understand such issues, but formerly there was a higher degree of trust between politicians and populations. The great majority may not have fully understood the issues, but they trusted politicians' saying that such-and-such would be beneficial for society overall despite the cost. But no longer. The panoply of new instruments of communication constantly undermines the trustworthiness of politicians and, more important still, it blurs the distinction between politicians and experts. Who is to be believed? The average person ends up believing no one and embraces simple solutions that are often populist.

This can be seen in the U.S. with the Tea Party and with various right-wing parties in Europe and, to a certain extent, in Asia. The result is that "hard" decisions become even more difficult to make. And, even once they have been made by governments and endorsed by parliament, forces outside the parliamentary system quickly move in to delegitimize the measures and reap the resulting harvest of confusion and discontent. Outside forces, very often populist in nature, use the new communication instruments faster and more effectively than the governing establishment to market simple answers appealing to the public, who may never realize that the wool has been pulled over their eyes.

The political system is forced into a defensive role. It has to respond to all kinds of criticism, claims, and loose allegations that often lack any supporting evidence but nonetheless convey the impression the system is hiding something. As the perception that the political system cannot be relied upon gradually gains ground, government's effectiveness crumbles. It is impossible for the established political culture to guess or foresee where and how the next attack will fall because the public is often guided by emotions, while the machinery of government depends upon reason and logic.

Formerly, the debate was steered by political parties. Now it is often dominated by unknown sources, each with its own agenda but without any responsibility for governing the country. It is almost comparable to a military superpower fighting a guerrilla war. One side has all the power to win but does not know where to apply it.

INEQUALITIES

Few dispute that economic globalization in the form of American-style capitalism delivers higher economic growth than any other imaginable model. The problem is that the flow of benefits it generates are not distributed evenly.

The Gini coefficient used to measure inequality has gone up for almost all countries in recent decades. In the U.S., the income share now going to the top 1 percent of the population is 20 percent, up from 8 percent in 1973. Simultaneously, the top 1 percent owned 33 percent of wealth, while the bottom 80 percent owned a mere 15 percent. For China, the Gini coefficient rose from 32 percent in 1978 to 50 percent in 2006. Note that the threshold for raising the red flag is about 40 percent.

Many people say American-style capitalism is great so long as high growth continues. But everyone expects to share in that growth. If they begin to feel excluded, why should they continue to support the model? Maybe they would be better off with a system that generates lower growth, but where benefits are more evenly distributed.

Add to this that we have seen that American-style capitalism has unquestionably negative side-effects on the environment and wastes resources even at a time when resources are becoming scarcer and more costly. This adds to inequality in its own way, as many of those who suffer from income inequality will also be harmed by environmental pollution, low labor standards, and use of hazardous substances.

Those left behind in the rush to maximize profits feel aggrieved and angry. They constitute an inviting field for recruitment by nationalist and populist extremists. In fact, it seems increasingly likely that such people form the core of the backlash against globalization.

Thus far, the upper segment of income earners have been unwilling to give up the privileges they enjoy — privileges which they often grant themselves, and which often appear undeserved. Their intransigence further deepens the feeling that the capitalist model of globalization is biased and lopsided.

Humankind is transiting from one era to another. Some would say that it is moving from the era of mass consumption to the era of "mess communication." Others say that the transition is from the era of plenty to the era of scarcities. Whatever its label, this transition calls for firm leadership, determination, and vision. Nothing of the kind is forthcoming. Instead, the system appears paralyzed by inactivity and long, drawn-out negotiations to make even incremental changes.

The political parties are baffled, and people smell this when reading vacuous statements. Even worse, many political parties vie for votes by calling for change, but then continue to pursue the same old policies once they are voted into office, thus depriving people of the hope that a change of government will improve their lives. It doesn't.

The current political system and economic model built up their roles over the last 200 years as the sole service providers to citizens of physical security, economic welfare, and employment. In the past industrial age, people linked their identities to the nation-state based on economics — standard of living, employment, etc. Being part of a nation-state secured access to the international division of labor. Without such access, growth would be lower, and merely regional and/or local communities could not successfully compete. A person would trade in some of his or her identity to achieve economic gains.

This is no longer so. A number of players — regional economic organizations, like the EU; multinational corporations (or let us use the label "supranational corporations"); and even the old sub-national regions, like Bavaria in Germany, Scotland in the U.K, and Catalonia in Spain — are now able to use the shifting architecture of the marketplace to take part in economic globalization circumventing the nation-state.

Instead of economics, people now look more to culture, values, norms, and ethics as the anchors for their identities, and they find them by joining groups inside the nation-state and beyond national borders. Migration, global mass communication, the disappearance of national media, and monopolies for transport and public services are among the elements explaining this trend.

An increasing number of people are choosing multi-identities. They see themselves not merely as citizens of a nation-state, but as belonging to regions, supranational corporations, and non-governmental organizations, to mention a few. Some of these deliver economic services, others human security, and still others make people comfortable being together with others who embrace similar cultural values.

In the industrial age, a public that was dissatisfied with the services provided changed the service provider by voting another party into office. In the future, a discontented public will seek better service providers from anywhere on earth.

THE CLASH

Inside the nation-state, a large number of people — perhaps the majority — trends towards nationalism. They adopt a more and more populist political agenda and table promises that cannot be fulfilled. In such an environment, inequality goes up, further aggravating social problems and undermining social coherence.

People look for strong social capital as the foundation for daily life. If the nation-state cannot deliver this, they seek it within groups, either national or international. This complicates the prospect of moving geographically or socially, because their individual identities are linked to the group and risk being lost if they move. Consequently, members of that part of the population tend to stay where they are. A decade ago, one out of five Americans moved every year. Now it is one out of 10.

A nation-state's intellectual and business elites tend to be increasingly international. They feel little common ground with the majority of the population, but identify instead with like-minded people in other nation-states. As a result, they become more and more mobile.

Thus we have on one hand the majority anchored in the nation-state, and on the other hand the minority elite going international and global. Supranational corporations and international non-governmental groups act as boosters for this growing dichotomy.

CONCLUSION AND SUGGESTIONS

What can be done to "unmix" this potentially deadly cocktail of nationalism, populism, and inequality? First, a stronger global governance — one that establishes links between the policy makers and those affected by policy measures, even if they find themselves in different nation-states — must be set up. We have economic globalization, but as yet no global economic policy. The regional integration agencies (EU, NAFTA, ASEAN, etc.) can be used as building blocks and gradually merged to make possible global governance. The advantage of beginning with regionalism is that we start at a point where confidence and trust are easier to achieve than on the global level.

Second, bring the new players — multinational companies, regions, nongovernmental organizations, and others with strong influence on policies and politics — inside the global economic system. Until now, and particularly in representative democracies, such groups have been classified as outsiders and relegated to lobbying to promote their special interests. This makes them automatically critical of the system, and prone to attack it and look for its flaws.

The recent financial crisis has revealed not only fundamental flaws in both corporate leadership and governance, but has drawn attention to the fact that they both operate without reciprocal support, fending for themselves often as antagonists. To bridge the gap, a redefinition of corporate governance is needed. The basic idea of business is not to make money, but to deliver goods and services to society. Money or profit serves in this context as an indicator of how well this task is performed. Those who are successful do make money, but their profits function merely as a traffic light, not an end in itself.

The borderline between private and public enterprises has shifted over the last 30 years in favor of private enterprises. Now it should be redrawn, with much more thought given to which enterprises are private and which ought to be public. In addition, remuneration of the elite should be brought into line with how well that the elite serves the interests of society as a whole and calibrated less to the profits that their enterprises garner.

Competition must be restored by breaking up enterprises that are "too big to fail." It is, in fact, quite simple. If an enterprise is too big to fail, it is too big to accommodate and should be replaced by a number of smaller enterprises competing freely with each other. This opens the door for those who do not serve society well to fail — and properly so.

Third, establish much better feedback among citizens, business, and the political system. The politicians must be better able to analyze and understand people's reactions to events and the reasons behind their dwindling confidence in governance and their growing sense of uncertainty and insecurity. These problems need to be addressed and not just brushed away.

And the political system must do a better job of setting the agenda. That agenda is now too often set by outsiders who criticize the system, forcing it to waste its breath defending itself and frequently conveying the impression that the system is fatally flawed or broken.

Representative democracy as we know it has run its course. It was based upon the assumption that people voted according to where they belonged in the industrial society (worker, farmer, civil servants, etc.) and on public confidence in their representatives' ability to represent their interest when voting. Average citizens were not expected to understand the complicated issues; otherwise, the system would not have been labeled a representative democracy. But today, information and communication technology has turned the tables. Now many people — and in some countries perhaps a majority of the people — follow closely what is going on and do not need to influence events indirectly through a representative.

This does not mean that democracy is on its way out. Looking around the globe, there is little doubt that fundamental rights and individual freedoms carry tremendous weight. A growing number of people today take active interest in how their community and/or country is governed. What many of them feel is that representative democracy no longer offers a channel to better exercise their influence, but instead constitutes a barrier. More and more are saying "I can do it much better myself via ICT." And in fact, they can!

Private Gain, Public Loss*

Behind the economics dominating the euro debate lurks a much bigger issue. Who is actually in charge? Are elected governments in control or do global financial institutions (banks, funds, hedge funds and the like) define the room for manoeuvre? Has the concentration of global capital gone so far that even the combined economic power of 17 European countries can be brushed aside? The markets know best. They keep the money they make if successful, but fall back on governments to bail them out if unsuccessful. Are we comfortable to watch this scenario unfolding?

These are pertinent questions needing an answer. If the euro zone should succumb, no country or government — whether it be the United States or China — would stand any chance of controlling their domestic economies; their role will be to read the markets and do what they are told to do.

The euro zone has, in recent years, implemented a number of austerity measures. Recent European Commission figures show that, in 2009, the general government deficit as a share of gross domestic product in the euro zone was 6.3 percent. It fell to 6 percent last year, and was expected to fall further to 4.3 percent this year and 3.5 percent in 2012.

Individual countries are turning around. Greece's primary deficit (the deficit excluding interest payments) is expected to be 1.3 percent this year. Italy has been downgraded by rating agencies even though its primary budget shows a small surplus. Just compare that with Japan's forecast deficit of 8.9 percent, the U.S. with 8 percent, and Britain on 5.6 percent.

Economists, columnists and reports from banks and funds alike have doomed the euro to failure without mentioning these figures. The same chorus has told us repeatedly that the European policy to cut the clothes according to the cloth would lead to deep recession. The figures tell a different story. One year ago, the International Monetary Fund forecast growth of 1.5 percent for the euro zone in 2011. Last month, it published a new forecast — of 1.6 percent.

---

*First appeared in *South China Morning Post*, 6 October 2011.

Admittedly, the euro zone is in severe difficulty due to flaws in the treaties and unwise economic policies, but it's clear that its policies work. The problem is that it takes time to turn economies around. Instead of allowing time for the measures to work, financial institutions take positions in the market that increase borrowing costs by pushing net interest payments up, thereby aggravating the crisis. They try to force weak countries over the brink, so they could earn a profit due to prior investment policies expecting such an outcome.

A few years ago, they cried out for help. Governments stepped in. Now they "pay back" by refusing to act as responsible stakeholders. A dichotomy has arisen between what they want (short-term profits) and government policies (to gain time to stabilise the economy).

Those sitting on the fence should know what the battle is about. Who do we want to be in charge: elected governments, despite their shortcomings, or financial institutions steered by the wish to gain profits and controlled by obscure funds and anonymous people? Transparency, accountability and legitimacy are key words for a political system. But where will they be if governments lose?

Making Profit at the Cost of Society's Interest*

According to business school textbooks, business power is not a problem in itself; the question is how that power is used. Problems arise if and when corporations exercise power contrary to prevailing social views, norms and values.

Most professors tend to add that competition constitutes a bulwark against malignant corporate behaviour and the whole panoply of catchwords such as corporate governance, corporate social responsibility and the so-called iron law of responsibility is rolled out to make the case convincing.

I have my doubts. Recent events illustrate that an enormous concentration of capital in the hands of a comparatively limited number of enterprises poses a problem because the risk of potential abuse is enough to unsettle many governments. Add to this the growing evidence that corporations do not act in conformity with the interests of society, but instead pursue profit regardless of the negative social impact and the picture becomes blurred and even murky.

The worries grow when you realise that some corporations gain enormous profits by deliberately trying to derail society and/or government policies. This is the antithesis of much of the conventional wisdom taught in textbooks.

When deregulation took off in the 1980s, the expectation was that it would produce more intense competition as barriers to entry would be lower. In fact, the opposite has happened.

Take the 1,000 largest global banks. The assets held by the five largest have, over the last decade, gone up from 8 percent to 16 percent of the total. From 1935 to 1995, the share of U.S. bank assets held by the three largest American banks was about 10 percent. But from 1995 to 2010 it has exploded upwards to about 40 percent.

At the same time, the number of financial institutions operating on Wall Street has almost halved. So we have not only a smaller number of institutions, but also a greater concentration of assets in a few.

---

*First appeared in *Business Times*, 5 May 2010.

If we turn to the high-technology sector, the picture is similar. Recently, the Financial Times published figures showing that the 10 top U.S. information technology companies had cash amounting to about US$250 billion. This roughly corresponds to 2 percent of total U.S. gross domestic product (GDP). What do they use this money for? To prevent competitors from entering the arena.

Over the last five years Oracle, to take but one example, has bought 62 companies, spending US$41.8 billion. But it's part of a pattern. As soon as a dangerous competitor is discovered, the big guys just buy it — either to kill its product or to integrate its research in their own product line. The small ones never get a chance.

And while many of the flagship companies used to do research and plough profits back into that activity, they now tend to use the money to consolidate their market position, with the unavoidable consequence that research suffers.

This colossal wealth among large business corporations is accumulated exactly at the moment when governments find themselves running large deficits and having to grapple with high levels of debt and not wealth. Who is going to finance research opening the door for new products in the future?

Business/government relationship in the past may not have been coloured by mutual love, but at least there was some kind of common understanding about reciprocal support and mutual interdependence. This is not the case any more.

Most big businesses have gone multinational. That may be good, because it gives them a wider horizon and a larger market, and helps to keep global inflation down. But the other side of the coin is that they do not really feel any connection or responsibility to any of the societies, nation-states or governments where they operate.

If they cannot find a satisfactory relationship in one place, they may go elsewhere. And they do — as the growing trend towards outsourcing, offshoring and international investment shows. Again, that is no bad thing in itself, but if it is used to escape common responsibility for the development of local societies, legitimate doubts surface about the social role of business.

The profit motive is understandable for the obvious reason that this is what keeps corporations in business. It proves that they are worthwhile producers remunerating not only employees but also owners. But profit alone cannot be the objective. Textbooks talk about a balanced relationship between profit, social responsibility and environmental concerns.

But reading the financial newspapers, one increasingly comes to the conclusion that the balance is tilting towards profit. This is borne out by economic statistics, which reveal a decreasing share of GDP going to wage earners. They also show the emergence of large and growing inequalities in many countries. The Gini-coefficient, usually accepted as a measure of inequality, has entered what is regarded as dangerous levels approaching the 0.50 mark in some of the major economic powers, including the United States and China.

The recently started investigations into the policies of the investment bank Goldman Sachs for allegedly gambling on a collapse of the U.S. housing market is another case in point. For how long can governments and society live with a situation where major economic players actually follow a policy to undermine the national economy and, indeed, the global economy?

Not very long, you would say. But the business sector does not seem to share this view. The concentration of power in the financial sector continues. The rating agencies are also part of the sad story. Of late, they have been busy communicating the view that Greece is not worth supporting. Thereby, they have accelerated a development which may be profitable for them and/or the financial institutions to which they are symbiotically tied.

It is notable that during the crisis, they failed dismally to raise the alarm about these financial institutions, but do not seem to hold back when it comes to warning about nation-states. You may, with justification, question their motives.

The time seems to have come for society and governments to step up and say enough is enough. The business sector cannot choose to live its life outside society, which at the end of the day is what they serve. There is a need for a drastic change of perception among business leaders. While it is good to make a profit, they must realise that the ultimate reason they are in business is to deliver goods and services to people.

The trend is clear in the U.S. and visible in Europe. Asia, however, still operates in the traditional mould where business feels responsibility for developing society and keeps friendly relations with governments. Seen in the perspective of governance and stability, Asia's great opportunity may be to hold on to this somewhat old-fashioned model.

Conventional Economic Theory — A Critique Highlighting Flaws in American Style Capitalism*,¹

For 200 years, we have lived with capitalism in its American style forged easy access to raw materials. Despite entering an era of scarcities, economics is still anchored in growth and distribution theories reflecting the world of plenty. Production theory does not recognize the significance of sharing of knowledge and group behavior introduced by ICT. Consumption theory is still about buying "more", neglecting the element of uncertainty. Competition has been eradicated and replaced by a limited number of gigantic corporations. Only recently has economics started to go interdisciplinary to incorporate psychology and brain research to explain behavior when confronted with economic choices and the difference between individual and group behavior.

Keywords: Capitalism; competition; burden sharing; social costs; interdisciplinary.

INTRODUCTION

The article looks at how assumptions of conventional economic theory still anchored in the thinking of Adam Smith and the market as an effective steering mechanism do not hold under current circumstances. We no longer live in the world of plenty with low prices on raw materials. Agents no longer work rationally. Markets are not competitive. All these cornerstones of conventional economic theory have failed to work as expected.

This leads to important deficiencies in the conventional economic theory. Conventional economic theory tends to be myopic, producing answers correct

---

*Reproduced with permission, Conventional Economic Theory — A Critique Highlighting Flaws in American Style Capitalism, Joergen Oestroem Moeller, *The Singapore Economic Review*, Vol. 56, No. 1 (2011) 1–18, Copyright 2011, World Scientific Publishing Company.

¹ Based upon a presentation February 3, 2010 at a seminar at Economic Growth Center, Division of Economics, School of Humanities and Social Services, Nanyang Technological University. My book *"How Asia can Shape the World"*, published in 2011, offers an elaborated version of these thoughts with subsequent application to Asian economies.

according to its own rules, but is of little use because it does not take into account how people react and how societies function. Production theory and consumption theory suffer under such lack of understanding of behavioral patterns outside the "science" of economics. Interdisciplinary analyses have never really been incorporated in theory and policies despite its obvious relevance.

These deficiencies have been most visible over the last couple of years when the American financial system canalizing global savings around collapsed, throwing first the U.S. and then most of the rest of the word into a global recession, which policy makers falling back on conventional theory found it difficult to deal with. The American capitalism was the highpoint of conventional economic theory, worshipping the market and reflecting many of the growing deficiencies of the model.

WHY DO WE QUESTION THE AMERICAN STYLE CAPITALISM?

Adam Smith's philosophy about the free market and competition with the invincible hand augured more than 200 years of a political and economic model where liberal democracy and the nation-state went hand in hand with the free market economy.

The plinth for this model to emerge was the saying that *pursuance by the individual for wealth coalesced into higher wealth for society as a whole because society's wealth is the accumulation of individual's wealth.* It worked because the world operated in an extremely propitious environment where access to commodities was unrestrained, productivity was measured as performance by the individual, and competition actually existed among individuals and/or enterprises.

All in all, the model was coherent and its various elements — consumption, production, the individual, enterprises, the state and the nation-state — supplemented each other in a win-win interaction.

At the start of the 21st century, hardly any one of the premises for the model are valid anymore.

Individuals may pursue wealth, but the assumption that the sum of wealth coalesce into societal wealth has been perforated. The wealth of individuals may be achieved by depleting resources society needs for the future, thus actually impoverishing society, and not enriching it. Individual wealth may still be measured in monetary terms, but this luxury is no longer at the disposal of societies facing scarcities and the growing demand for nonproductive activities inside the box of social welfare. Even if the wealth of individuals sum up to higher societal wealth, the question of distribution invalidates the philosophy of accumulating individual's wealth to get societal wealth. Societal wealth may be perceived as a combination of sustainability and ability in the long term of a dynamic society capable of answering the challenges felt by the various "stakeholders" in society.

The growing importance of values as a steering instrument for individuals and their adherence to groups makes social capital instead of economic capital decisive for economic development and political control.

The nation-state as the frame for economic activity and consequently for a political system capable of organizing society to that effect is crowded out by economic globalization. When economic activity is global or international, economic policy cannot be national, and when it is moved from the national level to the international/global level, the nation-state loses its grip on citizens as a provider of human security and economic welfare.

The nation-state worldview embodies symmetry between the citizens/voters benefitting or suffering from decisions made by politicians who are accountable at the next election. Until the last decades of the 20th century, the economy in the nation-state was still predominantly national. In the era of globalization, politicians in one country make a decision, which by openness of the economies, transcends to citizens in other countries who cannot react to the decision-makers, but only to their domestic politicians possibly not involved but trying through international meetings to transfer the heat to those responsible — with limited success. Political systems cannot be national when the economy is international. International political systems require an amount of pooling of sovereignty that only the Europeans have been willing to enter into.

Instead, groups, societies or communities forged by values and ethics take over as the provider of human security, identity, and economic welfare. It weighs more to be member of such societies/communities than to belong to a nation-state and/or be in possession of wealth measured in terms of money.

Sharing of knowledge will replace division of labor as the predominant factor determining productivity. Workers will no longer do only one thing — what they are best at, which is division of labor — but be partners in a team where their skills depend upon the skills of the other partners. The composition of the team overshadows the capabilities and competences of the individual. A number of individuals each surpassing individuals in other teams may still form a team with lower productivity if wrongly put together.

Consumption theory will evolve to incorporate the notion that people are willing to pay to prevent a clean environment and culture to be taken away from them. In more general terms, consumption will be less focused on material consumption as preferences change. Risk evaluation becomes more and more important in view of uncertainties about how much resources will be available.

Groups working together will constitute the plinth of economic performance and societal coherence, crowding out the drive of the individual to enrich him/herself with consequences for consumption where consumption reducing the potential of others will be penalized.

Interdisciplinary methods of thinking, analysis, and working will get the upper hand compared with specialization and individualization, diminishing the role of systematic learning that focuses upon a single discipline, probably raising doubts about the future of fundamental research. The time when economics served as an arbitration or judge of progress in other disciplines may well be over.

WORLD OF PLENTY

With the opening up of North America and other areas around the world, resources became plenty instead of scarce as had been the case earlier. Technology provided a tool for higher productivity, at first in agriculture. Transport revolution made it possible to bring the goods to the consumer and the new labor force to cultivate virgin soil and exploit natural resources.

This is what happened in America with the basic philosophy that resources are plentiful and more available right next door. Just go west and you will find more.

It fitted nicely with Adam Smith's theory of the invisible hand as an efficient mechanism for distribution. Everybody was better off in absolute terms. There were few if any scarcities disrupting the market mechanism. Darwin's theory of survival of the fittest and the observation that the fittest were those most likely to adapt fitted nicely into this picture.

Economics became a science, if that word can be used, for growth and distribution of growth. We all know all the production theories and distribution theories we have been exposed to when studying economics.

The core of economics and economics-political life switched to the distribution of more goods and services to a rising population.

Relative prices for production, cost of production and natural resources reflected what it costs to produce and extract natural resources and not the costs to societies of running down resources with consequences for future generations.

The wage rate should, according to neoclassical economic theory, reflect marginal value of added labor, but few will maintain that this is the case. Resources were priced at costs of extraction and loan/capital financing here and now without regard to the consequences for future supply. The result has been a price structure making labor expensive compared to resources, raising obstacles for conserving energy, and saving resources if it required use of more manpower. The inconvenient fact is, however, that labor is the only production factor that can be reproduced *ad infinitum* and consequently, the wage rate should be very low.

An illustration of how misleading it is to assume a continuous world of plenty can be taken from the current debate on rebalancing the global economy. Almost all economists are driving the point that private consumption in China needs to go up both as a share of GDP and in absolute terms. However, if there is something that is totally incompatible with a stable and sustainable global economic development over the next decade, it is Chinese and Indian consumption patterns gobbling up resources more or less like what took place for mass consumption in Europe and the U.S.

SCARCITIES AND BURDEN SHARING

The fact is that we are moving towards a world of scarcities and shortages: food, commodities, energy/oil, water, and environment/climate change. The drivers are larger populations and economic growth giving people more money to spend. Commodity prices augur this coming era. Measured in U.S. dollars, prices for all commodities have more than doubled over the last decade (while being broadly speaking, prices were unchanged in the period of 1990–2000) and so has food prices. China is now a net importer of food. Energy prices are holding at around US$80 despite the recession. Water is physically or economically scarce in almost all of India and most of China. The disappointment at COP15 in Copenhagen illustrates the impact of burden sharing on global negotiations.

These five problems are linked. Resources channeled to solve problems in one sector aggravate the problems in other sectors. They are all priced at "extraction" costs without having long term consequences incorporated in the prices. Relative factor prices do not reflect these scarcities. Raw materials, water and the environment have for a long time been priced at short term costs, while remuneration of labor has reflected the political preference for higher wages. Accordingly, it has been cheap to use resources and expensive to use labor with the inevitable and foreseeable effect that labor has been saved and resources used were at plenty. It makes sense in a short term, American style capitalism, but it makes no sense whatsoever in a long term scenario with rising population and gradual exhaustion of resources the consequences of which may be postponed, but from which we cannot escape.

The term "ecological productivity" may enter our vocabulary. So far, productivity has been defined as output per man hour or unit. In an economy ruled by scarcities, what matters is how efficient the economy is in producing per unit of commodities. The main idea is to look at production and productivity, trying to diagnose how we can squeeze more production out of one unit of resources.

Malthus predicted the same and was proven wrong because new territories were opened up, new technologies were developed, economics delivered a framework for managing these things, and industrialization and the nation-state combined. If it had not been for these changes, Malthus would have been proven right, and not wrong. We cannot hope for a similar conjecture of lucky circumstances again.

We probably have to move beyond economics to psychology and interdisciplinary analysis to find tools that can help us.

HOMO OECONOMICUS

The science of economics tells us that people behave rationally and are able to calculate gains and losses and act to reap an economic, tangible benefit that could be measured. Reality, however, is not like that.

Professor Jack Knetsch has lectured about the questions behavioral economics pose for a part of established economic theory.[2] This is, however, only the surface of a deeper questioning.

In 1954, the statistician, Leonard Savage (1954), demonstrated that if people follow certain axioms of rationality, they must behave as if they know all the probabilities and do all the appropriate calculations. They do not.

---

[2] At a number of seminars at Economic Growth Center, Division of Economics, School of Humanities and Social Services, NTU.

The conventional theory assumes that transparency reigns and that people or decision-makers have access to all relevant information, all facts, and can calculate correctly all probabilities and in fact do so to reach a rational decision. They do not.

Facts are rarely available in their entirety, probabilities cannot be gauged without uncertainty and people do not know whether the past will repeat itself or events will take another turn.

Research into how the brain functions and controls our decisions and subsequent actions tell quite a different story.

Two researchers, mathematical economist Donald Brown and psychologist Laurie Santos (2009), have come to the conclusion that maybe "bull markets are characterized by ambiguity-seeking behavior and bear markets by ambiguity-avoiding behavior". In other words, people go for much more certainty in bear markets than in bull markets and the market's behavior is not symmetrical. This fits in with thoughts about how people react when facing a potential gain or a potential loss — their behavior is not symmetrical.

However, brain research goes much further. Some researchers speculate that the reasons for herd behavior in markets is that the software installed in our brains has as a fundamental item learning by doing and learning by imitation. If that is the case, watching what others are doing leads people to imitate their behavior, which thus explains herd behavior, especially if the original actions were successful. However, what may have been successful when done by a few individuals may lead to disaster when done almost simultaneously by a large number of people.

Research suggests that every individual develops imitative ability by observing one's own actions and, first and foremost, through contact with others. Other research focused on the activation of the human brain. Research EU (2008) reports that "up to now, imitation was thought to be the most crucial ability for understanding the actions of others. A case of watch and imitate. EDICI research[3] suggests that the most important thing is the brain's intentional control over what it imitates". This means that humans are not automated copying machines. Brain imaging reveals that the area of the brain that is active during imitation is the exact same area that is active when we are aware of what is happening to ourselves or others.

A pension fund manager knows that over the next 6, 12, or 18 months the fund has to pay out a certain amount of money and he/she needs to be sure that the

---

[3] EDICI stands for Evolution, Development, and Intentional Control of Imitation, see http://www.univie.ac.at/edici/.

money is there. However, at the same time, the manager observes how other fund managers act in the market as the theory of imitation tells us. Even if he/she comes to the conclusion that operations running counter to what everybody else is doing, convincing the board that he/she alone is right and all the other managers are wrong is an almost insurmountable task. The result is that the fund manager normally chooses to play it safe not with regard to how well the fund is doing or how well-positioned it is to meet its obligations, but how it fares compared with other funds. This is avoiding risk which is defined differently from conventional economic theory. Risk avoiding is behavioral, and not economic.

In the same category falls the theories about wisdom of the crowd and many analyses outside the sphere of economics: "one ant is not intelligent, but an ant colony is", explaining how a large number of animals grouped together behaves in conformity with each other (a herd of wildebeest trying to confuse a lion) and completely rationally. We do not know how they communicate with each other, but certainly, there is some communication influencing their common behavior.

The point in talking about this, to a certain extent contradictory brain analysis, is not to find the truth, which is not, at least not yet, available, but only to underline that the fundamental assumptions of economic theory as we have known them over many decades and may be even longer, forming the plinth of the American style capitalism is actually not only dead, but completely wrong.

INTERDISCIPLINARY ANALYSIS

Economic theory has never really managed to incorporate Kenneth Arrow's (1974) basic observation that "virtually every commercial transaction has within itself an element of trust, certainly any transaction conducted over a period of time".

Admittedly, concepts such as social capital and social coherence have been the object of analysis over recent years, but this work is superficial and does not really take into account the massive importance of such factors.

If a society or community manages to establish common values, the cost savings are enormous. Based upon common values that cause people to trust each other, the financial system serves as an intermediary between savings and investment managing the savings, and the judicial system translates into rules what the population intends to do anyway.

If a society does not have social capital, people do not trust each other, and the financial system does not receive savings as it is hoarded in form of gold or cash, there are few links between savings and investment, and the judicial system serves to impose common rules interpreted differently by different social groups, leading to a cumbersome system gobbling up resources and needing a large "tail" to ensure compliance.

Without common values, there is no trust among people. Trust means that people accept that decisions of vital importance for them are made by other people. They only do so if they are convinced that the person in charge — institutions are not sexless so to speak, but comprised of people — decides on the basis of mutually shared values. Or in other words, if the roles were reversed, the decision made would be the same.

Even worse is the situation where a strong social capital is built up inside various groups, but not on a community wide or nationwide basis. In such cases, social capital becomes an almost insurmountable barrier for social and geographical mobility. If persons have to rely on groups instead of community/nation to deliver human security and/or social welfare, they dare not break out of the groups, starting to function like a kind of adscription hampering productivity and often building hatred among groups instead of furthering trust among groups.

Light on the risk that segmentation of social capital may affect society and the economy in a negative way has been provided by an Australian study (Spoehr *et al.*, 2007) that analyzes social inclusion and social exclusion in Northern Adelaide. The study looks at elements leading to social capital inside groups to constitute barriers for these groups to join economic life and take part in social activities of a broader character outside the groups inside which they find themselves comfortable.

The study selects three sub-locations: a disadvantaged area, a more affluent area and a relatively affluent town.

The conclusion is that people living in the disadvantaged area were more likely to have inward-focused relationships based upon neighbors and friends than outward relationships by taking part in economic and social life. In other words, these subgroups tended to live their own lives and keep a distance from the rest of society while the two other sub-groups had a lower social capital of inward-looking types, but on the contrary, a stronger degree of reaching outside their groups to society as a whole. (The study outlines a model for measuring social inclusion and social exclusion based upon a number of economic, social, and educational factors).

In the vocabulary of social capital, the inward-looking sub-groups were strong in bonding that focuses upon social relationships, making people share basic values of non-economic character to help and assist each other because they trust each other, but not outsiders. It is difficult to leave the sub-group and equally difficult to enter the sub-group. It also tends to freeze relationships preventing adaptations and adjustment to what is going on in society as a whole and constitutes a barrier — or at least can be — to building a nationwide social capital. The other two groups were less strong in bonding, but had a stronger social capital in bridging social capital that reaches beyond the sub-group being a tool for relations among people without common ethnicity and religion plus linking social capital that help people to interact with authorities, thus boosting economic growth and nationwide social capital.

All these are conspicuously absent from most main stream economics although they play a crucial role in explaining economic life.

SOCIAL COSTS

Interdisciplinary analysis leads us to look at how capitalism in its American edition or for that sake, any economic model, influences costs at running society — how much does it cost to maintain a well-functioning society, constituting a framework for economic activities. We single out three notions: social transaction costs, social opportunity costs, and net social costs of economic transactions.

Social Transaction Costs

Having lived most of my life in Denmark, I have witnessed nationwide social capital and saw how it works — not without flaws of course, but works — to promote creativity and lower social transaction costs perceived as the cost of managing the well being of society. The cost of running the Danish society is not high as compared to the costs of running the U.S. society even if a look at public expenditure may convey this impression. It is a mistake to believe that these costs can be measured *vis-à-vis* public expenditure. Many of them will be financed outside the public budgets by institutions or private persons. Activities not undertaken do not, of course, give rise to expenditure, but they may incur other costs on society and it is no foregone conclusion to say that money saved on the public budget is money saved for society as a whole.

Many items financed over public budgets in Denmark are financed privately in the U.S. Studies reveal that the total costs for social welfare does not differ much between the U.S. and Europe, but the number of people covered and the financing does. We only need to recall that with a large part of its population not covered by health care, costs in the U.S. are among the highest in the world as a share of the GDP. (Total health cost in 2007 as a share of GDP in U.S. is 16 percent, and Denmark 9.8 percent according to OECD statistics).[4] Adema and Ladaique (2009) have tried to compare Publicly Mandated Social Expenditure (as a percentage of GDP, 2003), which should, in principle, wipe out differences due to public versus private financing and come to the conclusion that the figures are 18.9 percent in the U.S. and 23.8 percent in Denmark.[5]

As an illustration of the costs incurred by a society forced to resort to a rule by law because social capital is low, lawyers can be brought in. The U.S. has 265 people per lawyer, Germany 593, France 1403, Denmark 1135 and Finland 2888.[6] The U.S. spends approximately US$70 billion annually on corrections reflecting that approximately 2.2 million people sit in jail, but this sum only shows the direct enforcement costs and not the colossal waste of resources knowing the alternative use of staff and non-participation in the economy of inmates.

Hacker (2002) points out that if corporate spending on health care and pensions (government spending and subsidized by tax breaks) the American "welfare state" is approximately the same size as other advanced countries measured *vis-à-vis* GDP.

Social capital also influences other important sectors such as education and may even influence life long education.

It is interesting to note that when talking about productivity and creativity, a number of analyses in Denmark (Lundvall, 2008) point to the existence of the social welfare system as promoting creativity while the mainstream thinking in the U.S. is that such a system constitutes a barrier, holding back risk-taking and ingenuity. We do not know the correct answer or explanation and maybe it is that creativity is linked to the social structure in each country so the way ahead is different from country to country.

It seems difficult to dispute that American capitalism increases the social transaction cost.

---

[4] http://stats.oecd.org/Index.aspx?DatasetCode=HEALTH).OECD.
[5] 15.6 percent for Ireland, 29.8 percent for France.
[6] Sources: http://wiki.answers.com/Q/What_country_in_the_world_has_most_lawyers_per_capita and http://www.ccbe.eu/fileadmin/user_upload/NTCdocument/table_number_lawyers1_1179905811.pdf.

Social Opportunity Costs

Social opportunity costs can be defined as the costs incurred by society of running inefficient systems of economic or social character — some would call it
waste. How much better could society be under the same cost level or how many
resources could we free for other purposes if we accepted same service level, but did
it more efficiently? To measure these costs, we can bring in cost-benefit analysis or
a benchmark by looking at other systems or common sense.

Unemployment is the first one that catches the eye, but the caveat is that some
unemployment may actually be good for society by allowing the labor force to
adjust. In some cases, it may be cheaper for society to accept that some people are
unemployed so that paying them social welfare is cheaper than forcing them into
employment, reducing productivity for the rest of the group.

Energy efficiency is clearly an item to be included on this list. Comparing how much
energy China uses for every unit of GDP, Japan remarked that China could get the
same productivity for almost 50 percent of the energy actually used. In addition,
the external diseconomies and the sum is very high.

The most interesting and difficult one is the education sector.

Goldin and Katz (2008) point out that technological development may have a
"dark" side in the form of adverse distributional consequences that may foment
social tension. Technological advances entails that the earnings of some groups
may increase more than for other groups. The condition for an equitable distribution of rising income/wealth is flexible skills and an educational infrastructure that
expands sufficiently to match demand for skills with supply of those skills. Growth
and the premium to skills will be balanced. If, on the other hand, the education
system does not conform to this recipe, imbalances will arise, unsettling not only
the education sector, but also the social fabric.

Goldin and Katz divide the wage structure and education in the U.S. in the 20th
century into three phases. The first one was from 1920 to around 1940, a period
when wage differentials narrowed and the earnings of the more educated were
reduced relative to earnings of the less educated. The second one was from 1940s
to the beginning of 1970s, a period when wage differentials widened only slightly
and income distribution was fairly stable. The third one was from the 1970s to the
end of the century, a period when inequality rose steeply, but productivity only rose
slightly (later, productivity rose sharply, but not in those more than 20 years). The
wage/income premium for college education went up. The interpretation of this

development is a mismatch between the demand for skills from industry and the education systems" ability to deliver students having these skills.[7]

First, we have the costs of mismatch between number of educated people and skills in demand. Second, we have the costs of inequality. Third, we have the costs (social and private) of having educated people out of jobs.

McKinsey (2009) looks at the American education system compared with a number of other countries taking part in the PISA (Program for International Student Assessment), and ranks and classifies what is termed educational gaps as the economic equivalent of "permanent national recession". If the U.S. had closed the achievement gap in education visible in the beginning of the 1980s and raised its performance level to the top level on par with countries like Finland and Korea, the U.S. GDP in 2008 would have been between US$1.3 trillion and US$2.3 trillion higher, corresponding to 9 percent and 16 percent, respectively, of total U.S. GDP.

American capitalism seems to have high social opportunity cost, leading to an inefficient societal system in several ways and blocking the full use of potential development.

Net Social Costs of Economic Transactions

We can take the analysis further and ask what the effect on society as a whole is of policy steps flowing from the economic system that obviously increases GDP, but at the same time, incurs social external diseconomies.

This is especially relevant when looking at the American model with a small public sector and activities referred to the private sector, but under the aegis of the public sector in other models (the European one as an example), not the least after the deregulation in the 1980s initiated by President Reagan and Prime Minister Thatcher.

The basic problem is that while many of these activities may be performed cheaper — at least in the short run — by private ownership, a privately profit-run enterprise may incorporate societal costs detrimental to the functioning of society as a whole.

---

[7] The works by Goldin and Katz analyze the U.S. education over the last hundred years and touches upon several aspects not relevant for other parts of the world, in particular Asia. Its basic message is, however, of crucial importance for other parts of the world, in particular Asia, spelling out that the education system is contributing to growth according to how well it is geared to society, but at the same time, is embedded with the seeds of disruptive forces if policies are out of tune with societal and technological development.

The best illustration of how uncontrolled market forces combined with disregard for environmental consequences and lack of understanding or lack of will to understand negative repercussions on the national economy of policies favoring big business dates from the U.S. in the 1930s. According to Newman and Kenwork (1999), a holding company bought the private electric streetcar system in 45 U.S. cities and then closed them down. It was owned by interests from the oil, tyre, and car industries. In 1949, a grand jury convicted General Motors, Standard Oil of California, Mac Trucks, Philips Petroleum, and Firestone Tires on a criminal indictment of antitrust conspiracy, but meanwhile, 280 million passengers had been chased from streetcars onto buses and cars. These big companies earned a fortune while the U.S. economy suffered badly and the U.S. was left with a transport infrastructure in cities wholly reliant on the auto industry.

A societal cost is that American cities over the last 70 years have been built so that workers need cars to go to work. An increase of the petrol price as an element of energy policy and/or climate change is simply not possible because that would lead to demand for higher wages, hollowing out American competition. So from this step, initially increasing U.S. GDP through higher car production etc. flows a series of highly negative repercussions on the economy and the social structure, locked into a given structure preventing change necessary for a number of reasons.

Another example is the discussion under the heading of "who killed the electric car", showing that environmental rules in California forced General Motors to offer an electric car (EV1) in the 1990s, but that GM combined with the oil industry and other pressure groups devoted most of its efforts to demonstrate that it did not work instead of trying to make it work.[8]

By highlighting the market in a business perspective, American capitalism forces upon society a structure with sometimes large societal costs, even if GDP in a narrow sense may benefit.

PRODUCTION THEORY

Production will increasingly be steered by science and knowledge as a production factor. It differs from conventional production factors (land, labor, and capital) in several decisive ways: it can be used again and again without any need for reinvestment, it delivers increasing returns to scale with the number of people using it, and most important of all, it can be used by several persons at the same time.

---

[8] Source: http://en.wikipedia.org/wiki/Who_Killed_the_Electric_Car percent3F.

Knowledge is the typical production factor underlining the switch from an individual or small group production to large groups, with productivity dependent upon the capability to work together.

The fundamental revolution comes from the observation of knowledge being used by several persons at the same time. It puts a finger on what is determining the shift compared to conventional production theory: sharing of the performance, skill or output embedded in a production factor. The faster knowledge is disseminated through society, the higher the total integrated value becomes. The higher the number of people using knowledge as a production factor, the higher total production becomes.

Consider the following example. A city has one million cars. The next car to be purchased may increase productivity somewhat for the owner, but reduce productivity for all others, and on top of that, bring along external diseconomies in the form of environmental damage augmenting anti-pollution costs. So all in all, the cost-benefit analysis leads to a negative result for society as a whole. The same city has one million mobile phones, one million PCs and several hundred of thousands on broadband and thousands on Skype. What happens when one more user makes his/her entrance? Productivity goes up for that user, but productivity/user value also goes up for all the other users of mobile phones, PCs, broadband registrants and Skype users. The effect is the reverse of the car case in an industrial society, and there will be little if any external diseconomies.

Unless people are convinced that the benefits from sharing — in this case knowledge — will be distributed in accordance with values and ethics, they will be reluctant to share. The key to sharing is trust — combined with privacy — and the key to trust is to build social capital inside and between groups. Social capital depends upon people adopting common values and ethics. Individuals network with others and groups build interaction inside the community with one another. This constitutes a break with existing (economic) distribution theory controlled by economic factors, ruling out values frequently leading to inequality and even worse, rising inequality, giving a part and sometimes a majority of the population the impression that they do not form part of society.

CONSUMPTION THEORY

The challenge for economics is to shift modeling from various alternatives, which can be quantified and reflect certainty to alternatives with alternatives based upon a high degree of uncertainty. This is especially the case for consumption theory, where not only economic parameters, but a whole string of societal and behavioral elements undermine the thinking behind *Homo Oeconomicus* and the ability to calculate various outcomes and compare them with each other.[9]

In general terms, the question can be put as: how will today's consumer react to reduced consumption when he/she is told that there is x percent risk for a major climate catastrophe 10, 20 or 50 years later? Even more crucial is that there is y percent probability that he/she will be affected? Or we can turn to probability about the public sectors' future financial clout to fulfill pledges about welfare and ask: how will the consumer react when he/she is told there is x percent risk that there will be no retirement help, or z percent risk that there will no land available for building?

Conventional theory says that a consumer with US$50,000 accepts to postpone the buying of a new car by five years provided that interest rate increases the sum to e.g., US$55,000. Consume now or later and if later, the consumer is compensated. Behind this theory lies the assumption that the goods or services will be available five years from now without major changes.

In new circumstances where resource scarcities make themselves felt as a constraint for material production, this is no longer sufficient. The equation needs to be reworked with built-in coefficients, transforming uncertainty into economics. The consumer contemplating to buy a car now may have to face choices like these:

Buy the car now for US$50,000 or invest to get US$55,000 in five years time to buy a similar car, but the following alternatives need to be taken into account. Alternative one: there is 25 percent probability that cars will be 50 percent more expensive, or even worse, that cars will not be sold according to today's practice. Alternative two: there is 50 percent probability that the car you look at will not be available. Maybe only cars meeting specific requirements for low consumption of petrol or hybrid cars or cars invested with new technologies will be on the market and they will be more expensive and perform less like a "genuine" car. Alternative three: restrictions for use of cars have been introduced, for example, stipulating that every car must not run more than 200 km per week.

In those cases, the consumer not only gets the choice five years later narrowed down, but also has to forego user value from year zero to year five, which cannot be recuperated. Some kinds of user value are simply confiscated by the authorities.

---

[9] In a working paper "Consumption Tradeoffs vs. Catastrophes Avoidance: Implications of Some Recent Results in Happiness Studies on the Economics of Climate Change", 2008, Professor Ng Yew Kwang discusses some of these aspects.

Normal consumption theory would tend to look at income and price elasticities for buying (acquiring or getting something), but what in the future may be decisive for the consumer is what he/she is not getting and as outlined above, the price a consumer is willing to pay for getting something is different from the price he/she is asked to give it up. In addition, the uncertainties about future consumption and the shortcomings of current consumption theory are obvious.

A similar line of questioning or reasoning might be applied to set out the preferences for social benefits. Where is the tilting point when having to choose between paying a sum of X now in taxes for no social benefit later in life or Z (a higher or maybe much higher amount now) accompanied by Q percent probability of a flow of social benefits with an annual magnitude of U? For most Western countries having had a social welfare system over many years, these equations have found a solution translated into politics, but that is not the case for most of Asia.

This line of thinking can be taken a long step further to look at how well, or rather how badly, consumption theory incorporates non-material preferences such as the environment and social welfare in its charts of behavior converted into income elasticities. The theory commonly estimates income elasticities by comparing the expenditures of people with varying incomes. In the case of environmental goods and services, as these are usually not priced in markets, people look at expenditures on things thought to be related to the environment, but these turn out to be things such as hiking equipment, travel to resorts, housing in nice areas, etc. Not surprisingly, these turn out to display very large income elasticities and conventional thinking makes the strong assumption that therefore, elasticities for the environmental services (clean air etc.) must also be large! The last assumptions seems to be unwarranted, or at a minimum, not demonstrated in any convincing way.

Instead, most environmental things (and reasons for doing something about them) involve losses, potential losses, or reductions of losses (more pollution, cleaning up pollution, preventing environmental health risks, etc.). And losses should be correctly assessed on the basis of what people need to be paid to accept them (willing to accept more pollution, and not to have pollution reduced, etc.). On the basis of this more direct and probably more correct measure, it is not at all clear that this would yield high income elasticities. It might be that the rich would demand more than the poor to put up with environmental degradation, but relative to their income, it is not certain that this would be the case that it leads to high income elasticities. And it is this that is the measure that guides policy. If this line of thinking is correct, the consequences for policies are significant especially when discussing the future of Asia. It transforms into repudiating the view that after becoming rich, people are willing to pay for reduction of pollution. The conventional view saying that the world cannot expect poorer countries to do something about the environment before they have reached a certain level of Gross Domestic Product per capita will be wrong. Maybe, after all, the poor Chinese peasants are as willing or even more willing than the rich Americans or Europeans to forego income gain to not see his/her environment being degraded.[10]

The necessity for adaptability becomes of critical importance in the years to come because the transition from a model based upon pure economies (money profits etc.) to a societal model incorporating social stability, use of resources, and non-material consumption ask for a transition not only in economic, but also in social terms. This poses problems for conventional economics in the sense that most of these investments run over a long time span of being profitable only after many years of and often providing benefit for society, which are not tangible.

Adaptability may compete with the other production factors as the determining factor in evaluating a society's future capability to deliver well-being for its citizens.

COMPETITION?

In 2006, the world's ten largest banks controlled 59 percent of global banking assets. This is an astounding figure by any account. Nevertheless, at the end of 2009, it has increased to 70 percent (Whitehouse, 2009). In March 2010, Colm Keller, co-head of Morgan Stanley's investment banking operations, went on record saying that "In the old days, before the financial crisis, there were 14 or 15 firms, now there are seven or eight. So perversely you've ended up with less competition" (Jenkins, 2010).

From 1965 to 2005, ownership of shares in the U.S. among households and institutions has almost reversed. In 1965, households owned 84 percent of all shares; in 2005, it was 33 percent. Institutions went up from 16 percent to 67 percent (Lawrence and Weber, 2008).

There is a lot of talk and a few examples can be mentioned about new enterprises entering the market, but the reality is that the large corporations sit on a war chest large enough to buy any enterprise threatening their position — and they do so. Fortune (2008) brought a list of the war chest among large ICT companies in the U.S.: Cisco US$26.2 billion, Apple US$25 billion, Microsoft US$23.6 billion, HP US$14.9 billion, Google US$14.4 billion, Oracle US$13 billion, Intel US$12.2 billion,

---

[10] I picked these thoughts up by listening to Professor Jack Knetsch, who has been so kind as to help me in formulating these two paragraphs.

IBM US$9.8 billion, Dell US$9 billion, and Motorola US$7.2 billion. Taken together, these ten companies had a cash pile of US$155.1 billion, equal to 1.2 percent of U.S. GDP or approximately 150 percent of Singapore's GDP. Since 2005, Oracle has spent US$41.8 billion buying 62 companies (Garner, 2010).

In the beginning of 2008, Microsoft was on the war path to buy Yahoo. Or so it looked, but Yahoo's largest investor, Capital Group's Capital Research Global Investors and Capital World Investors, managed 523.6 million shares of Microsoft compared with 154.8 million shares of Yahoo. T. Rowe Price, which ranks among Yahoo's top 10 investors, owned 136.5 million shares of Microsoft compared with 22.8 million shares of Yahoo. According to RiskMetrics, 90 percent of all Yahoo institutional investors also own shares in Microsoft. Of this group, 15 of the top 20 Yahoo institutional investors own more Microsoft than Yahoo.[11]

The Centre for Responsive Politics (2009) discloses that since 1989, the U.S. financial, insurance, and property sector have devoted more than US$2.3 billion to political parties and candidates. This is fully legal, provided that transparency is respected, partly telling why the figures are public. No other sector has gone close to such sums. Current lawmakers have collected US$661.6 million through appropriate channels. In addition, indirect sums channeled by the financial sector into influencing lawmakers through lobbying that since 1989 amounts to nothing less than US$3.8 billion. Through 2008 till November 2009, lobbying orchestrated by the financial sector can be calculated to US$803 million.

The plain fact is that since the Reagan–Thatcher era, the world has moved fast towards a corporate state of affairs with no genuine competition and the baton in the hands of a limited number of big companies.

GLOBAL ECONOMICS

We have a global economy, but no global economic policy. Looking at economic policies, it is clear that the game is about grapping employment and production from other countries, and not to control global demand and/or supply. In other words, we do see any attempts to move towards the general equilibrium, but a

---

[11] Source: http://www.zdnet.com.au/news/software/soa/Microsoft-shareholders-already-own-Yahoo/0,130061733,339286010,00.htm?omnRef=http://www.google.com/search?hl=en&rls=com.microsoft:en-us:IE-SearchBox&rlz=I7HPNW_en&ei=G95fS8OtIMqLkAXSuMj8Cw&sa=X&oi=spell&resnum=0&ct=result&cd=1&ved=0CAYQBSgA&q= shareholders%20microsoft%20yahoo&spell=1.

number of contradicting attempts often move towards partial equilibrium where a country has a balanced economy while others do not. The prime example is currency rate adjustment not doing much more than shuffling around with production and employment. Every country facing disequilibria tries to adjust by improving its economy, shifting the cost of rebalancing to other countries. The debate about the Yuan illustrates this. The problem is not the currency rate, but the overconsumption in the U.S. If the U.S. succeeded in forcing China to revalue the Yuan, the Chinese surplus on balance of payment would probably fall, but the U.S. deficit might not, and it would merely be shifted to other countries replacing China as main supplier to the U.S.

Unfortunately, in the era of the global economy, most if not all economic policies are still national economic polices, not taking into account the repercussion on other counteries, thus actually playing a musical chairs game about who is going to end up with the disequilibrium.

The global trade system seems to face two serious problems by this state of affairs. With no coordination of economic policies, stimulatory measures spill over in non-commensurate ways on production and employment among the various countries. Country A may stimulate more than country B, but does not reap the expected benefit because some of the demand leads to higher imports from country B.

The lesson is quite simple: the world cannot run primarily national economic policies while at the same time maintain a liberal trade system. Either the free trade system starts to crack because the countries losing employment carry out protectionist measures or a much better coordination ensuring equitable distribution of benefits among the stimulating countries is put in place.[12]

Furthermore, the coming era of scarcities finds the trade system unprepared for a new kind of trade policy in the form of export restrictions and/or export duties. The countries finding themselves in the enviable position of exporting scarce commodities will be tempted to tax the export, thus improving their terms of trade. Recently, there were rumors about a higher tax on mineral extraction in Australia, which amounts to the same.

The political system is asymmetrical perceived in the sense that people hurt by economic policy measures are, far from it, those who vote for the government introducing these measures. The U.S.-initiated recession hit millions around the

---

[12] I picked up this observation in a more elaborate way when listening to Razeen Sally.

globe left without any possibility of political feedback except directed at their own — innocent — politicians. This means that there may be transparency, but neither accountability nor legitimacy.

CONCLUSION

The market economy has not existed over the last few decades, but in many respects, the economy has been run as if it did — with disastrous results.

There is little chance to resurrect a genuine market economy. How can it be done with the mastodons we have built up?

Therefore, a move towards a kind of regulatory economy is likely, whose main task will be to tackle the problem that supply cannot keep up with demand for food, commodities, energy, water, and the environment. Recent price increases in various indexes indicate that we are in the first phase of this new kind of economics. The policy task will be the distribution of scarce goods and burden sharing perceived as smaller increases in wealth measured by traditional yardsticks. People normally measure increase in wealth by comparing with what they used to get. This opens the door to much more attention to find out how people react by NOT getting what they want or having to give up what they already have — all points not genuinely explored by economics.

If the task is left to the market mechanism, inequalities inside and among nation-states will continue to grow with predictable social instability and upheavals. Indeed, one may say that the rising inequality seen recently may be due to this mechanism working in economies still controlled by rules applicable for the market economy.

The logic points towards a distribution theory shifting from the individual and breaking from Adam Smith's dictum that "pursuance by the individual for wealth coalesced into higher wealth for society as a whole because society's wealth is the accumulation of individual's wealth". Instead, it may be other way around. The remuneration for the individual becomes a function of how much he/she contributes to the group they belong to, anchored in common and shared values. The closer the group is, the more likely it is that knowledge is shared and thus the higher is the output. A high willingness and ability to share enhances what we may term social productivity of the individual, even if personal productivity may be low. Productivity may increasingly be measured not traditionally, but against how much production the group and/or the individual can squeeze out of one unit of commodities (ecological productivity).

Taken together, groups that succeed in social productivity and ecological productivity will prosper and individuals good at contributing and sharing will be the most valuable group members, thus reaping the highest remuneration.

REFERENCES

Adema, W and M Ladaique (2009). How expensive is the welfare state. OECD, Paris.

Arrow, K (1974). Gifts and exchanges. *Philosophy and Public Affairs*, 1(4), 357.

Brown, D and L Santos (2009). http://www.project-syndicate.org/commentary/shiller66/ English.

Centre for responsive politics (2009). Crossing Wall Street. https://opensecrets.org/news/2009/11/crossing-wall-street-1.html, 16 November.

Fortune (2008). Fat wallets, 10 November.

Garner, R (2010). Oracle's sales forecast signals economic upturn. Bloomberg, http://www.bloomberg.com/apps/news?pid=20601204&sid=adaRUjtGcN8A, 26 March.

Goldin, C and LF Katz (2008). The race between education and technology. Cambridge, Massachusetts: Belknap Press.

Hacker, JS (2002). *The divided welfare state.* Cambridge: Cambridge University Press.

Jenkins, P (2010). Outsized risk and regulation inhibit entrants. Financial Times, http://www.ft.com/cms/s/0/7b7190c4-36ab-11df-b810-00144feabdc0.html, 24 March.

Lawrence, AT and J Weber (2008). *Business and Society*, 12th edn. New York: McGraw-Irwin.

Lundvall, B-Å (2008). The Danish model and the globalizing learning economy — Lessons for developing countries. First draft for the Wider-project, http://www.business.aau.dk/ike/upcoming/Danish_model_balrev.pdf, January.

McKinsey (2009). The economic impact of the achievement gap in American schools, summary of findings, http://mckinsey.com/clientservice/socialsector/achievement_gap_report.pdf, April. McKinsey Quarterly, Newsletter. The economic cost of the U.S. education gap. July 2009.

Newman, P and J Kenwork (1999). *Sustainability and cities — overcoming automobile dependence.* Washington DC: Island Press.

Research EU (2008). Special Issue November 2008, http://ec.europa.eu/research/research-eu/ani-mality/article_animality 26_en.html.

Savage, LJ (1954). *The foundations of statistics.* New York: Wiley.

Spoehr, J, L Wilson, K Barnett, T Toth and A Watson-Tran (2007). Measuring social inclusion and exclusion in Northern Adelaide. A Report for the Department of Health, The University of Adelaide. http://72.14.235.132/search?q=cache:24ogC2ynWBoJ:www.sapo.org.au/binary/ binary6522/Social.pdf+Measuring+Social+Inclusion+And+Exclusion+In+Northern+Adelaide&hl=en&ct=clnk&cd=2, February.

Whitehouse, M (2009). Economic crisis ebbs, systemic risks don't. Wall Street Journal. http://online.wsj.com/article/SB126014826015979385.html, 7 December.

Part II
Scarcities — New Economic
Thinking

Introduction to Part II

Traditional economics see the way out of the global recession through stimulating consumption in emerging economies in particular China, India, Indonesia, and Brazil. If so, the world is heading for a catastrophe. In the very short term, economic activity may go up and soothe somewhat the economic pain, but in the longer term the drain on resources will initiate an economic explosion and social implosion. There is, simply speaking, not enough resources to transfer mass consumption as a model for say 500 million people to one or two billions.

The counter–argument is that we have heard this before. Thomas Malthus 200 years and the Club of Rome 40 years ago. There are two differences that make reference to these — wrong — predictions irrelevant.

Firstly, they looked upon one or two sectors only. Malthus — food production. The Club of Rome — primarily energy. Secondly, they did not foresee the colossal jump ahead in technology and as far as Malthus is concerned, the opening up of new continents. Now we face scarcities in five sectors — food, commodities, energy, water, and clean environment. Even if contested by some, global warming is here, and there is close to unanimity that it is manmade. Price increases over the last decade are an incontestable barometer. Prices cannot go up, especially not during an economic recession unless scarcity is driving them. New technology cannot be ruled out and to a certain degree it will happen, but the world is far away from breakthroughs like electricity, new means of transport, and synthetic materials that we saw a little more than 100 years ago. The last real breakthrough changing daily life for mankind may be the Internet, although a large number of incremental improvements built on that platform have been seen. There does not seem to be a genuine new technology changing our use of or access to resources in the pipeline. Even if there were, it takes time to work through the system as it requires investment and adaptation of economic paradigms accompanied by a new mindset.

There is no golden escape hatch letting us off the hook. On the contrary, mankind has to tackle the issues and get through by adopting another economic model, another way of producing, another consumption pattern, and accept whatever that means for economic behaviour.

Whole panoply of measures needs to be mobilized, but in the first round, the price mechanism must be brought into play. This is already happening with commodity prices changing relative factor prices and influencing the behaviour of the consumer.

Two sacred cows are heading for the slaughterhouse: relative factor prices ruled by high wage rates and low commodity prices and, a tax system based on income instead of use of total resources.

Saving resources requires more manpower in the production process and a shift in innovation to that effect. This will only happen if the relative factor prices reflect that this is what we want through a price structure that rewards less use of resources plus more use of manpower and that penalizes use of resource and labour-intensive production. It is already happening. Comparing wage rates primarily in industrial-ized countries to commodities, the shift is underway — it is not so certain in many developing countries and emerging economies where the economic conditions are somewhat different. In fact, there may in many of these countries be a good case for higher wage rate to stimulate the economy and move toward a more equal income & wealth distribution.

Policy makers should reinforce that trend. The counter–argument is that interfer-ence in wage settlements is not good for the economy as the wage rate is set by parameters such as marginal productivity and marginal utility of labour. This is, however, not correct. The wage rate has for many decades been set through a mixture of policies going beyond economics to areas such as, politics, strength of unions, and preferred income distribution. The last one — income distribution — may be the most important one. If left to the market forces alone, the wage rate in industrialized countries would certainly have been different from what we have seen.

Therefore, it will not be a new phenomenon to see interferences in the way the wage rate is set. The political problem is that a lower wage rate will unavoidably have consequences for income distribution, which in most countries will not be welcomed. With an already high inequality, the risk of causing more inequality does not appeal to many. To prevent this, a whole string of policy measures to maintain income distribution at the preferred level should be brought into play.

One of them is the tax system. The income tax belonged to the industrial society where wealth was measured according to how much a country could produce and generate income from production. The higher the production, the more the wealth and income generated, so it was easy to adopt income tax as the answer to the question of how to finance the development of society.

However, in a system where there are scarcities, it is more sophisticated. Production in the physical and material sense is not welcome as it depletes resources, making the country poorer.

This makes a tax on total use of resources attractive as a brake on the use of resource and a factor in changing behavioural patterns. There are definitely difficulties of a technical nature, but economics through input-output tables and national accounting has a basis to move toward such a tax system. The road has already been opened by levies on use of water, energy, and several other goods and services — sometimes known as green levies to make them more palatable for the voters. They are, however, linked to improving the environment and see saving of resources as an instrument to do that. On the other hand, a general tax on the use of resources aims primarily to save resources and as a side-effect improves the environment — we change the order of policy objectives and policy instruments.

These will be some of the most important elements to be borrowed from the economic toolbox that we know of today that can launch a drive toward a society of no waste. Unquestionably, that can launch new economic instruments will be invented along the way.

Both domestically and internationally, burden–sharing will constitute the main problem.

Internationally, the main task will be a deal between the industrialized countries and the developing countries plus the emerging economies. The first group favours the argument that the rise in use of resources is due to rapid growth among countries in the second group who take the view that this may be correct, but the high level for current use of resources is due to the irresponsible behaviour of industrialized countries in the past.

The way out of this is to shift the burden to the consumer who is ultimately responsible for use of resources irrespective of where production takes place. It is a nonstarter to postulate that because production shifts from the U.S. to China to be sold anyway to an American consumer in Walmart, China has to bear a larger burden. A kind of global-polluter-pays principle converted to resource-use global-tax system will eventually be adopted.

Key Events Driving the Future of Chinese Economy*

Chinese economy is not export oriented. Its growth is a consequence of public investment — for example in research and development. China has no debts like Western countries; portable communication and a less materialistic consumption will cause more growth. This will open the door for a new style economics not counting upon mass consumption. The author reflects this scenario of economical growth considering Chinese values and culture.

The wonder story about the Chinese economy is well known. For the last three decades annual growth has rarely been below 10 percent. China has become the place for global manufacturing driven by labour intensive and low cost manufacturing sectors. It is often heard that Chinese growth is export oriented, but that is in fact not true. Composition of growth over the last decade gives average net export about 20 percent. By far the most important element is public (not private) consumption and investment.

Now China is heading into the middle income trap with a national income of about USD 4.000 per capita. Experience indicates that the large majority of countries moving into that bracket do not manage to move on, but find themselves trapped. On one hand wage costs make labour intensive manufacturing too expensive. On the other hand there are not sufficient skills to adopt technology, quality, and service as competitive parameters. Lost manufacturing is not replaced by goods and services higher up the value added ladder.

The question is whether China will make it? If yes continued globalization looks likely as Chinese growth will boost the global economy. If no the threat of protectionism and a gradual break-down of the existing global system looks like a genuine risk.

Before analyzing China's prospect let us look at the three most important elements shaping future global economics.

---

* First appeared in *Swissfuture* 02/12.

The rich countries have run up a historically *high debt* that must be repaid. Many people do not fully understand that debt means that we have encroached into future consumption with the inevitable result that future consumption must be "lower" corresponding to how past consumption was "too high". The outcome is lower growth among the established and debt ridden countries, in this order: the U.S., Japan, and the E.U.

It happens at the same time as the global economy is going through a transition from the industrial age spanning over more than two hundred years character-ized by mass consumption framed by easy access to all kinds of commodities and raw material to a low price. Ruthless exploitation followed. Material consump-tion was the key word. Now we move into an era where mass consumption is replaced by mass communication and the era of plenty gives way to the era of scarcities.

Portable communication makes it possible to communicate with anybody, any-where, anytime about anything. China and India have each close to one billion subscribers to mobile phones. China has close to 500 million people with access to the Internet. This will without doubt change our lifestyle, consumption pattern, and behavioural attitudes. In an economic and technological context numbers create.[1]

Productivity will rise as knowledge becomes the most important production factor, but only if societal structure allows, yes, encourages people to share knowledge. Knowledge is worth nothing if kept "secret" by persons; they must communicate with other persons to reap the benefits, thus societal structure is imperative.

Even more important may be the enormous data stored and exchanged not among human beings, but among "machines". IBM's Chairman Samuel J. Palmisano offers these observations:

> We have a trillion interconnected and intelligent objects and organisms — the Internet of Things. — One billion transistors for every human being on the plane. — Intelligence now embedded in the systems that enable services to be delivered. — Physical goods to be made and sold. — All of this is generating vast stores of information. — Estimated that there will be 44 times as much data generated over the next decade, reaching 35 zettabytes (a 1 followed by 21 zeros) in 2020. — Advanced computation and analytics makes sense

---

[1] The British Admiral Nelson coined the words "numbers annihiate" for military doctrine — the exact opposite.

of that data in something like real time. This enables very different kinds of insight, foresight and decision making.

The winners will be those who master the skills of managing these big data, build systems that make them useful and manageable for corporations and organizations. Big data will empower the economic system and change rules for competition to an extent not seen since the industrial revolution.

Scarcities of food, commodities, energy, water, and clean environment change the paradigm for economic activities. Distribution of benefits pursued over two hundred years will be replaced by burden sharing. As for mass communication and sharing of knowledge, burden sharing works only if people get together in groups and communities anchored in shared and common values. Otherwise people fear that others will wriggle out of burden sharing so why should they weigh in. The political systems have not realized this; the economic models put forward as instruments to solve global economic problems are still driving in the lane of growth and distribution of benefits while in fact the challenges are quite different.

Production processes change because productivity ceases to be a question of producing more per man-hour instead being how to squeeze more output out of one unit of resources. A completely different ball game. Hitherto innovation has focused upon saving labour classified as the scarce production factor. In the future the focus will be upon savings resources. The whole thinking behind research, development, technology, and innovation is reshuffled.

Consumption shifts toward less materialistic because resources will be more expensive. One element is durability of consumer goods where the well known recipe of short term use cannot any longer be applied. The same hardware will stay with us for longer time may be combined with possibilities for substituting the software keeping the performance of the durable consumer goods up to standard.

Taken together these elements form the basis for future global economics. Tomorrow's winner will be the countries — or corporations — understanding this and drawing the consequences. The key is the ability to form groups and communities where people pursue analogous goals on the basis of common and shared values. It constitutes a complete break with the industrial age where the wealth of society as defined by Adam Smith was the accumulation of individual wealth.

China is still far behind the U.S., Europe, and Japan (G-3) with regard to income per capita, but the Chinese leadership seems to be much more aware of these threats than the U.S. and Japan while the Europeans despite all the current problems look to be someway in between.

China's economy has been well managed with a fairly low debt ratio to Gross Domestic Product (GDP) and low deficits on the government budget. Interestingly the Chinese government stimulated the economy in 2007/2008, but kept the brakes on in 2011 to guard against overheating and bubbles. There are uncertainties about debt for local and regional communities, but as far as can be judged by available data China is far from debt ratios comparable to the G-3 providing more room of manoeuvre for channelling funds into projects for the future.

The Chinese leadership is beefing up R&D (Research & Development) expenditure very fast. It is, however, not a foregone conclusion that this will give the expected results as the jury is still out whether societal structure will facilitate transformation of breakthrough in technology into new products. The Chinese attitude toward use of the Internet looks incompatible with efforts to turning mass communication into an asset for the economy. Statistical evidence tells that Japan is the top R&D spender compared to GDP. The number of Japanese researchers is very high. Until 2011 Japan filed the largest number of patents in the world. But, and this is a crucial but, actually very few NEW products have come out of Japan not only questioning the societal profitability of this investment, but telling that societal structure may be more important than money invested in R&D.

There is legitimate doubt whether China will be able and willing to build institutions opening the door for innovation and creativity. Many Western observers see democracy as a political system and market economy as economic model linked together as indispensable conditions for moving into the stage of an innovate economy. This verdict rests upon the observation that all innovative countries run such "twin systems", but it is not the same as concluding that it can not be done applying a different formula. China is as far as can be seen searching for such a formula. The worry is what happens to China and the global economy if it is not found, while China's political leaders continue to be unwilling to shift tack.

China is a heavy polluter not the least because approx. 70 percent of the country's energy comes from coal with no prospect for a tangible reduction. This is the bad news.

The good news is that the Chinese leadership is aware of the dangers embedded in pollution and further degradation of the environment for economic growth and social stability. The World Bank has calculated that approximately half of China's growth needs to be channelled back to redress distortions and harmful effects in the slipstream of growth.

Before meetings of the National People's Congress in 2011 and in 2012, Prime Minster Wen Jiabao stressed that economic growth was not an end in itself and focus should increasingly be switched to qualitative economic growth. There are indications of ambitions to create 30 million new jobs over the next decade in what is termed sustainable jobs.

Many observers question whether China actually means it when talking about qualitative growth and if the leadership does whether it can be implemented in view of opposition from regions, local communities and state owned enterprises all of whom see their legitimacy through the lens of delivering growth and higher material welfare to the people. This is indeed a valid argument — highlighting again societal structure. The counterargument is that China like the rest of Asia adopted Western values and in particular mass consumption to catch up with the West at a time when the Western model (Washington consensus) model stood undisputed and unchallenged as THE model for economic development. Now when it is discredited through the global financial crisis and the subsequent recession it does not look so attractive anymore.

This opens the window for China, the rest of Asia and other emerging economies to ask whether the time has come to switch to another model and the sentiment is gradually pointing to yes as the answer. If so the next question is what will form the basis for such a model?

Working on the assumption that mass communication and burden sharing push people to work in groups to produce less material wealth it is natural to investigate how Asia stands if indeed economics and societal structure swing toward values instead of money.

"BOTH" INSTEAD OF "EITHER-OR"

The Asian concept of yin yang reflects that contrary forces are interconnected and interrelated and one of them may give rise to another one. They cannot be separated. In this context the point is that Asian values are much more "both" instead of "either-or" as in the Western world.

Asian way of thinking is more syncretism than Western thinking trying to reconcile various lines of thought into one line of thinking avoiding to choose which one is the right one instead amalgamating various elements. A Western court of Justice will almost always rule that one of the parties are right and the other one wrong, while in Asia it is more likely that a court of justice will weigh arguments against each other finding a sort of compromise giving each party "something" — syncretism and yin yang applied in practice.

The traditional Asian religions and philosophies gives the same story painting a much more complex picture of the relationship between man and nature then what appears in the Abrahamic religions with God nominating man as the custodian of nature thus removing philosophical inhibitions for abuse and exploitation of nature.

Asia was for many centuries dominated by rule by man, which means that societal norms were respected. In such a society there is no need for rule of law as everybody follows established norms and values. The law applied primarily to individuals outside society who could not be expected to know and understand the common values.

LESS INDIVIDUALISM, MORE COLLECTIVISM

Thus there is a firm basis in Asia for switching to an economic values based on groups and communities pursuing less materialistic welfare instead of individualism, profits, and mass consumption.

It is not the same as saying that this will happen. We do not know. But we do know that the existing model has run its course and must be replaced by something else focusing upon saving resources. An economic model doing this may come out of Asia under pressure from high and rising populations, scarcities, and drive for economic growth.

Saving Resources with a Tax on their Total Use*

The gloom about a potential global recession has opened the door for a cascade of recommendations to stimulate private consumption. An almost unanimous chorus advocates transfer of the Western mass consumption model to Asia - overlooking the fact that if their advice is heeded, the global economy will implode under the weight of resource demand.

We are running out of resources (commodities, raw materials, food and water), making the longer-term economic outlook uncertain at best. Physical shortages are obvious for several resources — as we saw with rare earths, indispensable in the making of, *inter alia*, cell phones. Economic shortages push prices up, opening the door to supply-side inflation even under a low-growth scenario.

A higher gross domestic product is synonymous with higher production and a wealthier society because there are more goods and services. But this is a short-term view, not taking into account, even neglecting, the fundamental observation that a higher GDP signifies more use of limited resources. Societies become poorer in the longer term by depleting limited resources.

A society's wealth depends on the ability to save resources while maintaining or even increasing production. The more output a society can squeeze out of one unit of resource, the wealthier it becomes in the longer run.

Higher commodity prices must be allowed to change relative factor prices, making labour less expensive and resources more expensive. There are too many examples of countries resisting this by subsidising commodity prices. In fact, we need exactly the opposite.

The change in relative factor prices needs help to get underway. The way to do it would be to revamp the tax system, replacing income tax with a tax on total use of resources. Arguments and protests will mushroom, but this was also the case when the income tax and the sales tax were introduced.

---

* First appeared in *Business Times*, 9 December 2011.

Politically, a tax on total use of resources can be made progressive with a rising scale depending on resource use. It can be geared to influence the production processes applying different tax rates on various resources.

Economically, it would not be too difficult to measure total use of resources for a product. Economics already has a tool in the input-output tables disclosing where the input to make a product comes from. It may need some fine-tuning, but could be adapted to serve as basis for such a tax.

In a global context, the tax would facilitate negotiations about climate change and make burden sharing easier as it would end nations negotiating with other nations on this issue. Instead, the burden would be passed to the consumer who ultimately is responsible for emissions of carbon dioxide. Assuming that the tax takes the form of a levy, working more or less like a general sales tax, it would introduce the "polluter pays" principle on a global scale.

Now it is impossible to cut through the heated political arguments because the issue very soon boils down to which countries are going to pay more and which countries to pay less. A shift in location of production (outsourcing) from the United States to China means that China is being penalised even if global emission of carbon dioxide is the same.

Such a system is doomed to fail. Efforts to reduce global emissions of carbon dioxide should be neutral *vis-a-vis* localisation of production and consumption. A tax on total use of resources would meet that requirement.

If production is moved from the U.S. to China, total use of resources might change a bit because production processes in the two counters differ somewhat, but not fundamentally. Consumption and, consequently, total use of resources will not change though.

Efforts to push consumers to use fewer resources might not stop with a tax, but it surely is the most effective way of getting there. Mandatory labelling might be envisaged to disclose resources used in the total production process, supplementing existing labelling about ingredients.

Producers would undoubtedly argue that it might not be possible or difficult to do this, but there seems very little evidence for repudiating the idea on such grounds.

If we know how the end product is made, we also know the inputs and it should be possible to turn that into some kind of common measurement for use of total resources.

We might go one step further. As at now, many consumer products are produced deliberately to last a limited amount of time. Technological obsolescence is often given as a reason, but that does not sound convincing.

It is much more likely that the business sector wants to boost revenue by forcing the consumer to buy a new product even if the one we have is still useful.

A tax system as proposed could reward products with a longer life span and punish products with a shorter one. It could be done by stipulating that a product with a guaranteed lifetime would be taxed less than a product with a shorter life span.

Just look at the market for many electronic products (cell phones, for example) or washing machines, dryers, fridges etc. It seems evident that most of these machines could easily last longer than they actually do.

The argument is sometimes put forward that the new model saves energy, but just keep in mind how many resources were used to produce the new model - it far outweighs the savings on the energy bill.

Want a Way Out of the Recession?
Create Jobs by Saving Resources*

The outlook for the global economy crystallises around two trends: lower growth and quality growth. The trend growth of the U.S., the Euro-zone and Japan (the G-3) shifts downwards and is estimated to fluctuate around 2 percent, perhaps a little bit more, with luck.

It is highly unlikely that U.S. annual growth will get back to the 3–4 percent levels of preceding decades. Job creation in the tradeable sector, which finances the rest of the U.S., was dismal over the two previous decades and nothing points to a turnaround. Productivity seems set to fall from the earlier annual trend of around 2.5 percent to 1.5 percent. The cost of welfare, health and similar services are bound by demography to rise faster than gross development product (GDP) this year.

Almost every day, the forecasts for public debt worsen — with current prognosis revealing public debt crossing 100 percent of GDP a couple of years before expected. Net interest payments account for 1.4 percent of GDP currently and run to 3.4 percent in 2020 — and that on overly optimistic assumptions.

The Euro-zone is fighting its own battle to solve a sovereign debt crisis and even if forecasts for the strongest economy, Germany, are rosy with more than 3 percent growth for 2011, the other member states lag behind.

Europe's demography is worse than America's — although better than Japan's. However, Europe's population outlook is not good enough to form a stable basis for growth much above 2 percent.

Japan is unlikely to get out of low growth shackling the country over the last 20 years. Demography and debt have locked the country into a path of close to zero growth even if the statistics may show ups and downs. The country has never really got out of the bind imposed upon it by the financial crisis more than 20 years ago.

---

*First appeared in *Business Times*, 29 June 2011.

ENORMOUS SOCIETAL COST

Consequently, employment cannot rely upon growth to get out of the doldrums. To catch the wind, policymakers must understand how quality growth driven by the environment and rising commodity prices influences employment.

In some countries, almost half of economic growth has to be channelled back to address environmental deterioration generated by the conventional growth process. The societal cost is enormous.

First, a lower quality of life combined with health problems reduces productivity, which points to a future lower growth path.

Second, an enormous opportunity cost hollows out the economy as it is more expensive to restore the environment than to prevent its degradation in the first place by incorporating parameters to prevent external diseconomies.

Rising commodity prices reinforce these negative effects. Many large multinational companies report how commodity prices depress their operations. Swiss giant Nestle, the world's largest food company, stated a few weeks ago that higher raw-material costs will weigh on first-half profitability.

The way ahead is to cut down on use of raw materials by understanding what productivity means nowadays. In the industrial age, it was about production per man hour: how much more could one worker produce. In the new age of scarcities, it becomes a question of how much more output can be squeezed out of one unit of input.

COHERENT POLICY FRAMEWORK

Such an approach will reduce waste and thereby may help improve the environment and contain global warming. Tomorrow's winners — countries, regions, megacities and corporations — will be those knowing how to do that and use it as a competitive parameter.

Therefore, these two trends — lower growth and quality growth — do in fact support each other and promise synergies if put together in a coherent policy framework.

So far policymakers have detected very little of this on their radar screens — which are still in search of conventional growth. The debate in the U.S. is all about whether the economic stimulus was strong enough or whether the second round of qualitative easing (QE2) should be followed up by a QE3 — how to produce more without questioning the underlying trend shift.

The failure of these policies over the last couple of years certainly indicates that such an approach won't do. Jobs are not coming back. We cannot put the clock back and reinvent the economy as it used to be. Established economic theory and conventional economic policies do not work anymore.

The core is high labour costs with low prices on protecting the environment and saving resources. This reflects a perception of scarce labour and abundant resources.

The result is efforts to save labour (increase conventional productivity) and hold the floodgates open for use of resources. And it worked; that's why unemployment refuses to fall — we are successful in our endeavours to reduce labour per unit of output.

On top of that, current wage levels make it cost-effective to invest in emerging economies. Resources are still priced in as a plentiful factor irrespective of recent hikes in commodity prices telling a different story.

The price mechanism does not punish, as it should, using more resources than necessary per unit of output. Despite various financial incentives, it is cheap to pollute; consequently, waste flows into the environment. The combined result is unemployment, resource waste and deterioration of the environment. Getting back to high growth patterns does not alter this equation.

The new paradigm calls for exactly the opposite. Rising scarcities of commodities make it profitable to cut down on use of resources in the production process. Abundance of labour — yes, labour is abundant; just look at the number of people in the age bracket 19–65 years — calls for more use of manpower.

The key is to face the music and start the politically agonising, economically necessary and ecologically imperative process of changing relative factor prices. Labour costs (wages) must fall relative to commodity prices — otherwise it won't happen and we will stay where we are right now, like it or not.

A look at commodity price indices and political support for the environment shows this is already happening in the real world. The main problem is that current policies are holding back (or preventing outright) changes in the production process and a new consumption pattern favouring goods and services gobbling up fewer resources over their lifetime.

The reasons are that an adjustment of relative factor prices to the disadvantage of labour is regarded as politically unpalatable. But in the long run, it may be even more unpalatable to confine millions of people to unemployment, while at the same time aggravating global warming, polluting the environment uncritically, and wasting resources. We should stop digging, as we already are in a deep hole.

The Era of Scarcities*

The world is experiencing a seminal shift, the kind that comes every couple of centuries and fundamentally changes the way we think and act. The business world is undergoing tremendous upheavals. The economic model created and perfected by thinkers and economists from Adam Smith to Paul Krugman is fading away almost as fast as the polar icecaps.

The existing model — let us call it American Style Capitalism — catapulted the world into the industrial era, phenomenally improving the standard of living globally and lifting billions out of poverty. Unsurprisingly, we forget that this model was tailored to the circumstances 200 years ago: the opening up of North America, Latin America, Africa and large parts of Asia, an unparalleled evolution in transport combined with formerly unthinkable technological breakthroughs and a new mindset focusing on business and economics.

To this should be added the easy access to the raw materials used in industrial production. The whole structure was founded on cheap commodity prices. We could and did produce without considering the possible impact on our future supply of raw materials. Why bother? The world is infinitely abundant. Just go West, young man and you shall find.

We now realise the error of this philosophy. Suddenly, we are standing on the brink of an abyss, coming to grips with a harsh reality. There is not enough of everything. Raw materials are increasingly scarce. Global warming and climate change top the global agenda. Whole nations like the Maldives risk literally going under. Millions and millions of people living in coastal communities risk displacement — just look at Bangladesh, Indonesia, Thailand and Vietnam to feel a shiver.

HOW DO WE COPE WITH THIS CHALLENGE?

The great British historian and philosopher Arnold Toynbee coined the phrase 'response to challenge'. Only when confronted with circumstances threatening survival do civilizations respond by generating new technology or societal models.

---

* First appeared in *Copenhagen Cleantech Journal*, June 2011.

Some say the European age began about 500 years ago in response to the challenge posed by the closing of the Silk Road, the traditional trade route to Asia through the Asian heartland. This forced the Europeans to take to the sea if they still wanted their precious spices.

In his brilliant book, Collapse, Jareed Diamod describes how civilizations fully aware of the environmental dangers threatening their survival refused to respond and consequently perished, for example the Norse settlements in Greenland.

We are still in control of our own destiny. We can respond as the Europeans did 500 years ago or we can close our eyes and perish as the Norsemen in Greenland did.

The choice is ours. Let us look at the challenges before we look at responses.

Food Scarcity

The FAO reports that 40 countries already face food shortages. Just to maintain the status quo for nourishment, world food production must increase by 40 percent by 2040 and 70 percent by 2070. Robert Zoellick, President of the World Bank, repeatedly asserts the urgent need to tackle the food problem. Even optimistic forecasts project a sweeping decrease in agricultural production that will affect South Asia, most of Southeast Asia, parts of China, the Middle East, Africa, except for Egypt, the southern USA and Mexico plus Latin America, with the exception of Argentina — areas covering three quarters of the world population.

The commodity price index conveys an equally gloomy picture. For years remaining constant, it is now sharply rising, more than tripling since the turn of the millennium.

Energy Looks the Same

Assuming global growth in the coming decades, a steep rise in energy consumption, primarily in Asia, will translate into higher energy prices. There is much talk about renewable energy, but the truth is that coal is predicted to substitute for oil in the wake of almost inevitably increasing oil prices. Thus fossil fuels will continue degrading the environment, fuelling not only growth but also climate change.

Water is a real horror story. Physical or economic water shortages are affecting about half the world population in the Southern USA, Mexico, Africa, the Middle East, South Asia and Northern China.

A Clean Environment is the Fifth Scarcity

The World Bank has calculated that half of China's economic growth needs to be checked to address the problems engendered by that growth. This makes net growth only half the amount that we read about in the papers. These five scarcities are interlinked. To grow more food, we need more water, which is already scarce. Desalination is a solution, but that requires more energy — already scarce. To generate more energy, we have to use more fossil fuels, especially coal, one of the few non-scarce resources (75 percent of China's energy comes from coal), but that impacts the environment and precipitates climate change.

We need to change our way of thinking, make reducing our resource consumption a far higher priority. To achieve this, we need a new economic and societal model that lets us leave the era of plenty behind and enter the era of scarcity.

To manage this turnaround, we have to go beyond economics and technology. Cleantech is a commendable and imperative solution, but a true change in the composition of energy sources will require a far more determined effort. Look at China. It wants to increase the share of renewable energy from 7.5 percent of primary energy consumption in 2005 to 15 percent in 2020 — a period of 15 years to achieve a relatively modest increase of 7.5 percentage points. Already now, China is devoting USD 35 billion annually to clean energy, a figure almost double that of the USA and larger than the total EU expenditure.

A wide range of measures are being deployed. Grid power companies are required to buy power produced by renewable energy generators. Grid companies attain tax benefits for using renewable energy. A set of preferential prices is taking effect. R&D subsidies are being granted for various new technologies like wind power and solar photovoltaics (PV). Households in western China receive subsidies for using renewable energy. These are only examples, but illustrate the vast panoply of measures that we need to marshal in an effort to impel a visible change towards a sustainable energy supply. The Chinese example underscores how the world must change its economic paradigm and, even more so, its societal structure to tackle the era of scarcities.

Established economic theory operates with productivity as production per man hour. In the future productivity should be defined as the maximum output per unit of input. The equation must include the entire lifecycle of a product. Most of us feel good when buying a new fridge with a label declaring that it is more, say 15 percent, energy-efficient. We fail to consider the fact that manufacturing that fridge required resources that effectively negate the advertised energy savings. Many products, mobile phones for example, are "programmed" to last for a limited time because they become technologically obsolete long before they physically break down.

Established consumption theory operates with increased consumption as a function of economic growth. We materialistically focus on gobbling up resources regardless of mounting scarcities. Our future consumption must be less materialistic and more founded on the results of recent economic studies that tell us people's well-being — let us call it happiness — depends more on what we do for others than money. Today, newspapers carry advertisement after advertisement encouraging us to buy new products and more of them. Some decades from now, whatever media we are using will tell us to buy less, go for durability and find satisfaction somewhere beyond the material.

Can It Be Done?

We do not know. What we do know is that the current economic model and societal system venerating material consumption and resource exploitation are simply unsustainable. We must conceive a new model and start to work on its premise.

Asia Redraws the Map of Progress*

Balance of economic, if not political, power is shifting from West to East. A diplomat and scholar argues that, if Asia is to rise to the challenges that this power shift will bring, it must not emulate the more destructive, materialistic values of industrialized society.

Over the last 30 years, unique opportunities for high and persistent economic growth have blessed Asia, and policy makers grabbed them with both hands. Global growth was high, commodity prices were low, and a growing labor force turned China into the world's top manufacturer. Meanwhile, there was not much pressure to heed environmental warnings. The policy challenge for Asia's political leaders was primarily to manage economic growth.

All that is changing. Global growth is slowing, commodity prices are expected to continue rising, and oil supplies are declining. Alternative energy sources are available — but for a price. Starting in 2015, the labor force will shrink in China while it continues to rise in South Asia. Environmental problems demand far more resources, and the United States can no longer be counted on as a stabilizing power. Indeed, there is a risk of Chinese-American tensions catapulting the Pacific trade and growth engine into trouble. So creating the conditions for economic growth becomes a policy challenge — and it's a whole new situation.

Asia cannot do without economic growth. Over the preceding decades, a large part of the population has become accustomed to an almost permanently rising living standard, considered to be a kind of prescriptive right. Many political regimes find that their legitimacy in the eyes of their people depends on constantly rising prosperity. But the demographic composition is changing, with more elderly people calling for more welfare, more pensions, and better health care. Large infrastructure investments are necessary, not the least in South Asia, which is destined to take over from China as the next home of low-cost, labor-intensive manufacturing. Meanwhile, investment in research and technology is becoming more costly as Asia moves from catching up with the West to searching for new breakthroughs — a more laborious and costly exercise than simply improving existing technology.

---

* First appeared in *The Futurist*, September–October 2010.

The weaker fundamentals will force Asia to find a growth pattern other than the mass consumption of America and Europe, which, if pursued successfully, would result in an implosion of Asian societies as natural resources become unavailable. Mass consumption for a couple of hundred million people in the West cannot with a stroke be extended to between 1 and 2 billion people. Something has to give, and that something is the perception of economic growth, which makes people feel that their living standard is improving.

For the last 200 years, the world has lived and lived well with what may be termed American-style capitalism, which hit full throttle in the twentieth century. It was a combination of economic and political elements that fit admirably well together. Adam Smith's dictum that the pursuit of wealth by individuals coalesced into higher wealth for society as a whole, because society's wealth is the accumulation of individuals' wealth, proved largely correct.

Easy access to natural resources gave the impression that they were unlimited. Transport opened up for new markets, giving access to raw materials hitherto out of reach. Technology improved productivity, keeping inflation in check. Population growth boosted the economy. The nation-state served as the political framework and mechanism for distribution and as the administrative infrastructure for industrial growth.

Asia accepted this worldview at the peak of its ascendancy during the second half of the twentieth century. The rise of Asian economies has depended primarily upon using this Western model as a guide to growth.

Nothing is more striking than Asia's jump into the global political-economic system forged after 1945. This system was not truly global, but an institutional setup designed to further American preponderance and to secure American interests all over the globe. It worked because the American model was regarded as attractive and, in the eyes of a large majority, had proved itself. It is no wonder that a "Washington consensus" embracing an economic free-market model like the American one was forged at the end of the twentieth century and adopted by the two leading global economic institutions, the International Monetary Fund and the World Bank.

Now, as Asia gradually takes over as the global economic powerhouse, people are beginning to realize that this model was and is a Western one — suited to Europe and America, but not able to sustain global development. Asia has achieved as much as possible by emulating that model and borrowing from its principles. Now, however, awkward challenges not inscribed in the textbook of American-style capitalism must be tackled. In short, Asia must find and develop its own way ahead; it has to invent a new economic and societal model.

ASIAN DEMOGRAPHY AND THE NEW ECONOMIC MODEL

Over the next 25 years, demographic factors will bring tremendous changes and challenges for the whole of Asia.

First, three groups of countries emerge: (1) those with a falling population, consisting of Japan (still the world's second-largest economy), South Korea, and a few others; (2) those nations with a stagnant and gradually falling population (notably China); and (3) those with a rising population, including India, Pakistan, Bangladesh, Vietnam, Indonesia, and the Philippines.

Demographic divergence is not a recipe for stability. Economically, it almost certainly starts a transfer of labor-intensive, low-cost manufacturing from China to countries with a rising population requiring investment to equip and house new industries; China will experience a swing from low-cost to more value-added production, putting strains on the education system. On top of that, there is the sensitive question of whether skilled workers will be allowed to migrate among countries according to where they find the highest wages. If yes, productivity will go up; if not, productivity will be held back, and animosities of ethnic and/or religious character may pop up. The first omen of these problems will soon be seen, as the Chinese labor force starts to shrink in 2015 and the size of total population follows between 2025 and 2030.

Second, the number of people in the age bracket above 65 years will rise markedly in China. The surging increase of the elderly, which has already happened in Japan, will put an enormous strain on society and will require services that are not embedded in the current societal system. Today, Chinese society presumes that the family takes care of the elderly. That arrangement worked well for a long time, but now with the smaller core family and more singles, the younger generation is not willing to shoulder this burden. The fact that the savings rate in China continues to be well over 40 percent suggests that people expect to pay for social welfare themselves. The problem, however, runs deeper: People may be able to pay for the services, but the services have to be provided by somebody — the public sector or private institutions. Meeting this demand will require large investments in infrastructure and training of people to perform care functions. So far, these preparations have hardly started.

Third, the difference in fertility among ethnic and religious groups will change the composition of Asia's population. Twenty-five years from now, there will be fewer ethnic Chinese and more ethnic Indians and Malays. There will be more Muslims and Hindus, and a smaller share for religions and philosophies rooted in Chinese culture. The most significant development takes place for the share of Muslims. Globally, Muslims increased from 16.5 percent in 1980 to 19.2 percent in 2000 and are forecast to be 30 percent in 2025. As 69 percent of the world's Muslims live in Asia, it is a certain conclusion that the share of Muslims will go up. The impact will be most visible in India, where 13.4 percent of the population currently adheres to Islam, but concentrated in the north of the country. It is conceivable that sometime between now and 2040 one or more of the Indian states will have a majority of Muslims and be governed by Muslims.

This is not necessarily synonymous with problems, but if the emerging trend of religions holding stronger command over behavioral patterns remains in place, tensions among groups inside and between countries may intensify.

TRENDS IN TECHNOLOGY AND EDUCATION

Asia may be an economic powerhouse, but it is not yet a technological pathfinder. Admittedly, Asia excels at improving existing technology and has taken over much manufacturing, but so far very few inventions can trace their roots back to Asia.

Having said this, there can be little doubt of Asia's growing technological strength. The three top spenders on R&D are the United States, Japan, and China. China is publishing 120,000 scientific articles annually, an achievement only surpassed by the United States, with 350,000. The strong upward trend in patents and scientific articles augurs a future leading position for China. Japan is filing the largest number of patents worldwide, but China's filing rate is increasing explosively. Most of Japan's patents are filed by companies that make them dormant unless they intend to use them — which often is not the case. Selling to competitors that may turn the patents into new products is simply not "on." Many of the Chinese patents are held by a very limited number of companies, notably telecom giant Huawei, casting doubt over how widespread innovation and invention is.

This raises a broader question of how well technology and innovation are embedded in Asian societies. To reap the benefit of the heavy outlays in R&D, a country must be geared to turn technological novelties into new products, refine them, achieve high-quality goods, and finally set up organizations to market, sell, and deliver after-sales service. Here, almost all Asian countries seem to be behind the curve. Moving into high tech calls for a societal effort encompassing education, the financial sector, government services at both the local and national levels, protection of intellectual property rights, corporate governance, and a domestic market guaranteeing increasing returns to scale as a platform for global expansion. Many Asian countries have some of these assets, or soon will, but not the whole panoply; moreover, the true art of the game — to combine these assets based upon long experience — is yet to be acquired.

MATCHING EDUCATION TO NATIONAL NEEDS

A tremendous effort has been put into universities, but with mixed results so far. The number of graduates rises fast, but doubts persist about the quality of their education.

Asian countries have long sent a large number of students to the United States. These students used to opt for staying in America after graduation, but the pendulum is now swinging the other way. A majority of Chinese and Indian students in the United States now say they want to return home to pursue careers, according to several reports. The reason they give may be a barometer for the future of technology in Asia: Career prospects are judged to be better in their home countries than in the United States.

Much will depend on how well Asian education systems cope with the challenge of matching future skills with future demand for those skills. The education system must work under the pressure of turning out students now with the skills necessary for the future.

The system must anticipate what the economy needs tomorrow and adapt curricula before it happens. That means schools must offer training and skills not in demand now, but judged to be so in 10 or 20 years. That is very difficult, and the stakes are high. The U.S. experience shows heavy costs for failing to anticipate future skills needs: Productivity fails to reach its full potential, undermining competitiveness; meanwhile, people in possession of the sought-after skills reap a premium, deepening social inequality. The combined result is an underperforming economy and growing social problems.

In countries with large and growing populations moving upward on the economic and technological ladder, the performance of the education system will be pivotal for stable and relatively harmonious growth. Otherwise, imbalances jeopardizing social harmony will result. An enormous number of dissatisfied people due to training with no economic value and an economy desperate for skilled workers and technological staff is a recipe for economic weakness and social unrest.

FIVE SCARCITIES: FOOD, COMMODITIES, ENERGY, WATER, AND A CLEAN ENVIRONMENT

A common thread in analyses of the global economy is a focus on the need for higher personal consumption in China to replace U.S. consumption as the driver.

This thinking may be correct in the short term, but it is catastrophic when looked at in a broader context.

There is ample evidence for a forthcoming era of shortages in five vital areas governing economic activity: food, commodities, energy/oil, water, and clean environment. These resources are interrelated, and efforts to solve one problem with existing methods invariably lead to deepening problems for one or several of the other shortages.

The Food and Agriculture Organization reports that global food production will need to increase by more than 40 percent in 2030 and by 70 percent in 2070. China, Japan, and Korea are net importers of food, and India is just above self-sufficiency. A number of geographical areas around the world have potential for higher food production, but few are found in Asia.

China, India, Japan, and Korea all depend upon imports of commodities. Little can be done to change that, apart from investing in overseas mining, which reduces the economic — but not the political — uncertainty.

Energy needs have pushed all major Asian economies into becoming heavy importers of oil, but oil is not the main source of energy — coal is. About 70 percent of China's energy supply comes from coal, as does 55 percent of India's. Relying on coal with existing technology aggravates the already dire environmental prospect, explaining why China is pouring billions of U.S. dollars into clean coal technology. However, forecasts indicate that China will continue to be the world's largest emitter of carbon dioxide, and in 2015, India will have moved into the number-three position.

Large parts of China and India are already in the grip of water shortages; the Chinese government is drawing up a financially ambitious (but environmentally dubious) plan of turning some of the country's main rivers around to channel water toward the dry northern regions.

Degradation of the environment is threatening continued economic expansion. The World Bank estimates that the costs to China of air and water pollution range up to 5.8 percent of gross domestic product — an enormous sum that swallows up about half of China's economic growth.

If prevailing forecasts turn out to be correct, global warming will aggravate these problems. Under a pessimistic scenario, the decades ahead will see declining agricultural output in all of China, all of South Asia, and most of Southeast Asia. Even if crops can be made to benefit from increased carbon dioxide, agricultural output will still decline in all of South Asia and most of Southeast Asia.

FORCES THREATENING ASIA'S FUTURE

Strategists have often pondered the prospect for war between two or three of the juggernauts — China, India, and Japan. In fact, however, none of them threatens another's vital interest. The three nations may compete for influence and play the good old game of being a nuisance by seeking influence in each other's backyard — as China is doing in Myanmar and Sri Lanka, much to the chagrin of India — but basically it stops there.

Over the last few decades, the threats to nation-states have changed completely. Threats emanate from non-nation-state players aspiring to delegitimize the political system. One vehicle for doing so is to undermine the government system's ability to function, thereby opening a window of opportunity to establish control over populations and to impose a different societal model. This is the lesson from Iraq, Afghanistan, the Taliban, and al-Qaeda. Threats may also come from disruptive nation-states (rogue states), terrorists, and criminal organizations aiming to disrupt the functioning of global systems.

The legitimacy of the political systems in China and India rests upon their ability to ensure rising living standards and human security. Political stability requires social stability, which requires adequate numbers of jobs, which requires economic growth, which requires a firm anchoring in economic globalization. So it is no coincidence that first China and then India have joined economic globalization and its institutions.

There is much talk about China and its growing military muscle, but all indications are that China's leaders worry more about domestic unrest than military aggression. Foreign powers enter this equation only as instigators of social unrest, which explains the Chinese sensitivity about the Dalai Lama, Tibet, Taiwan, the Uighur people, and the Falun Gong religious movement. India seems to be more relaxed, but behind the curtain the same kind of problems harass policy making: The Indian states go their own way, and terrorist groups of both political and religious nature cast doubt upon the state of human security.

Political leaders do not see war as a continuation of politics by other means, but rather as the ultimate catastrophe throwing their nations into chaos and wiping out decades of hard work that gave their populations a better life. They do not harbor aggressive designs toward any other nation-states or see gain of territory as a reasonable objective. They have enough already on their plates. The Chinese perception of Taiwan is that it is part of China, and as long as this perception is not disturbed, things can go on as they have for years.

Only one point may trigger an armed conflict, and that is a Chinese attempt to divert the water flowing from the glaciers in the Himalayas away from the Indian rivers to China. If China does this, India will see its survival under threat, legitimizing any action it takes to ensure that the water still flows to India. China is well aware of Indian concerns.

Some observers see a future war between China and the United States as an almost certain result of the U.S. decline and Chinese ascension. This projection is based on the theory that no superpower has ever been replaced by another one without a war. That observation can be disputed, but suffice it to note that, if such a war erupts, the trigger will likely be declining interest in economic globalization. That cannot be ruled out, especially if the U.S. economic downturn continues and allows China's economy to knock the United States off its perch. And even if the United States were to win a war, the costs would be tremendous and in a best-case scenario only postpone the ultimate decline of American power.

A NEW PARADIGM FOR GROWTH

We often take present social structures for granted and forget that the architecture of societies undergoes change all the time. The industrial model — with mass consumption as the economic driver, freely using raw materials, focusing upon the individual, and built on the nation-state — has been with us for 200 years, but is by no means an indispensable part of human civilization. The successor to the industrial model is in the wings, and we may not have to wait long for it to emerge.

New trends may emerge and shape a new societal model. A more likely scenario, however, is a comeback for classic values that are embedded in traditional societies but have been lost in industrialized culture. Based on its cultural heritage, Asia is much closer to supporting such a reversal than the Western world, especially the United States.

The Abrahamic religions (Judaism, Christianity, and Islam) tend to view nature as of secondary importance because God is regarded as above nature and God created man. So the exploitation of nature and its resources introduced by industrialization met no religious obstacles.

Asia's religions and philosophies take a different view. One of the key messages in Hinduism is the presence of God in everything. A river or a tree can be holy. Buddhism does not set human beings above nature, as the Abrahamic religions do. Confucianism and Taoism teach that people are part of nature, and so human beings do not have the right to exploit nature.

Both China and India have long been governed by the "rule of man" instead of the "rule of law." By adopting a common set of values, people knew how to behave *vis-à-vis* others and did not rely on written texts such as laws or regulations. Values and ethics governed relations among citizens. Conflicts were rare, and most of those that surfaced were solved by mediation, such as by elders or highly esteemed individuals who could find common values in opposing views. Typically, there was no "winner," but rather an attempt to resolve disputes in a way that all parties can live with.

The Confucian Code of Rites (*Liji*) controls civilized behavior by laying down norms, ethics, and values. The law is only brought into the picture when dealing with people who do not respect shared values and therefore fall outside civilized behavior. Relations between civilized people are governed by ethics and values, while the law and litigation are for non-civilized people — those who do not know or who reject common values. In Japan, the equivalent code is a mix of Buddhism and Shinto called *syncretism.*

The two crucial challenges to the current worldview — to change the pattern of materialistic consumption and switch from individualism to group behavior — find support more in traditional Asian values than in Western ones.

That Asia can and perhaps will find solutions to its problems by invoking traditional values may be countered by the fact that, so far, very little of this has been seen. Asia has happily jumped into the box of Western values, adopting them almost unchanged.

However, there is little doubt that continued application of this model will lead Asia — and the world — into disaster. Arnold Toynbee taught that civilization is built upon "response to challenge." To avoid a meltdown in the maelstrom of environmental degradation, social unrest, and competition for ever scarcer resources, Asia must respond. It is possible — maybe even plausible — that this response will take the form of reintroducing cultural values that have been dormant — but not forgotten — during Asia's industrialization.

What has not yet fully been understood is that the modern worldview is moving away from distribution of benefits — ingrained in the industrial model and mass consumption — to burden sharing imposed by increasing scarcities. The societies that find the key to doing this, minimizing friction among their citizens and with the rest of the world, will be the winners.

Tax on Commodity Profits Could Postpone Scarcity*

With the Great Recession, the red-hot commodities market has cooled, but that may not last long as the era of scarcity nips at the heels. One of the world's top mineral holders — Australia — is proposing a tax on "super profits" of mining companies, or profits beyond what's needed for reinvestment. The proposal signals a new backdrop for commodities, with far-reaching consequences for resource use, foreign trade and investment, and the global power balance. Irrespective of all arguments, such a tax would change relative prices in favor of commodities and against manufactured goods.

Norway already has such a tax, it's been on the agenda in Canada and some states of the U.S., and China contemplates testing the water as the era of scarcities takes over from the era of plenty. However, Australia is among the top 10 countries worldwide in production of 13 minerals — ranging from common iron ore to niobium, a superconductor when lowered to cryogenic temperatures and relied on for scientific breakthroughs such as the Large Hadron Collider. In the oligopolistic market for minerals, Australia is potential price setter, market leader and trendsetter.

The tax triggers political and economic arguments about tax policies, tax reform, income distribution and effects on how mining companies may reallocate activities to avoid paying the tax.

Resource-rich countries would benefit and worldwide efforts to conserve resources would be more profitable. Both effects are a turnaround from more than 200 years of downward pressure on commodity prices relatively to manufactured goods that benefited manufacturing countries and encouraged waste of resources to save the more — relatively — costly manpower.

The emergence of China and India as manufacturing countries increases demand, changing the established supply-demand equation in favor of supply. Even with more efficient technology, the pendulum swings in favor of higher prices thus for the first time auguring steadily better terms of trade for commodity-exporting countries.

---

*First appeared in *YaleGlobal online*, 10 August 2010.

For the long term, this might be exactly what the world needs. Higher commodity prices would spur an intensified, maybe even frantic development of production methods that reduce use of commodities. Hitherto we have measured productivity as production per man hour because manpower was scarce. In the future, we may measure productivity as the ability to squeeze more output out of one unit of input conserving as much as possible of what will be regarded as the scarce production factor — resources.

With luck, rising commodity prices would work their way through the system and through the pricing mechanism, reduce deterioration of the environment and boost efforts to slow climate changes. Global negotiations have not been up to the task, tabling not-so-workable administrative, even bureaucratic schemes based upon country quotas.

To ensure conservation, countries should put the burden — and true costs — on the ultimate consumer, regardless of where consumption takes place. And a tax on mining would help to accomplish this.

In the industrial era, the era of plenty, the game was about customs duties, and negotiators exchanged gifts called concessions — "You lower your customs duty, and I'll lower mine."

In the era of scarcities, distribution of benefits will be replaced by burden sharing. To reduce pollution and stop climate change, to conserve oil/gas and water, to use commodities more efficiently and sparingly, the challenge becomes how to make cuts in resources and distribute these cuts without disrupting fundamental competitive patterns driving the global distribution of labor. This augurs a new way of conducting business that most politicians have not fully grasped, as many still hope for a return to the more attractive system of distribution of benefits.

Two groups of countries will emerge as winners.

First, those who realize what is happening and consequently switch to a new economic model and production methods focusing upon the idea of how to squeeze more output out of one unit of input. This is not only a question of economic policies and energy conservation, but requires a total restructuring of how a country or a society operates with repercussions on all societal sectors. The educational system will be in the forefront as teaching needs to tune into this phenomenon and make sure students understand and can apply new principles as they enter economic life.

Second, the countries exporting commodities, raw materials and energy that recognize they must husband these resources carefully over the coming decades. Under the current economic model — no longer sustainable — the industrial countries set a price for manufacturers looking for optimal economic gain, and the commodity-exporting countries look for the optimal commodity price. The difference, however, is that manufacturing countries wanted to sell to create jobs, and a low price to stimulate consumption was the answer.

Commodity-exporting countries are aware that they sit on top of a resource base that ultimately will be depleted, which explains why their optimal price will be high instead of low. A super tax is attractive, providing these nations with a tool to step in and influence price in an upwards direction.

Manufacturing countries will try to resist this tidal change. The first battlefield will be found inside the global trading system. They will try to enact rules — postulating that free trade is at stake — giving them influence over the behavior of commodity-exporting countries. They may go so far as to try to outlaw resource taxes. In the same vein, they will try to get or keep ownership of mining companies and licenses to exploit resources, even buy geographical areas having resources to channel the windfall back to their own coffers. They may succeed for a while, but not for long as realities win over formalities. Then they will work in earnest to introduce technology-saving commodities — the new concept of productivity – and adjust their domestic economy by tax systems and other instruments available to rush new production methods into use.

The losers will be those countries not having commodities or late in understanding what's going on.

Interestingly, China is trying — at least for the moment — to play both cards. The Chinese government is looking at a resource tax for the north-western part of the country while at the same time launching an almost gigantic financial effort to step up use of sustainable energy. It's doubtful whether China will win this race against time in a short-term scenario, but the prospect for a new Chinese economic model taking the changed environment into account offers potential for the long term, not the least because nobody else has started. Also giving China a good start is its share of world savings and funds to invest in the competition that this new economic model will entail.

Several global heavyweights like China and the U.S. are both manufacturing and mineral-producing countries, with an interest in securing a permanent supply of minerals at reasonable stable prices, which could help move the tax forward. China's exposure to environmental degradation pushes policymakers in that direction. The U.S., accustomed to ample resources and having implemented the economic model and transportation infrastructure based on old premises, may be less ready. To a certain extent, Europeans may for a variety of reasons — tighter space, fewer resources — be ready for a tax.

Regardless, times have changed. As the global population grows and demands more comforts, as resources decline, new economic patterns are thrust upon the world. Those nations that come to grips with this stark realization early could fare best.

Part III
Debt

Introduction to Part III

Debt among the rich — industrialized — countries and in particular, among them, the three biggest economies — the U.S., the Euro-zone, and Japan (G-3) has grown to more than 400 percent of GDP. This is the case for Japan, Britain, the Euro-zone, and the U.S. in that order. In all these economies, debt burden is harassing major sectors of the economy: households, the corporative sector, the financial sector, and the public sector.

There are differences in the structure of the debt. Japan has by far the biggest public debt measured to GDP and no deleveraging in sight. The U.S. displays all sectors engulfed with households as main debtor in the past being relieved by the public sector and deleveraging starting and confined to all three private sectors — households, corporations and financial sector. In Britain the financial sector accounts for the largest share albeit the picture is a bit blurred by London's status as a global financial centre. The main Euro-zone country, Germany, has a debt ratio below 300 percent and a fairly even distribution among all four sectors. For France and Spain, the leader of the pack is the corporate sector and for Italy, it is the public debt followed by the corporate sector.

Looking at how these countries tackle the debt crisis over the last five years, there is one major difference between the Euro-zone and the U.S. The Euro-zone has focused on bringing public debt and deficits under control and seems in the course of 2012 to have come close to meeting this target. The U.S. has made progress of substantial size in bringing debt down — deleveraging — for the three private sectors, but not for debt — moving up — or deficit — still around seven percent of GDP — for the public sector.

The decisive difference between the U.S. and the Euro-zone is, however, size of debt for the household sector. In the U.S. it runs above 100 percent of GDP even after some, but limited deleveraging is serving as a drag on the economy. In the Euro-zone, France and Italy have household debt below 50 percent of GDP, Germany about 60 percent and only Spain gets close to the U.S. figure although below with a household debt ratio of around 80 percent of GDP.

This is the flywheel for predicting what will happen when these countries are coming out of the tunnel into daylight. The U.S. households still need to increase their savings to pay back the debt. If they do so, private consumption will fall keeping the growth rate down as consumption account for about 70 percent of GDP. If they don't, debt continues to go up not only for the public sector, but also among households auguring some kind of economic "Armageddon". For the Euro-zone, despite the visible and tangible difficulties, the promising factor is that household debt is so low that no fear of future debt will hold household spending down. With such a low debt ratio, they are far more likely to spend than is the case for American households, not only guessing that future taxes will go up to bring public debt down, but also facing a debt burden of their own.

Consumption theory spells out why. It says that people consume portions of their anticipated lifetime income steadily throughout their lives. Lifetime horizon means that temporary fluctuations in income do not influence consumption. Instead the consumer absorbs fluctuations by building up or running down wealth. Young people borrow, anticipating higher incomes, the middle-aged save more and the elderly exhaust their savings.

When asset prices in particular property prices, were going up in the U.S. and consumers expected that to continue, they consumed beyond what their running income warranted. They borrowed in expectation of being able to pay back loans from asset inflation. When asset prices turned around they were caught out of balance having accumulated debt, forcing them into savings instead of consumption. No such mechanism was seen in the Euro–zone where consumption was sustainable, financed out of running income instead of borrowing anticipating future capital gains.

Debt has to be repaid. The only way to do so is less future consumption compensating for overconsumption in the past. The Euro-zone has chosen austerity meaning that debt is paid back with unchanged purchasing power. It is a difficult process, but if it works the economies will come out of the fire much stronger. The U.S. seems determined to meet the debt issue taking the view that the largest economy in the world has nothing to fear and that debt somehow will not stand in the way of recovery.

Neither the Euro-zone nor the U.S. can decide on these matters alone. They need to draw in the reaction of the creditor — the country, financial institution, or corporation that provided the loans and keep a vigilant eye on the behaviour of the debtor to be sure that repayment will take place. The creditor for obvious reasons tilt toward an approach that keeps the purchasing power of outstanding debt stable, which means that their choice is austerity and not eroding purchasing power by inflationary policies through massive monetary stimulus. The game is however complicated as the creditor has a vital interest in seeing the debtor through the difficulties being able to repay not suffocating itself in the process. China is often spoken of in the context of helping the Euro-zone. China is not helping anybody other than itself and invest in the Euro because it suits its interests for a variety of reasons. China and the U.S. have locked themselves into a situation of main debtor and main creditor, which means that if it goes wrong, both parts will suffer. Next to the U.S. itself, China is the country in the world most interested in a strong American recovery.

The power of creditors will also be felt in international investment. Until the global financial crisis, the main creditors in particular China thought that the expertise for global investment was found at Wall Street. They do not have the same feeling anymore, taking a much more active role in how their money is invested. In the future, the world will see not only creditors taking a share of ownership in established global financial institutions, but also new institutions working out of the creditors and owned by them.

There is nothing new or strange in this. Economic history shows that the mantle of main global investor follows rising economic power. So it was with industrial Britain and with the U.S. having global superiority when the world economy transited from manufacturing to a new economic era. And so it will be for Asia, where we find the new economic powerhouses. Transfer of financial power takes time as it is rooted in networking, know-how, trust, and many other factors than just sheer financial clout, but the Western financial institutions have helped the transition to get underway through their behaviour prior to and during the financial crisis.

New operators such as sovereign wealth funds have entered the arena over the last decade(s). There is some suspicions, even fear, that these funds are not managed according to pure economic or market guidelines, but used as a vehicle for political purposes. There is, however, very little evidence to support this.

There is a growing apprehension among Western countries about the role of China and some other creditor nations, but these new creditor countries do not behave differently from what Western nations did when they were in control. What apparently is "wrong" is that it is China and not them who is doing it. This is a dangerous shift in outlook. The global system must be based on equal rights for everybody. If Western economic powers try to put spanners in the work for Chinese overseas investment because they are Chinese, the global system built around the International Monetary Fund (IMF), the World Bank (WB), and the International Trade Organization (formerly GATT) will be questioned with potential risks for economic globalization.

As long as there is no global economic policy and no genuine global institution to lay out the guidelines for the world economy, there will be no international monetary system in the true sense of that word.

The world will go on relying on national currencies to be used internationally. It has worked quite well over the last 200 years. First under the industrial age with Britain as the strongest economic power accompanied by Pound Sterling as the international reserve currency and then the U.S. Dollar performing when the U.S. took over.

The role as international currency cannot be separated from being the world's strongest economy. The U.S. Dollar worked well as a global reserve currency because other countries wanted to hold it for possible use to buy goods or services in the U.S. — and they were available because the U.S. was the strongest economy having what people wanted — or investing in the U.S. — and the U.S. as the strongest economy offered attractive investment opportunities.

From this follows that eventually the U.S. Dollar will follow Pound Sterling into semi-oblivion later to be fully 'retired' from the international system analogous to declining economic power of the U.S. As the U.S. continues to be the largest and strongest economy for a decade or two, it is not on the agenda to see the U.S. Dollar being replaced by either an artificial currency such as the SDR issued by the IMF or any other national currency. This is not the same as saying that the U.S. Dollar is the sole international currency. The Euro has carved out a respectable role for itself and the Japanese Yen is also playing a role. Smaller currencies such as the Swiss Franc and the Singapore Dollar might also be mentioned.

By far the most likely candidate for a future role is the Chinese Renminbi. But there is a long way to go. First of all it is not yet fully convertible and it may take some years before the authorities relinquish the last control instruments. Secondly, even if China might be — do not yet take it for granted — the largest economy by 2030, it does not mean that the Renminbi will take over.

The world will probably see a gradual phasing out of the U.S. Dollar within an interim phase where several currencies fulfil the role subsequently to be replaced by the currency of the strongest economy — and let us assume it will be China — if China is sufficiently much stronger economically in the same way as was the case for Britain and the U.S. compared to other countries. The alternative is a genuine international currency and that is only likely under global governance far exceeding what we have seen yet.

Meanwhile the U.S. Dollar will linger on, fluctuating around a falling trend *vis-a-vis* most other currencies. It will lose some of its attractiveness. It may also start to be phased out as a denominator for international trade in commodities maybe even oil, which would pose economic and monetary problems for the U.S.

The Way Out of the Debt Trap*

How to get out of the debt trap? The figures are terrifying. U.S. sovereign debt is close to 100 percent of gross domestic product (GDP) and apparently on an unstoppable trend irrespective of what happens at the fiscal cliff. The federal deficit was, for the fourth consecutive year, above US$1 trillion and is running at 7 percent of GDP. The Euro-zone is doing somewhat better with debt/GDP at 87 percent. Forecasts point to a gradual, albeit small, decline from 2013/14 and a fall in the zone's budget deficit from its current level of 3.3 percent of GDP.

Analyses of debt burdens in the past highlight limited inflation as the magical stick hollowing out purchasing power, reducing the share of GDP needed to honour outstanding debt. Countries trying manfully to pay back the debt by austerity and low inflation — as the Euro-zone is doing now — have rarely been successful.

BURDEN OF ADJUSTMENT

This may be true, and if it is, the omens for both the U.S. and the Euro-zone — as well as Britain and Japan — do not look promising. The public has grown used to low inflation over the last 25 years and do not seem ready to surrender that privilege, least of all the creditors knowing that it would shift the burden of adjustment to them.

So what to do? The answer may be that these analyses speak the truth, but not the whole truth. Debt does not go away. It has to be repaid — eventually, but not necessarily now or within a short time span. The alternative to start paying back here and now is to leave debt levels (the principal) where they are, renewing debt when it is due, and focusing on an economic policy that diminishes the net interest burden. Japan has done so over the last 20 years. Italy too. Admittedly, neither of these two countries can flag a good growth rate, but nor have they suffered some kind of cataclysm.

---

* First appeared in *Business Times*, 24–25 November 2012.

First, the debt level must be under control to instil confidence among households and private investors to encourage them to spend without fear of further tax increases. John Maynard Keynes is often invoked in this debate. What he said was that if private demand falters, the public should step in to bridge the demand gap to maintain aggregate demand. But this policy only works if private demand does not react negatively to public policy as it may when debt levels and public deficits go up.

Second, low interest rates to reduce the net interest burden, and low inflation should be the main objective of monetary policy. In past crises, countries may have relied on inflation to reduce the payback burden, but as the interest rates followed the price level upwards, the real interest rate was kept steady and the net interest burden did not fall.

What we see now in the U.S. Japan, and the Euro-zone is a monetary policy pursuing low interest rates by pumping money into the system. Many observers have predicted inflation, but they are wrong. There is no demand pressure, so consumer prices have been steady and it is unlikely that this trend will be reversed. Liquidity goes into commodities, property, and stocks and not to the market for goods and services.

The net interest burden for even the heavily indebted countries will not be insurmountable. If we assume — not unreasonably — that for the Euro zone including weak countries real trend growth will be 1.5 percent per annum and inflation 2.5 percent, nominal GDP growth comes to 4 percent. Recent debt auctions for Italy and Spain show that the yield is falling. At the end of October, Italy sold eight billion euros (S$12.6 billion) of six-month T-bills at an average yield of 1.347 percent. At the end of September, Spain saw strong demand for the 10-year bonds, with investors bidding for nearly three times the amount on offer with an average yield of 5.66 percent. Investors bid for three-year bonds, with an average yield of 3.85 percent.

The current net interest burden on government budgets compared to GDP is, for France, 2.6 percent; Italy, 4.8 percent; and Spain, 3 percent. For the U.S. the corresponding figure is 1.5 percent. These figures may, however, not give a correct picture of the burden on government budgets as public budgets among the Euro-zone countries are double the size of the U.S. federal budget, generally speaking. The tax burden thus amounts to almost the same among the heavily indebted Euro-zone countries and the U.S. Forecasts point to a rising burden in the U.S. and a smaller burden for the Euro-zone countries.

BLESSING IN DISGUISE

The next step is to figure out where to find the tax revenue to finance net interest payments without stopping the recovery. The answer is: institutional investors. For the Euro-zone, institutional investors account for 40 percent and in some cases almost 50 percent of public debt-holders. A shift in the tax system to increase taxes on remunerations from bonds held by these investors would in reality mean that you give with one hand and take back with the other one.

The losses would in due course be borne by retirees, but as the Europeans try to make people stay longer in the labour market, this may be a blessing in disguise encouraging people to work longer to get the same pension.

This model would clearly work for the Euro-zone — even for countries such as Italy and Spain. For the U.S., it is not certain. Forecasts signal continued rising debt/GDP ratio. A higher share of public debt is held by foreigners (50 percent of treasury bonds) compared to 31.5 percent for the Euro-zone (Italy and Spain at or below 40 percent). Institutional investors do not account for much more than 15–20 percent of treasury bonds with the Federal Reserve and foreigners taking about 75 percent.

As for any prescription to get out of the blind alley, there are weaknesses. It would require adroit economic and, in particular, monetary policy to balance nominal growth, nominal interest rates, and the size of debt/GDP. Creditors might unexpectedly ask to get their money back, but as this would ground the global economy including their own, it is unlikely that they will do so.

Debtor countries will not find room to do much else than servicing the debt — but do they have any freedom of action now? The alternatives — starting to pay back or inflation — are worse, so the way outlined above may be what we are going to see either because policy-makers choose it or by default.

Global Debt Picture Not Very Pretty*

The deleveraging of debt among OECD countries will lock the global economy in a decade-long low-growth scenario. It will also change the ranking among the industrialised countries to the detriment of the U.S., Japan, and Britain while the Euro-zone, despite current difficulties, will fare better.

Debt (household + corporate sector + financial sector + public sector) amassed by OECD countries over preceding decades amounts to about 300 percent of their GDP.

Among the top five we find the U.S., Britain, and Japan. The public, the households, and the financial sector all contribute to the calamities in the U.S.

The main culprit in Japan is the public sector, and in Britain the financial sector. The big four Euro-zone countries (Germany, France, Italy, and Spain) have a lower debt/GDP ratio than the U.S., Japan, and Britain. The debt is spread more evenly among the four sectors mentioned above.

The deleveraging has started, as it must. There is no way around it; this augurs lower growth as repayment of debt is irreconcilable with rising demand. Judging by historical experience, it will take quite a while before households and corporations feel confident enough to spend.

A number of studies are available, but are of little relevance as they suffer from the weakness of looking at isolated case such as Sweden in the early 1990s compared to the present situation of all major OECD countries in hot water. Unavoidably, the consequence is a much longer time needed because no major OECD country stands ready to act as a locomotive.

After all the rescue efforts, it would be permissible to think that the financial institutions in the U.S. were back to form, but they aren't, acting as a serious brake on the policies to break out of the low growth debt trap.

---

*First appeared in *Business Times*, 5 July 2012.

Under normal circumstances, the money market ensures that banks loan freely among themselves using liquidity in an optimal way (a bank that temporarily has too much liquidity loans to another bank that is in need of liquidity).

UNDIGESTED LESSON

Unfortunately, banks nowadays either sit on their liquidity to improve the balance sheet or put it into speculative financial derivatives. Yes, you would assume that the crisis had taught them a lesson, but they haven't digested it.

Over recent years, the U.S. has put in place a massive public stimulus programme, but only managed a paltry growth rate for 2011 at 1.7 percent with the prospect of the same for 2012. According to orthodox economic thinking, growth should have been higher. The fact that it isn't has puzzled many economists; some say the stimulus should have been even greater.

The explanation is found in the deleveraging process. By definition, public stimulus leads to higher public debt/GDP ratio. Households anticipating higher taxes to repay the public debt react by increasing savings so they have the money for the taxman at a later date. Private consumption is put on the backburner. The implication is that aggregate demand in the economy will not go up as much as expected.

This observation falls in line with analyses showing that if public debt passes a level of around 90 percent of GDP, further stimulus does not work because households lose confidence in the economy. The households are no longer spending, but saving; policymakers are stuck.

The Euro-zone situation is almost the opposite. The public debt/GDP ratio has been stabilised through austerity. The households and the corporate sector have not really started to deleverage (their spending has not fallen much), but they do not need to do so, because their debt/GDP ratio is more favourable than for the U.S. — especially in the case of households.

The combined result of fiscal austerity and no real deleveraging in the private sector has been a less than feared fall in demand. Last year, the Euro-zone managed 1.5 percent — not much different from the U.S. growth. 2012 will probably show zero growth.

The prospect for higher private demand is, however, brighter with falling public debt/GDP ratio, augmenting confidence among consumers and investors, making it more likely that aggregate demand will go up. Looking at the figures, it seems that the Euro-zone is bottoming out this summer. Thereafter, growth will begin — the official forecast for growth in 2013 is one percent.

Figuring in the financial sector reinforces the picture of a better medium-to-long-term prospect for the Euro-zone than for the U.S. A couple of weeks ago, we learned that JPMorgan had lost up to US$9 billion on speculative trading in derivatives; it may be higher. The bank has also revealed that US$50 billion in losses could hypothetically bring it down.

Its total balance sheet is valued at about US$2.3 trillion and a good deal of it is in derivatives of doubtful quality. Bank of America has over the last four years lost US$40 billion on its failed acquisition of the mortgage lender, Countrywide.

The financial press is brimming with news about the Euro-zone banking system, but seems oblivious to Bank of America's losses even though they amount to about two-thirds of what is required to recapitalise the entire Spanish banking system (estimated at US$64–78 billion).

The European banking system is not in fantastic shape, but the measures agreed at the summit last week goes a long way towards recapitalising weak banks.

Over recent years, German and French banks have reduced their exposure to the weaker European countries. Continental European banks are much less engaged in financial derivatives than their U.S. counterparts.

Japan's problem is the public debt — close to 240 percent of GDP and still counting. Household debt is small, while corporate and non-financial corporate debt measured in percent of GDP is not far from the U.S. figure.

The Japanese parliament's lower house recently endorsed a hike in the sales tax, but even if also adopted by the upper house, it will only take effect in 2015 and is already deemed insufficient to address the debt problem.

The high public debt has forced Japan to engineer a monetary policy with zero interest rates; otherwise, the debt burden would destroy public finances.

With rising debt, this will obviously not change. The role of the financial system (to channel savings into profitable investments) cannot be fulfilled with zero interest rates, given that interest rate is the mechanism used to separate profitable from unprofitable investment projects.

This cannot go on — although this has been said many times. The day of reckoning will come if or when Japan's balance of payments swing from surplus to deficit.

For Britain, the public debt/GDP ratio is still going up despite strenuous efforts by the government to turn around public deficits. Households are only just starting to deleverage.

The fact that this is only beginning now explains the comparatively well-functioning of the British economy until a few months ago when it became clear that the country is heading into recession.

The governor of the Bank of England has demanded immediate and far-reaching action to reform the structure and culture of the UK banking industry.

He said: "That goes to both the culture in the banking industry and to the structure of the banking industry, from excessive levels of compensation, shoddy treatment of customers, to deceitful manipulation of one of the most important interest rates and now this morning to news of yet another mis-selling scandal."

DYSFUNCTIONAL U.S.

The statement came after Barclay's bank was fined £290 million (S$576 million) for manipulating a key interest rate.

The medium-term outlook for global debt deleveraging will be strongly influenced by what happens to the Bush tax cuts in the U.S. They expire at the end of 2012 unless a decision to the contrary is made by a political system that truly deserves the label "dysfunctional".

The U.S. is caught between the devil and the deep sea. If the tax cuts are extended, surely public demand will go up, but so will the public debt/GDP ratio with the result being households and maybe the corporate sector would deleverage even more, keeping aggregate demand low, preventing full positive effect on growth.

If they are not extended, public demand will fall and even if it is difficult to gauge the reaction by households and corporations, it looks unlikely that they would step in to compensate for the falling demand, raising the prospect of a recession. There is no way out of this trap. Damned if you do it, damned if you don't.

Of course, the U.S. can approach its main creditors (China, Japan, and some countries in the Middle East) for a restructuring of its public debt.

Some people would call it a default, but wordsmiths will be busy inventing another word. China with allegedly US$1.3 trillion and Japan with US$1 trillion in U.S.

treasury bonds would hold the fate of the U.S. economy, and indeed the global economy in their hands.

As long as the U.S. debt problem has not been addressed, the world will not get back to higher growth. The risk is that it won't, which will take us into uncharted waters and make the Euro-zone problem look like a picnic.

Inflation or Deflation? Both!*

The jury is still out on the question of inflation or deflation for the global economy. Those who see an inflationary trend point to the almost enormous amount of liquidity pumped into the economy by the U.S. central bank (Federal Reserve) through qualitative easing and the European Central Bank (ECB) doing more or less the same by supplying banks with cheap loans. The contrary opinion gets ammunition from forecasts telling that the global economy, in particular for the established industrial countries, will run below capacity (caught in a supply gap situation) making inflation very unlikely if conventional economic theory holds.

In fact, the world may be heading into a kind of economic situation not seen before. The goods market — the real economy producing and selling goods — will certainly not get out of the supply gap in a foreseeable future.

With low demand it is difficult, indeed impossible, to see what can push prices upward. So yes, even if there will be pockets of rising prices due to high commodity prices, consumer prices will not rise very much, may be somewhere between 2 and 4 percent for most mature economies. Not exactly deflation, but near enough to warrant this label especially at the lower end.

Rising labour costs in China accounting for a high share of global manufacturing will be nullified by transfer of production to countries with lower labour costs such as Vietnam, Indonesia, Myanmar and, in particular, India and Bangladesh.

In principle, some of the extra liquidity should enhance the willingness of banks to lend to the business sector; thus stimulating investment and subsequently consumption. It does not work like that though. The banks, mostly in Europe but also in the U.S., have been hit so hard by the financial crisis that they are using the money to improve their balance sheet by buying assets and paying back debt.

It is fine for them, but does little to help the economy. The money gets trapped in the banking sector that is not willing to take risks. The lifeblood of a well-functioning economy — lending among banks to smooth out individual banks' need for liquidity — has stopped and so has growth. Going by experience, this state of affairs is not going away any time soon. But the money used to improve the banks' balance

---

*First appeared in *Business Times*, 11 April 2012.

sheets must go somewhere and it does. It goes into the market for assets — commodities and equity.

Those who determine where the money goes (fund managers) have lost confidence in the political system and central banks. More than 30 years ago, financial institutions on Wall Street discovered the opportunities offered by commodity markets. They did not directly enter these markets, but invested in warehouses and storage facilities.

When the financial crisis struck, these investments took off and over the last six years banks have acquired such physical facilities having little or nothing to do with their proper business — lending and borrowing. This has gone largely unnoticed, among other reasons, because there has been enough on the plate calling for regulatory action, but now the Fed is on the warpath looking at the activities undertaken by JPMorgan Chase, Morgan Stanley, and Goldman Sachs.

They make large profits by selling storage facilities to clients who see investment in commodities as the way to safeguard purchasing power of their investments. The commodities are stored by speculators and not channelled into production. It is a strange unholy alliance with one sure result: a continued demand for commodities decoupled from the real economy.

The equity market is also doing very well. After a dramatic fall from end-2007 to mid-2009, the Standard & Poor's index is back almost touching the level before the eruption of the financial crisis in 2007. This sounds strange recalling that global growth has shifted downwards and shows no sign of getting back to the former trend of 4.5 percent.

Buying equities may not look like a fantastic business opportunity, but with reasonable profit rates the downside risk seems limited. It even looks good compared to the bond market. U.S. 10-year treasury bonds offer the investor a nominal interest rate of 2.2 percent, which, taking the inflation rate into account, means a negative real interest rate.

Add the growing discomfort about the U.S. debt situation and one wonders how long any investor will be willing to buy these bonds. Over the next five years, the U.S. has to roll over 71 percent of its debt standing near 100 percent of gross domestic product (GDP).

The prospect of a possible U.S. default that seemed laughable some years ago, now pops up on the horizon as a risk that cannot be disregarded. U.S. corporations are a safe haven compared to this world of uncertainties and risks under the control and command of policymakers having forfeited what remained of credibility.

Under normal circumstances, central banks would change tack and withdraw liquidity from the system to get back to how things looked before they injected money into the economy. But things are not normal. The culprit is the debt.

Servicing the public debt requires that the U.S. and Japan, less so for the Euro-zone, keep interest rates at a very low level. Otherwise, the net interest burden will kill the economy. A forecast by the Congressional Budgetary Office (CBO) a couple of years ago came to the result that from 1.4 percent of GDP, net interest payments on the federal budget would rise to 3.4 percent in 2020. Since then, the underlying assumptions have turned worse as the growth rate is lower than expected.

Recalling that 71 percent of debt, incurred when the interest rate was low, has to be rolled over in the next five years, it does not require much arithmetic to spot an unsustainable burden if interest rates start to go up. Japan with a higher debt and net interest payment ratio is even more locked into a low, yes zero, interest rate policy. There will be no withdrawing of liquidity. Indeed, further easing is more likely to keep the interest rate as close to zero as possible.

Two almost certain results are in the pipeline. First, commodity prices and stock markets will look good. Second, bond holders will react by asking for a positive real interest rate to lend money to the U.S.; opening the door for turmoil in this market — one more reason to stay with commodities and equities.

U.S. More Worrying than Europe*

A few days ago, the consulting firm McKinsey's published a report telling that the U.S. has started deleveraging its debt; the Euro-zone has not. A look at the figures shows, however, that the U.S. household sector, pivotal for private consumption that accounts for 70 percent of GDP, is still showing debt at 87 percent of GDP compared to 58 percent as an average for France, Spain, and Italy.

McKinsey's adds that 'the (U.S.) households could face two more years of deleveraging'.

Two-thirds of the deleveraging has taken the form of defaults on home loans. Even if optimism prevailed, it is difficult to see the American consumer back in business, while the prospect of rising private consumption in Europe looks better — at least from a debt perspective.

The latest IMF forecast for U.S. growth in 2012, set at 1.8 percent, may prove to be too optimistic, while the forecast for the Euro-zone — a mild recession — may prove too pessimistic.

Hard won experience tells that austerity takes time to engineer a turnaround, but at the end of the process a sounder economy and social balance emerges. Inflation destabilises the social fabric. Confidence in a country not willing or able to maintain stable prices becomes shattered. This was why both the U.S. and the EU in the 1980s changed course to get out of the inflation trap that caught them in the 1970s.

Figures and forecasts are difficult to trust these days, but the Euro-zone's public debt is set to 87.9 percent of GDP in 2011 and expected to rise marginally to 88.9 percent in 2012. Thereafter, it will fall, auguring a levelling off and then a smaller gap to be plugged by borrowing. Exactly the opposite holds for the U.S.: Total national debt reached 100 percent of GDP in the third quarter of 2011 and will continue to rise — according to some forecasts, alarmingly so — raising borrowing requirements over the next decade and probably longer.

The global financial press is highlighting the Euro-zone's difficulties in getting the needed funding even with a positive real interest rate that rewards creditors, but

---

* First appeared in *Business Times*, 7 February 2012.

the U.S. picture is much more worrying. U.S. treasury bonds offer an interest rate a bit above 2 percent. With inflation running at 3.4 percent, lenders to the U.S. bag a substantial negative real interest rate. With an ever increasing borrowing need and further inflationary pressure embedded in monetary policies through quantitative easing, there is no prospect of seeing a turnaround.

One wonders how long creditors will be willing to invest in assets with in-built erosion of purchasing power. When — not if — creditors get enough of this and ask for a positive real interest rate, servicing of the debt will blow a gigantic hole in the already leaking federal budget. Indeed, foreign central banks, mainly those from China, Hong Kong, and Russia, have over the last six months sold almost US$100 billion and, as far as can be deduced from statistics, the selling has accelerated since November 2011.

The rating agencies are basking in their false glory — downgrading or threatening to downgrade or upgrading. We do not need them. It is very simple. Creditworthiness depends on a country's willingness and capability to tax its citizens to service the debt.

The Europeans score quite well. All members of the Euro-zone have adopted painful measures. We do not know how effective they will be, but we do know that the Euro-zone governments are willing to do it. The expected riots in the streets have not materialised except in a few cases, although one cannot rule out that the threshold for suffering will shift downwards. But so far so good. Not many are ready to put their heads on the scaffold and predict that the U.S. Congress will do the same.

Many economists have sought refuge in John Maynard Keynes and his prescriptions from the 1930s on how to deal with a depression. We all have our own interpretation of what Keynes meant; no one knows what he would advise today. We do know, however, that he advised the public to step in counteracting negative effects on the economy from faltering private demand. To my mind, that selects aggregate demand as the crucial factor. Public spending does increase public demand, obviously, but not necessarily aggregate demand. If the private sector loses confidence in the economy, it may react by holding back on consumption and investment and if that happens, aggregate demand may not go up. Public debt erodes confidence.

The U.S. public stimulus has boosted aggregate demand and the Euro-zone restraint has cut aggregate demand, but in neither case to the extent one would have expected. For 2011, growth was marginally higher in the U.S. than for the EU (1.7 percent versus 1.4 percent). Low confidence keeps U.S. private sector spending down. The personal savings rate (savings as percentage of disposable income) being around 2.5 percent in 2006 has since, as shown in the McKinsey's report, risen sharply.

The U.S. economy is caught between the devil and the deep blue sea. If household and corporate sector debt falls to rebalance the economy, aggregate demand is held back, diminishing tax revenue, pushing public deficit and debt up, further eroding confidence.

If private consumption and investment goes up, keeping savings low, the already high deficit on the balance of payments may explode. There is no room for manoeuvre for the U.S. economy. Debt in all four main sectors (household, corporate, financial, and public sector) is near record levels, while the deficit on the balance of payment is running at around 3–4 percent of GDP and showing no signs of going away.

The Euro-zone may look bad, but is in fact much better. Figures for individual sectors and/or individual countries may rightly give reason to worry, but overall deficits and debts are lower than is the case for the U.S. and Britain. The crucial point is a near equilibrium on the balance of payments, revealing that overall savings and investment are in balance — giving room of manoeuvre.

We may know more in the course of 2012, but it is frightening that the Euro-zone and the U.S. find themselves so far apart from each other in choosing economic policies to get them out of the slump.

They cannot both be right. My instinct tells me that the winner is "you spend what you earn" and not "you spend what other people will lend you".

Why Debt Does Not Go Away*

After World War I, global sovereign debt was 70 percent of global gross domestic product (GDP). After World War II, it was 100 percent. In both cases, war devastated economic activity while at the same time calling for a colossal financial effort.

There was no other way than to resort to borrowing. Nation-states brought global debt down to 30 percent of GDP in the early 1970s, whereafter it exploded upwards over the first decade of the 21st century to reach — again — 100 percent. And that after two decades with historically high economic growth, which should have made it possible to save for rainy days.

Exactly the opposite happened, primarily among developed countries that put the foot on the accelerator with disastrous results. Politically, it was almost criminal; economically, it stoked irresponsible behaviour and it explains the financial crisis and the subsequent Great Recession.

Debt means that the current generation has encroached upon the next genera-tion's consumption. It turns into a problem when the size of debt (claims on future GDP) surpasses the ability of GDP to redeem these claims while at the same time meeting the next generation's expectation of consumption and investment. If so, realignment must be undertaken. Debt must fall or GDP must go up or a mixture of both.

Traditionally, a sovereign debt below 60 percent of GDP is regarded as man-ageable, but the threshold differs from country to country, dependent upon circumstances.

In a European context, it is almost pathetic to read comments that Greece can solve its problem by leaving the euro, reintroducing the drachma and letting it float on the currency market — as if that removes the debt. It doesn't. It is one of many ways to bring about the necessary realignment. A depreciation of the currency means rising inflation that erodes real income, thereby reducing consumption through a lower standard of living.

---

* First appeared in *Business Times*, 28 July 2011.

The same can be achieved by lowering domestic wages and income — a so-called internal depreciation. A third way is fiscal tightening (lower expenditure and higher taxes) combined with a tight monetary policy. They all amount to the same: debt is repaid through lower future consumption.

The difference lurking behind the veil is burden sharing — who is going to live with lower consumption: creditors or debtors? With economic globalisation, it becomes a bit more complicated because creditors and debtors are found in different countries. Japan is an exception with a debt problem looking awful, but confined to redistribution among Japanese citizens and institutions. Therefore the Japanese problem is less bad than it looks and surprisingly sustainable.

The European problem turns around the future of European integration because the creditors/debtors are found inside the European Union (EU), but not inside the same nation-state. Greek assets are mainly held by German and French banks. It automatically becomes a question whether the EU can build a mechanism that channels funds around among financial institutions such as inside a nation-state or whether failure to do so will push a genuine union, the end goal, further into the horizon with each member state fending for itself.

The European case illustrates economic policies and how they affect burden sharing. Cutting public budget deficits through austerity puts the lion's share of the burden on the debtors who benefited from the overconsumption, but now have to accept lower consumption over a number of years (citizens mainly).

CONSUMER SENTIMENT

If a more inflationary policy is adopted, rising prices will eat away purchasing power of the assets shifting a part — the rate of inflation tell how large — to creditors (in the Greek case German and French banks), allowing debtors to escape more lightly.

It is disputed how economic growth will fare under these two policies. Conventional wisdom has it that the first option leads to low growth, but so far this is not borne out in Europe. Consumers seem more ready to open the purse with falling deficits and debts, enhancing confidence in long-term prospects for the economy. The International Monetary Fund (IMF) has upgraded Euro-zone growth for 2011 three times; the forecast for Germany, the economic powerhouse, is 3.2 percent — pretty good by any standard. Austerity depresses public demand, but prodded by consumers holding up spending, aggregate demand controlling the growth rate is not falling.

The United States has been downgraded three times by the IMF, now forecasting growth for 2011 at 2.5 percent. Despite rising public demand, aggregate demand is not going up; consumers are holding back sensing that federal borrowing inevitably will lead to a tax hike so better keep the money to pay future taxes than to spend now. For the first time in several decades the household savings rate is up.

U.S. debt is not a closed system where redistribution among Americans can do the trick. The U.S. is heavily indebted to China, Japan and the oil-exporting countries in the Middle East, ruling out a unilateral U.S. burden-sharing decision.

These things do not work out in an explicit and transparent way, but it is quite obvious that any steps by the U.S. are scrutinised by its creditors wanting to safeguard the value of their assets.

The U.S. can choose austerity like the Euro-zone in which case Americans will have to shoulder the main burden; logical because they enjoyed the overconsumption. The creditors may not, however, be happy, facing the prospect of slow growth depriving them of a buoyant export market.

American citizens and the political system also seem miles away from selecting this option. Inflation, eroding the purchasing power of outstanding assets, will certainly lead to falling U.S. dollar, hitting foreign creditors.

BITING THE BULLET

A good many observers openly or tacitly support this course, but may have overlooked that a lower U.S. creditworthiness hikes the costs of financing the rising debt. Politically, inflation may be unpalatable for the American public and undermine the prospect of re-election for the incumbent president. Can the world's mightiest power choose such a shabby way out of living beyond its means?

The argument is often voiced that there is no alternative for China to hold on to U.S. Treasury bonds. If they are dumped on the market, the U.S. dollar will plummet and that will make the creditor worse off. Yes maybe, but it also means falling bond prices synonymous with rising interest rates in a sluggish economy with a fragile property market — not really what you look for.

The only way out of this impasse is to bite the bullet and acquiesce with debt repayment. Forget the economic jargon and countless technical analyses. It means depriving Americans of a share of potential future consumption, opening the door for foreign creditors to redeem claims on consumption earned by past abstention. As analysed above the transfer of consumption can be facilitated by various economic policies, but they all have one thing in common: a lower future American standard of living.

The longer this issue is skirted the more brutal will be the awakening. A concerted effort with its creditors through a genuine global economic policy may help. High growth among creditors will keep demand for American goods and services up, allowing debt repayment by transferring part of rising U.S. production, possibly preventing an absolute decline of living standard.

This becomes even more attractive if accompanied by a gradual, managed and mutually agreed depreciation of the U.S. dollar. Low growth among creditors makes such a scenario unlikely, raising the prospect of an absolute decline of the standard of living over a number of years, which undoubtedly will have strong repercussions on U.S. domestic policies.

Global Economy Faces Wealth Redistribution*

The forecasts for the global economy published by the International Monetary Fund promise steady but hesitant recovery. Global trend growth will be well below what it was in the golden years that are behind us and may never really come back.

Recent events in Japan and the Middle East not only confirm such a lower trend, but augur a looming battle for the redistribution of global wealth with unpredictable consequences for global economic growth and political stability.

The disasters hitting Japan and its economy will unquestionably affect growth negatively. Optimists point to a speedy Japanese recovery, even a kind of renaissance. However welcome, this view is based upon hope with no evidence to support it. On top of the impact on Japan itself, the consequences for the global supply chain are severe, especially for electronics. Companies such as Nokia and Sony/Ericsson have announced problems. The car industry is also affected and both Japanese and American producers are in a similar situation.

There are rumours that the Boeing Dreamliner 787 will be further delayed as about one-third of its components come from Japan. The disruption of several nuclear power stations in Japan, combined with uncertainty about the future of nuclear power, will push up oil prices.

As if that was not enough, the disasters struck Japan at the same time that social and political unrest cast a spell of doubt over the future of Middle East oil-exporting countries such as Libya and Bahrain. Their exports are at least partly out of the equation and no one knows when they will come back. The situation in several other countries seems uncertain at best.

In short, the control of a large part of the world's oil reserves is gradually being transferred from the ruling elite whom we know and who have integrated their countries in Western-style economic globalisation, to political forces and movements of whom we know next to nothing.

---

* First appeared in *Business Times*, 8 April 2011.

We do not know whether the new political forces in the Middle East want to keep their countries in the existing global system or whether they want to change course and maybe seek another road for development. Maybe they do not know themselves. From our point of view there may be no alternative to current policies, at least not very attractive ones, but that may not be how they see it.

What is happening in the Middle East is an omen of growing discontent among people around the globe with conditions agreed by their rulers when integrating their countries in the global economy.

Allegedly, the uprising in Egypt was triggered by inequality, corruption and nepotism, which resulted in the lion's share of Egypt's wealth being allocated to a small elite. In Bahrain, the background may be confrontations between Sunni and Shiite Muslims. In Libya, it is a kind of tribal war with tribes in the west supporting Muammar Gaddafi and tribes in the east in revolt against him.

The common denominator is that in each case, the elite brokered a deal with the Western world about exploitation of natural resources and subsequent distribution of the resulting benefits — to the advantage of the elite and the West and at the expense of the majority of the people living in these countries.

UNCHARTED WATERS

Especially in the Western world, recent events are seen and presented as a kind of popular uprising against dictatorships controlled by people or groups of people wanting to introduce a more liberal governing system, maybe even a liberal democracy. But there is little evidence to support such a posture.

This is not the first time in history that policy-makers see what they want to see instead of coming to grips with reality.

It is much more likely that we are witnessing the starting signal to redistribute global income and wealth. Hitherto the global system has favoured manufacturing nations. Rising commodity — food and oil — prices indicate that the pendulum is swinging in the other direction favouring commodity-exporting countries.

The commodity-importing countries suddenly find themselves at the mercy of the commodity-exporting countries after 200 years where the opposite was the case. In such circumstances it comes as no surprise that populations in the commodity-exporting countries react or even revolt, demanding new deals allocating more to them and less to the elite which are seen as part of the Western world and, indeed, less to the Western world.

Their populations look upon their rulers as part of the existing global jetset benefiting from rules agreed previously and not interested in changing these rules.

In the eyes of the people, the ruling elite is not "one of us" but "one of them", where "them" is the global elite still dominated by Western rules and mindsets; and even more important, channelling the main part of economic benefit flowing out of globalisation to them.

It is still early days and much may happen, but if this interpretation is correct, and there are many signs that it is, the world is sailing into uncharted waters, totally unprepared to tackle the demands for another distribution of income and wealth between manufacturing countries and commodity-exporting countries.

One of the surest predictions is that this will push global growth lower at least in a transitional period until a new system has been agreed upon and set up. The manufacturing countries will try to hang on to the current system, which will make the transition longer and more painful than if they realise what is going on instead of misinterpreting the unrest, seeing it as a sign of moving towards the Western-style political system.

Has the Fed Got it Wrong Again?*

A few days ago, U.S. Federal Reserve chairman Ben Bernanke made a statement explaining current monetary policies. As might be expected, the risk of inflationary trends figured prominently.

What did he say? First, that if inflation persists or if inflation expectations begin to move, then there's no substitute for action. Second, that inflation was being boosted by high commodity prices and there was not much the Fed could do about rising oil prices.

This does not inspire much confidence. What kind of action can be envisaged if the cause for inflation comes from outside and "there is not much the Fed can do about it"?

It actually highlights that the Fed apparently has not yet fully understood the underlying causes for inflation in the United States and why a national monetary policy is ineffective addressing inflation worries.

Twenty years ago, inflation in industrialised countries started to fade away after having reached double-digit figures in the early 1980s. New monetary policies and in particular inflation targeting, that spread like a prairie fire, were presented as magic inventions by central bankers and monetary economists.

In fact, they had nothing to do with it. The integration of China in the global economy gave rise to a steady flow of low-priced industrial goods that put a lid on prices and suppressed wage demands in industrialised countries, thus adding an indirect effect. Had the central banks got things right, they would have tightened monetary policy much before they started to do so in summer 2004 and that might well have prevented the subsequent financial crisis.

Instead their belief in having solved the riddle of non-inflationary growth opened the door for the biggest asset bubble ever seen — and a global one at that. They thought that this time monetary policies were sophisticated enough to do what had never been possible: reconcile low inflation and high growth, so there were no reasons to part with a fairly loose monetary policy.

---

* First appeared in *Business Times*, 29 April 2011.

They did not notice that liquidity pumped into the economy had nowhere else to go than into assets, which it did, and we all know the result: booming asset prices cutting the economy into two separated sectors, the real economy (production, employment doing fine) and a financial sector harassed by disastrous investment decisions.

The ghost that haunts them now does not look very terrifying on closer inspection. The annual rise in consumer prices is 2.7 percent both for the U.S. and the Euro-zone — historically fairly low and about the same level as 10 years ago.

But central bankers want to move, so what to do about it? Hike interest rates, make credit tighter and more expensive, keep demand in check, and avoid bottlenecks runs the standard recipe coming out of economic textbooks. And this is what they are doing or on their way to do.

Except for a limited number of industrialised countries, however, demand pressure has nothing to do with the embryonic inflation. How can it be with unemployment in the U.S. at 8.8 percent and 9.9 percent for the Euro-zone, revealing a substantial output gap?

It is China again. First, through rising labour costs due to a growing shortage of skilled people pushing up wages. Come 2015 and the labour force starts to fall. Productivity is going up, certainly, but not sufficiently to wipe out higher wages. The relentless pressure, mainly from the U.S., on China to appreciate the yuan reinforces this development.

Second, the Chinese demand for commodities heralds a supply side inflation not seen for a very, very long time and consequently off the radar screen of most policy-makers. A supply-side inflation generated by emerging markets does not respond to tightening of monetary policies in industrialised countries.

The lesson to draw from the 1980–2010 era is unequivocal. Economic growth, employment and inflation inside nation-states are mainly determined by supply and demand on a global level. Chinese wages are more important for prices in the U.S. than monetary policy.

The Fed has missed this point in the midst of all kinds of technical analyses and modelling, leading to managing liquidity and setting interest rates' levels as if the business cycle can be managed by national policies. Driving in this lane has delivered and will continue to do so unbalanced national economies.

The only way ahead is to phase in a mechanism for synchronised national policies applying global policies to address the effects of economic globalisation.

The Markets Prey on Debt-Laden Nations*

Select reported figures on growth show improvement, yet global recovery seems as elusive as ever. The U.S., the Euro-zone and Japan still show disappointing growth, and the three have something in common: All are mired in debt, sucking their capabilities and constraining their efforts at remedial measures. Until the West finds a way out of its stifling and growing debt, genuine recovery is out of reach.

Some regard the financial markets as a culprit, but this is the wrong approach, suggesting misunderstanding about how the market functions and reacts. The markets are governed by selfish behavior, focused on financial gains. Markets care about politics only to the extent they affect profit-making ability. The markets analyze behavior and draw conclusions — to earn money!

The omens for 2011 are not good. The year starts with a toxic cocktail of nervous investors scared by debts and deficits, excess liquidity nourished by the U.S. Federal Reserve System, and financial institutions stoked by this liquidity and chasing profits. This is a recipe for instability, ill-founded decisions and reckless behavior. The global financial system lacks steering. No leading institutions point the way ahead, marshalling market forces for a course other than profits.

The market neither supports nor rejects the euro, but smells gains if the Euro-zone can be broken up or weaker member states forced into default, thus forcing higher interest payments on loans. The Euro-zone responded reasonably well to the attacks, though the authorities were mostly behind the curve, raising doubt about their abilities despite the political will.

Sensing that battle over the euro is yet not won by either side, the market can be expected to renew its attack before the end of summer, testing the resilience of Euro-zone member states. The potential profit by driving down bond prices, keeping them low, thereby augmenting the cost of borrowing for deficit countries remains attractive. During late 2010, institutional investors such as pension funds were

---

*First appeared in *YaleGlobal online*, 17 January 2011.

unwilling to purchase bonds issued by weakest Euro-zone members, thus letting more speculative institutions control the game.

A combination of reform, austerity, slightly falling euro values and modest growth that's sustainable will carry the Euro-zone through for now, giving it breathing space to implement stronger fiscal coordination. Speculators may make life uncomfortable, but as long as the European Central Bank, strong countries like Germany, and weaker ones like Greece, Ireland and Portugal do not lose their nerve, the speculators — irrespective of enormous funds at their disposal — cannot squeeze a sizeable profit out by hammering the Euro-zone.

So attention will turn to where profit is possible with lectures on debt and that's the United States.

The debt/GDP ratio for the Euro-zone stabilizes around 85 percent, but continues to rise for the U.S., anticipated to break the record set at the close of World War II — 109 percent — before 2020. According to the U.S. General Accounting Office and the Congressional Budget Office, taking into account likely policy changes, the federal debt continues to rise, reaching 200 percent around 2030. The federal deficit may improve slightly in the short term, but will balloon again by 2015, as baby boomers retire and social security payouts climb.

Federal debt is not the only U.S. problem: 48 of 50 U.S. states had shortfalls in fiscal 2010 and anticipate more in the years ahead. Stimulus funds distributed to the states under the American Recovery and Reinvestment Act will be spent before 2012. The possibility is real of one or more states going into default and sharply curtailing education, health, transportation programs. Turning to major U.S. cities, the outlook darkens: More than 100 American cities face soaring debt and bankruptcy, including New York City, Detroit, San Francisco and Los Angeles. Combined, U.S. states cities confront a $2 trillion mountain of debt. Incidentally, the year 2010 recorded the largest number of bank failures since 1992.

Economists have theorized just how much fiscal tightening the U.S. needs to reduce the federal debt/GDP ratio to 60 percent. One calculation — made before the extension of the Bush tax cuts — is an annual effort of 2.8 percent before 2020, amounting to a total of 22.4 percent, in tax increases or program cuts, or a combination of both. By comparison, the tightening required of Greece is similar, 3.0 percent annually for a total of 24.9 percent. Unlike the U.S., which boosts its deficit to higher levels, the Greek government has already introduced measures to reduce the deficit. The rating agencies, consistently wrong in recent years, allegedly contemplate downgrades for France and Spain. The annual fiscal tightening required for these two countries to achieve 60 percent is 1.8 percent for France and 1.7 percent for Spain — less than two thirds of what the U.S. needs to do.

To restore the global economy, debt restructuring must take place, pitching the creditor nations like China against the U.S. and other debtor countries in a tough fight of burden sharing. History suggests the debtor often loses, so it would be wise for the U.S. to contemplate what China will ask for and what the U.S. can and will offer. Secretary of State Hilary Clinton has few illusions, as noted to former Australian Prime Minister Kevin Rudd, according to a leaked cable, "How do you deal toughly with your banker?"

The U.S. has one card up its sleeve. China does not want a weakened U.S., certainly not with low growth patterns for the rest of this decade. The U.S. market remains valuable for Chinese exporters though talk of China's dependence on its U.S. exports is off the mark — with net exports accounting for less than 25 percent of Chinese growth as an average over the last five years. The U.S. could offer the quid pro quo prospect of a global recovery for restructuring U.S. debt. Already China is helping stabilize Euro-zone by extending credit to Greece and promising help to Portugal and Spain.

The U.S. must admit how its debt has weakened its global role, making it dependent on other countries and undermining its ability to lead.

For China, an equally difficult barrier is realization that dependence on the global economy requires responsibility.

For the Euro-zone, the crisis is a wake-up call that the U.S. can no longer automatically be counted upon to support Europe. Europe must undertake what will be agonizing reappraisal of its global role.

Around the world, some will initially express glee at the prospect of seeing the U.S. served the same medicine it has forced upon other countries. But that's short-sighted, overlooking how much the world still needs the U.S.

The debt problem, in particular U.S. debt, is one more sign that the established world order of the late twentieth century is fading. And if not dealt with promptly, the debt problem could bring world order down crashing.

The U.S. and Europe may still initiate a new world order, but only by putting their own house in order and realizing that neither the global financial system nor control over global natural resources are exclusively in their hands. Power and influence must be shared. Otherwise creditor countries will do it their way.

Nationalism or Capitalism? Sovereign Wealth Funds of Non-OECD Countries*

INTRODUCTION

For many years sovereign wealth funds (SWFs)[1] lived a quiet life without attracting much attention. They were regarded as "normal" investment funds shuffling the world's savings around like other financial institutions. The interest started to grow a few years ago for two main reasons: First, a total amount of SWFs — a potential of US$6–10 trillion by 2013, and US$12 trillion by 2015 — started to look big enough to influence international investment. Second, SWFs proliferated from a limited number and 20 new funds were set up between 2000 and 2008 (Jen, 2007; Regling, 2008). Finally, the Chinese government's decision to launch China Investment Corporation (CIC) triggered particular attention despite its limited size — US$200 billion. It did not take long for statements about the potential risks of sovereign wealth funds from leading politicians to reach the headlines, accompanied by various initiatives by international institutions "to do something" about SWFs.

When the global financial and economic crisis erupted in 2008, these initiatives were put on the backburner. In the last year or two, activities to establish a regulatory framework for SWFs have waned, being replaced by frantic endeavours to get the financial markets back to normal, as SWFs stepped in and helped save the near collapsing Western financial system by injecting US$60 billion into U.S. and European banks (Fotka and Meggtson 2009).

Currently SWFs are not a hot issue among European Union/Organisation for Economic Cooperation and Development (EU/OECD) countries, but the situation might change any time because the fundamental issues concerning SWFs remain. They touched a

---

* First appeared in *The Political Economy of Sovereign Wealth Funds*, edited by Xu Yi-Chong and Cawdat Bahgat, Palgrave MacMillan: 2010. Reproduced with permission of Palgrave MacMillan.
[1] The EU literature normally defines SWFs in this way: SWFs are generally defined as state-owned investment vehicles that manage a diversified portfolio or domestic and international financial assets.

raw nerve and caused serious concerns about the future role of EU/OECD countries in the global economy — the word "angst" may be used in this context.

The main problems embodied in the policy stance in EU/OECD countries towards SWFs are:

- questions about the management and investment policy of funds not subject to normal financial supervision (risk of politically motivated investment decisions).
- worries that countries operating SWFs wish to accumulate assets through deliberate low currency rates, thus distorting comparative competitive advantages.
- unease that the shift from liabilities (bonds) to equities leads to opaque changes in corporate governance.
- feelings that national security may be jeopardised.
- presumed risk that the "brain power" of enterprises would be moved out of home countries relegating them to "producing" Instead of "inventing" countries.

The question this chapter tries to answer is whether the underlying skepticism and negative attitude towards SWFs is directed against the funds themselves or radiates a deeper anxiety among Europeans about the long-term position of Europe in the global economy.

THE FIGURES

At the beginning of 2009, the size of SWFs worldwide was between US$1900 and US$2900 billion (CRS, 2009). This corresponds to a maximum of 44 percent of global currency reserves standing at US$6531 billion (IMF 2008) and is equal to the combined assets of all hedge funds and private equity firms as of February 2008 (House of Commons 2008). Global equity market capitalisation is estimated to be approximately US$50 800 billion and bonds, equities and bank assets US$190, 400 billion (IMF 2008); SWFs therefore represent only 5.8 percent and 1.52 percent, respectively, of these funds.

The EU (Eurostat, 2007, 2008) was investing far more abroad in non-member states than it receives in inward investment. In 2006, outward foreign direct investment (FD1) was €206 billion and €157 billion inward FDI. At the end of 2006, EU outward FDI stocks were €2649 billion and EU inward FDI stocks were €2057 billion — a net position of €592 billion. For the year 2005, outward FDI rose 16 percent and in 2006 rose 11 percent, while inward FDI flows rose 10 percent in 2005 and 13 percent in 2006. From 2002 to 2006, outward FDI rose 42 percent and inward FDI rose 63 percent.

Looking more closely at the composition of inward EU FDI stocks from 2001 to 2004, important changes emerge. North America's share falls from 62 percent to 51 percent, a significant change in a relatively short time span. Those having increased their share are non-EU countries from 16 to 20 percent, South and Central America from 11 to 14 percent and Asia up from 8 to 9 percent. This trend continued in 2006, with North America's share falling to 50 percent and non-EU countries rising to 22 percent.

A further breakdown reveals that at the end of 2006 the top investors in the EU were:

Investor	Stocks in euro (€) billion	Share in percent
USA	953.7	46.4
Central American countries	261.3	12.7
Switzerland	247.8	12.0
Japan	99.3	4.8
Canada	81.0	3.9
Norway	63.0	3.1
Singapore	40.0	1.9
Near and Middle East Countries	35.2	1.7

Another classification reveals that offshore financial centres account for €393.8 billion, which explains the high figure of Central American countries and Singapore. Hong Kong, with €16.4 billion, also falls within that group.

The picture changes completely when one looks at growth rates for inward FDI. The following list shows absolute amount of FDI stocks at the end of 2006 (in parenthesis):

Turkey (€11.6 billion) with 300 percent growth tops the list, followed by Brazil (€10.5 billion), Singapore (€40 billion), Norway (€63 billion), Russia (€12.7 billion), Iceland (€6.29 billion), Lichtenstein (€7.7 billion), Korea (€7.6 billion), Canada (€81 billion), USA (€953.7 billion), Japan (€99.39 billion), Switzerland (€247.89 billion), Mexico (€8.4 billion), Hong Kong (€6.4 billion) with a growth rate of nil, and at the bottom of the top 15 comes Australia (€17.3 billion) — the first country whose FDI in the EU indeed declined.

There is little evidence that SWFs have controlled or are in the progressing of controlling a significant share of total economic activity in the EU, whether it is about the total stocks of FDI, or investment flows or specific economic sectors. Only Norway and Singapore among the well-known SWFs appear to be the large investors in Europe. Near and Middle East countries account for only 1.7 percent of inward FDI stock. What attracted attention to the SWFs was probably the *growth* in their size and activities rather than their absolute size.

An analysis by The Monitor Group (2008) suggests an increasing difference in investment patterns by SWFs located in the Middle East and North Africa (MENA) versus those located in Asia. Those from MENA tend to direct their investment more towards North America and Europe than the Asian SWFs, which tend to invest in Asia. Since 2000, MENA-based funds have invested US$100 billion, out of which US$72 billon went to North America and Europe. There were 205 deals, with North America and Europe accounting for less than half of their total investment activities. SWFs domiciled in Asia invested US$150 billion, with US$74 billion going to North America and Europe; a total of 573 deals with 74 going to North America and Europe.[2]

Looking at the picture in the perspective of EU/OECD positions/reactions, the following observations are pertinent:

- the EU is and will continue for the foreseeable future to be a net creditor and a net investor abroad.
- the size of SWFs may look large, but in the context of global equity markets they are not.
- EU outward FDI stocks are at least equal to their total; they are not a significant share of EU inward FDI stock.
- their limited size rules them out of having any consequence for EU/OECD economic policies.
- the trend over recent years may disclose a somewhat stronger investment by SWFs, but this is not significant, and 2008 — dominated by the financial crisis — saw a sharp decline in SWFs' investment in OECD countries, which fell from US$37 billion in the first quarter of 2008 to US$9 billion in the second quarter and US$8 billion in the third quarter (Fotka and Meggison 2009).
- any concern about foreign direct investors and their possible impact on economic activity and business life in Europe should be directed towards offshore financial centres and hedge funds rather than SWFs.

The author is often struck by the apparent oddity that these funds are more acceptable than SWFs. The explanation may be that the Europeans feel that the money

---

[2]Total figures are available for the first quarter of 2008 revealing US$58 billion, more than for 2000 to 2005 taken together. The figure for 2007 was US$92 billion.

invested from offshore centres is European money — in reality recycled — making this a circuit to evade European tax, but still under European control and steered by commercial objectives.

THE EUROPEAN REACTION

The essential point is that the attitude of the EU and its member states towards SWFs inscribes itself in the normal political framework and manoeuvring of the Union. The logic of the integration imposes constraints on national policies while offering the benefits of common policies. Largely, the member states seek to pursue national interests inside the EU framework by influencing EU decisions. The European institutions (Commission, Council and Parliament) play a similar game to compete with each other and with the member states too.

The EU originally foresaw that movements of capital could cause, or threaten to cause, difficulties and a clause allowing precautionary measures to be introduced as a temporary measure was part of the Treaty of Rome of 1958. After the implementation of the Economic and Monetary Union, this clause was directed solely towards movements of capital to or from third countries. With the entry into force of the Lisbon Treaty, the scope of the Common Commercial Policy — where member states have pooled sovereignty to exercise it in common — is extended to cover "foreign direct investment, the achievement of uniformity in measures of liberalization".[3] This is one of the explanations why EU institutions have taken an active line on the issue of SWFs.

The EU position towards SWFs was set out in the Presidency Conclusions, endorsed at the meeting of the European Council on 13–14 March 2008 (Council of the European Union 2008)[4]:

> The European Council welcomes the Commission Communication on Sovereign Wealth Funds (SWFs).[5] The European Union is committed to an open investment environment based on the free movement of capital and the

---

[3] I am grateful to Horst Krenzler for drawing my attention to this point.

[4] The European Council is the highest political body of the EU. It comprises the Heads of State or Government of member states along with the President of the European Commission. It is assisted by the Foreign Ministers of the member states and one member of the European Commission. It meets at least twice a year, normally three times a year.

[5] Communication From the Commission to the European Parliament, the Council, the European Economic and Social Committee and the Committee of the Regions, Com (2008) 115. *A Common European Approach to Sovereign Wealth Funds, Brussels,* available at http://ec.europa.eu/internal_market/finances/docs/sovereign_en.pdf.

effective functioning of global markets. SWFs have so far played a very useful role as capital and liquidity providers with long-term investment perspective. However, the emergence of new players with a limited transparency regarding their investment strategy and objectives has raised some concerns relating to potential non-commercial practices. The demarcation between SWFs and other entities is not always clear-cut. The European Council agrees on the need for a common European approach taking into account national prerogatives, in line with the five principles proposed by the Commission, namely: commitment to an open investment environment; support for ongoing work in the IMF and the OECD; use of national and EU instruments if necessary; respect for EC Treaty obligations and international commitments; proportionality and transparency. The European Council supports the objective of agreeing at international level on a voluntary Code of Conduct for SWFs and defining principles for recipient countries at international level. The EU should aim to give coordinated input to this ongoing debate, and invites the Commission and the Council to continue work along these lines.

The question of financial stability, the capital markets, international cooperation and a common EU position was on the agenda for the meeting of the European Council in March (Council of the European Union 2009a) and June 2009 (Council of the European Union 2009b). In both occasions, SWFs were not an important issue and they were actually conspicuously absent from the conclusions. This suggests that the global economic and financial crisis shifted parameters and attention, at least temporarily.

The same pattern is visible when looking at statements by leading European politicians who had discussed the possibility of setting restrictions on inward FDIs from SWFs. Since the spring of 2008, however, these voices have calmed down albeit they may still be espoused by left-wing political forces in particular.

French President Nicolas Sarkozy initially launched a vigorous attack on SWFs, but little more than six months later, he established such a fund to defend France's own interests. In January 2007, President Sarkozy stated: "France must protect its companies and give them the means to develop and defend themselves" (Emmanuel and Hepher 2008), and "I believe ... in globalisation but I don't accept that certain sovereign wealth funds can buy anything here and our own capitalists can't buy anything in their countries. I demand reciprocity before we open Europe's barriers" (Reuters 2009a). These are strong statements; Sarkozy does not mince words. In November 2008, the French government announced a strategic industries fund estimated at €20 billion to invest in France's key industries to defend them against takeover bids by SWFs (EUobserver 2008). It became clear that the French government meant business when, in July 2009, 20 stakes in companies amounting to €14 billion were made public (Reuters 2009b).

German Chancellor Angela Merkel stated in July 2007: "With those sovereign funds we now have new and completely unknown elements in circulation .... One cannot simply react as if these are completely normal funds of privately pooled capital" (Dougherty, 2007). In Germany, but also in other European countries, the prospect of the Russian company Gazprom taking a share or buying national energy companies raised fear leading to proposals to block such plans (Twickel, 2008; Walker, 2008).

In Britain, Chancellor of the Exchequer Alistair Darling publicly distanced himself from the French position of defending selected key sectors and stated: "Sovereign wealth funds or companies owned by governments need to play by the rules. We believe in a liberalised trade system. One of the reasons London is the number one financial center in the world is because we have a very open economy .... [The worry is] if a company is behaving in a way which some might regard as not commercial but political" (Conway, 2007). A few days later he was prompted to clarify this statement and did it in the following way: "When a company is not acting in a commercial way or we have reason to believe it is going to make an investment where there is an issue of national security, then we have powers to take action".[6] An article in the *Sunday Times* added: "Behind the scenes, his advisers were rather more explicit: if Russia's Gazprom has ambitions to take over Centrica, the parent of British Gas, then it can think again. No deal" (Laurence and Armstead 2009).

Analysing the French, German and British views, while they all pay lip service to the freedom of capital movements and maintaining the current international system, they all:

- focus upon national security as a concern that legitimises restrictions.
- explicitly or implicitly mention the energy sector as an example of national security (it is interesting to note that the deregulation wave starting in the 1980s — that privatised what used to be public utilities — has brought, among other things, the energy sector in reach of private instead of public ownership).
- require the money spent by SWFs to be invested with them, beefing up their industries with more capital, provided that they have a hand in how the money is used — a somewhat conflicting policy as the investors obviously want a free hand themselves.

---

[6]The Enterprise Act 2002 (House of Commons Library 2008).

Behind these policies there seems to be a fine line of balancing fundamental economic interests with the activities of SWFs.

The British are influenced by London's role as a major financial centre. A large part of British industry has ceased to be competitive and/or has been sold to foreign investors (for example, the car industry), transferring the role as driver for the economy to oil and services. Britain is vulnerable to steps that might tempt international investors, including SWFs, to question their use of London as a destination point for their investments. Despite various attempts, neither Frankfurt nor Paris has succeeded in establishing themselves as a credible alternative.

Germany is a traditional supporter of a liberal global economy. A tough German line towards SWFs would not fit this image, and German industry may also welcome capital from abroad. Accordingly, Germany is soft-pedalling on restrictions while at the same time expressing anxiety about key industries. It is, however, careful to mention only the energy sector in this regard, not its manufacturing industries. The spring of 2009 saw a major investment (Reiter, 2009) in what may be labelled Germany's most precious industrial asset — its industrial jewel — when Aabar Investments PJSC (an Abu Dhabi-based SWF) took a 9.1 percent share in Daimler AG. Adding its shares to those already held by Kuwait (6.9 percent) gives SWFs from the Middle East a 16 percent ownership share. This was not regarded as a threat to national security, more an important boost for car production, research and development, and employment for the whole German economy. The reaction was unanimously self-congratulatory, with Daimler Chief Executive Officer Dieter Zetsche saying: "We are delighted to welcome Aabar as a new major shareholder that is supportive of our corporate strategy .... We look forward to working together to pursue joint strategic initiatives." "It's a win-win situation for both companies", stated Ferdinand Dudenhoeffer, director of the Center for Automotive Research at the University of Duisburg-Essen.

France's strategy is more difficult to gauge, possibly because it is more subtle. By asserting its position early on to establish its own fund and safeguard key industries in French hands, France conveys the message that any investment in France would have to sound out the French government prior to taking any initiatives. By applying such a policy, the French government wants to have its cake and eat it too. The SWFs have tempted to go along with this as there certainly must be French companies that are interested in their investment while at the same time they do not wish to antagonise the French government. Judged on the structure of political systems among the large European nation-states, France can get away with this; the British and the Germans probably cannot.

What these moves signal about France's economic and industrial policy is still open for interpretation, but it seems possible that the alleged threat of SWFs is used as a pretext to take state-owned shares in a number of key industries. Referring to SWFs may make these measures more palatable to the skeptical French public because the European Commission and other international organisations have been given the job of ensuring competition.[7]

The European Commissioner for Internal Market and Services, Charlie McCreevey, in January 2008, outlined a European approach:

> The freedom of capital movements is too precious to be jeopardised on the grounds of sudden unrest .... Some have argued that new legislation is needed to protect national security concerns of EU Member States. In reaction to this, I would like to stress that investments which have the potential to compromise national security can already be blocked. It is often forgotten that a Member State is entitled to restrict Treaty freedoms on the basis of legitimate national security concerns .... We must not allow the discussion on Sovereign Wealth Funds to be used as an excuse to raise unjustified barriers to investment and the free movement of capital .... I do believe there are issues relating to transparency and governance that we need to engage on with certain Sovereign Wealth Funds .... We need Sovereign Wealth Funds, to be transparent in their operations, preferably on the basis of an international code of best practice.
>
> (McCreevey, 2008)

The European Commission (European Commission, 2008) sees benefits as well as concerns of specific relevance to the EU connected with SWFs, enumerates reasons and proposes five steps for a common approach.

- Benefits: SWFs have helped to keep the global financial system stable by recapitalising other financial institutions in difficulties and will probably help to strengthen the euro's role as an international reserve currency; even if this is not mentioned by the Commission, the bid of Frankfurt and Paris to be global financial centres may thus improve.
- Concerns: the opaque way of management of some funds. There, is uneasiness that the funds want to give lower priorities to pure commercial purposes and accord higher priority to other purposes such as acquiring high technology or getting control over distribution channels. Political motivations could influence investment

---

[7] To put the size of these investments by the strategic industries fund in perspective, the total FDI liabilities for France at the end of 2005. were €144.5 billion, whereof €14.5 billion is held by the Near and Middle East countries and €4.4 billon by other Asian countries (Eurostat Pocketbooks, 2007, 2008).

decisions spilling over into negative consequences for recipient countries. The Commission does not mention it, but abrupt selling of shares in a company trying to casts doubts over its viability tails into this category of potential uneasiness.

- The Commission is not oblivious to the strong interests of member countries, in particular the major member countries and enumerates the following three reasons for a common EU approach instead of letting member countries act on their own. First, multilateral solutions offer greater advantages than individual national responses. Second, maintaining a well-functioning internal market and non-discriminatory rules requires a common approach. Third, It will be difficult to open third country markets to EU investors if the EU or individual member countries were to be seen erecting barriers.
- A common approach should be built around five steps: First, commitment to an open investment environment. Second, support for multilateral work. Third, use of existing instruments. Fourth, respect for EU Treaty obligations. Fifth, proportionality and transparency.

In July 2008, the European Parliament, assuming more and more responsibility in shaping policies for the EU, adopted (with 661 votes for and 11 against) a resolution (European Parliament, 2008) highlighting that:

> SWFs have not caused distortion of capital markets ... is concerned about the lack of transparency ... welcomes the Communication from the European Commission but regards it as a first step ... requests the Commission to conduct an analysis of tools at the European Union's disposal in either Treaty provisions or existing legislation — such as transparency requirements, voting rights, shareholders" rights and golden shares — that would allow some reaction in the event of ownership problems due to SWF intervention.

The final phrase is the crucial one as it opens the door for "reaction in the event of ownership problems" without specifying what kind of problems might give rise to the reaction.

At the OECD Ministerial Meeting in June 2008 (OECD, 2008a) the chair summarised the discussion about SWFs in the following way:

> SWFs have become a key player in the new financial landscape. Ministers welcomed the benefits that SWFs bring to home and host countries and agreed that protectionist barriers to foreign investment would hamper growth. They recognised the rapidity by which the OECD has responded to the mandate given by the G7 Finance Ministers and other OECD Members. Ministers praised the Report by the Investment Committee on SWFs and the guidance they give to recipient countries on preserving and expanding an open environment for

investments by SWFs while protecting legitimate national security interests. They expressed their support for the work at the IMF on voluntary best practices for SWFs as an essential contribution and welcomed the continuing coordination between the OECD and the IMK. Ministers looked forward to future work on freedom of investment by the OECD, including surveillance of national policy developments. They adopted the OECD Declaration on SWFs and Recipient Country Policies and were joined by Ministers from Chile, Estonia and Slovenia, who adhered to the Declaration. This Declaration constitutes another example of the OECD's capacity to set international standards.

Since 2006, the OECD (OECD, 2008b) has "provided a forum for intergovernmental dialogue on how governments can reconcile the need to preserve and expand an open international investment environment with their duty to safeguard the essential security interests of their people" and finalised its work on guidance on sovereign wealth funds in October 2008. It consists of three parts.

- Declaration on recipient countries' policies with the core element that OECD countries should not erect protectionist barriers to international investment, should not discriminate among investors, and safeguards for national security reasons should be transparent and predictable, proportional to the concern and subject to accountability in application.
- A confirmation of investment policy principles reflecting the need to keep markets open and transparent.
- More detailed guidelines for recipient countries investment policies relating to national security aiming to strike a balance between legitimate concerns for the investor and the recipient countries by enumerating a number of steps to be complied with in case of restrictions motivated by national security.

The OECD guidelines are more complex and go indeed deeper into the matter than is the case for much of the work done in the EU. This can be explained by the non-binding character of OECD guidelines compared with the more intricate task of drawing up legal Acts for the EU fitting into the existing or planned regulation of the European capital market. The common denominator is the concern for national security where the EU concern goes deeper and further includes consequences for economic activity and ownership of investment under the auspices of SWFs.[8]

---

[8] As this paper deals with the EU/OECD attitude, the "Santiago Principles" (Generally Accepted Principles and Practices) agreed October 2008 among 26 countries with SWFs including one member country (Ireland) of the EU and eight member countries of OECD is not incorporated. The paper, however, attempts to accommodate the concerns of recipient countries where of 13 including the European Commission participated. The report also contains a useful list of SWFs. Available at http://www.iwg-swf.org/pubs/eng/santiagoprinciples.pdf.

EU/OECD SWFS

The non-EU/OECD countries' funds are normally fed by strong export earnings that are expected to continue with an overall objective to invest over a long-term horizon without any specific purpose. The EU/OECD[9] countries' funds cannot count on export earnings, but are normally fed by public funds to act as a reserve when in a decade or two a higher absolute number and share of people above 65 years of age will shift the burden of financing to a smaller share of the population in the productive age.[10]

Australia. The Future Fund. Set up in 2006. Objective: to build up a buffer in view of the expected demographic evolution. Management through an independent board. As of 30 June 2008, the total portfolio was A$64 billion.

Belgium. Zilverfond. Set up in 2001. Objective: to fund claims for expenditure from 2010 to 2030 flowing from an ageing population. Management is linked to the Minister of Finance, who issues guidelines. Flexibility is limited as the fund invests exclusively in Belgian Treasury Bonds. As of 31 December 2009, the total portfolio was €15.5 billion.

France. The Strategic Industries Fund is mentioned above, but France also has Fonds de Reserve pour les Retraites (FFR) set up in 2001. Objective: to fund old age pensions. Management is under the supervision of a board composed by, *inter alia*, parliamentarians and representatives of ministries, but aiming for independence and transparency. As of 31 December 2008, the total portfolio was €27.7 billion.

Ireland. The National Pensions Reserve Fund (NPRF). Set up in 2001. Objective: to meet as much as possible of the cost to the state of social welfare and public service pensions to be paid from 2025 until at least 2055. Management is performed by seven members of the NPRF Commission appointed by the government. As of end-2007, the total value of NBRF was €21.150 billion.

---

[9] In the following SWFs, those established by Canada (Alberta), Norway and Mexico are excluded as their operations are comparable to oil-exporting countries' SWFs and not EU/OECD countries' funds. It should not be overlooked, however, that the underlying idea behind the Norwegian, Canadian and may be also the Mexican funds are somewhat similar to funds in EU/OECD countries: namely to build up a reserve to finance social welfare in particular pensions.

[10] Sources for the following short description are — unless otherwise specified — the "Santiago Principles' and websites for the national funds.

Korea. Korea Investment Corporation (KIC). Set up in 2005. Objective: to manage public funds entrusted by the government and the Bank of Korea. Management is in the hands of a nine-member steering committee with public and private sector members. Initially KIC was entrusted with US$27 billion and as of end 2007 US$14 800 million was invested.

New Zealand. The New Zealand Superannuation Fund. Set up in 2001. Objective: to meet the cost of an ageing population. Management is handed over to a board (Guardians) who must manage the fund consistent with best practice portfolio management, maximising returns without undue risk and avoiding prejudice to New Zealand as a responsible member of the world community. The government plans to allocate about NZ$1.5 billion a year over the next 20 years. As of 31 May 2008, the value of the fund was NZ$14.7 billion.

Almost all the funds were established around 2001 to accumulate reserves deemed necessary to meet future pensions and possibly other social welfare expenditure, and they are institutionally linked to government supervision or guidance. As they belong to the public sector and are supposed to finance future public expenditures, they are basically an instrument for siphoning off some funds from the normal budget to special institutions that are allowed to invest in a different manner to the way in which they would invest if the money was kept inside the budget, where it would have improved the budget balance and public debt position.

The political consideration must have been that a deterioration of public finances *ceteris paribus* is worthwhile compared with another policy for disposal of public finances. This is of course why investment policies and transparency, in addition to accountability, become an interesting question. Whether or not it is a profit-able or beneficial policy for society depends simply upon the portfolio perfor-mance compared with conventional management of the public debt/public assets. It looked a safe practice in 2001, but after the upheavals on global capital markets in 2007–2009 (and the volatility will probably continue for at least another two years) many of the funds have suffered substantial losses that have to be recouped in the future.[11]

The philosophy of the funds may be to buy into tomorrow's production by shifting from bonds (mainly more conservative treasury bonds} to more aggressive equity shares as an investment objective. Without doubt, equity markets rise over the

---

[11] France's FFR informs in its annual report for 2008 that the result for 2008 was minus 24.8 percent and the annual performance since the fund's inception In 2001 is plus 0.3 percent (see http://www.fondsdereserve.fr/IMG/pdf/FRR_RA_2008_version_fr.pdf).

long term, but there have been long spells — several decades in fact — where the market did not move and of course not everyone selects equity shares that are going to grow in value.[12] It is not a foregone conclusion that a switch to new investment methods will increase the value of a country's savings allocated to meet future claims. Many governments were carried away by the euphoria of the equity market in the 1990s and decided to enter the market; they often did so when it had reached its peak.

WHAT MAKES AN SWF INVESTMENT DIFFERENT FROM OTHER INWARD FDI?

This section will analyse European skepticism, fear and outright negative attitudes towards SWFs compared with other kinds of inward FDI. SWFs appear to be easy to identify, but when we look at their effects from a recipient country's point of view, it is less simple. First, SWFs are different because of their country of origin. Second, what is the difference from the recipient country's point of view between an investment undertaken by an SWF or company that is fully or partly owned by a SWF? One of the least analysed but most important issues is the blurring of distinction between SWFs, state-owned enterprises and other enterprises in a country that has set up SWFs.

Defensive Actions

1. Many EU/OECD countries have announced measures to protect themselves against FDI inflows, which might threaten national security or similar interests.[13] It is, however, an open question whether national security is threatened more or less by SWFs than by private investors. If a private foreign company obtains high technology that is vital for national security, it may not hesitate to sell it to other countries. Many countries need to defend themselves against industrial espionage gradually evolving into a policy instrument.

---

[12] The U.S. Standard & Poors index hardly rose in 15 years from 1965 to 1980. From 2000 to 2007 it fluctuated around a stable trend and then fell to about the 1997 level.

[13] Here I have chosen to focus on the political, economic and psychological aspects and do not enter into a discussion of limitations for discriminating between domestic investor and foreign investors, be they private companies or SWFs written in international treaties such as commitments undertaken under the World Trade Organisation (WTO) or Free Trade Agreements.

Suppose that private funds pursue a policy of maximising profits; then they would not hesitate to jeopardise a country's national security by, for example, selling "high-tech" information. They might even postulate that such selling/buying is part of natural commercial operations and that inhibitions go against commitments undertaken by international treaties guaranteeing free trade in goods and services.

A sub question is the argument that SWFs would be more liable to steer investments towards companies having "interesting" technology and offer a higher price than other bidders to acquire that technology. Such a policy would crowd out competitive bids for a "high-tech" company pushing it towards SWFs as the only serious bidder on the price level set by its (allegedly) too high a bid. An "unfriendly" SWF may prevent, for example, defence-related national companies from consolidating into one large company and in so doing, it may stand a better chance of surviving international competition. The remaining small- or medium-sized companies could subsequently be "conquered" one by one.

There is little evidence to support the view that domestic, privately owned companies in possession of high technology or the knowledge and ability relevant for national security are open for outside bids.

Again, the question arises as to what the implications would be to national security of a takeover by a SWF instead of by a foreign privately owned company. The question can be posed differently in that a government might have more leverage in negotiation or in discussion with another government about national security than if it negotiated with a privately owned company.

National security may be threatened by outside FDI, but it is far from obvious that it is threatened more by SWFs than by foreign privately owned companies. If there is a need to protect national security it should be done by other measures, not by discriminating between SWFs and private investors.[14]

Until now, national security has been considered only in a conventional sense. We need to broaden the analysis and examine national security in terms of securing supplies, guaranteeing effectiveness of infrastructure, maintaining competitiveness and knowledge of ownership.

2. The question of securing supplies is much in the forefront of the debate on SWFs, but the focus is mainly on oil-exporting countries in the Middle East buying, among

---

[14]The EU when setting up rules for the internal, later single, market was aware of the need to build in a safeguard for security even if the words used are "public security" and not "national security"; see Articles 36 and 224 of the original Treaty of Rome.

other things, agricultural land or in the case of China, buying minerals and oil. The large scale of Chinese investment in natural resources in Africa and Latin America and the latest controversy surrounding the Chinese investment in Rio Tinto (Cimilucca *et al.*, 2009) highlight how important this issue will be. An increasing scarcity of commodities, such as food, means higher prices and more profitable investment in these sectors. EU/OECD countries, however, do not seem to be a target, as few of them possess energy resources and/or commodities. What they might fear is SWFs investing in third countries and eventually taking over traditional suppliers to EU/OECD countries.

3. The case of a Dubai consortium wishing to take over the operation of a number of U.S. ports illustrates how sensitive EU/OECD countries might be, fearing that vital infrastructure could come under the control of a foreign government. It is difficult to gauge what foreign ownership would mean for ports and other infrastructure if a recipient country wanted to "mobilise" them to defend national security, but this is probably one of the few cases where SWF ownership might jeopardise national security.

At various points in the twentieth century, the British government subsidised the building of liners for the two main transatlantic ship owners — Cunard and White Star Line — conditional upon these ships being deployed as armed merchant cruisers in the event of national security. During World War I and World War II, the liners were used extensively as hospital ships and troop carriers. As late as 1982, *RMS Queen Elizabeth II* served as a troop ship in the Falklands War. Similarly *USS United States*, a passenger liner built in 1952, was a joint enterprise between the U.S. military and United States Lines transatlantic shipping company and was designed as a troopship with a capacity of 15,000 soldiers, although the ship served only as a liner until it ceased operating in 1969. These may or may not exist similar arrangements between governments and private companies in selected areas — not necessarily confined to shipping — and they might not be publicly known, but SWFs would not be allowed to invest in them.[15]

4. Maintaining competitiveness, or keeping what is regarded as a country's assets or "crown jewels", can evoke, and has evoked a national security issue. An example

---

[15]This is mentioned as an illustration only. For the shipping sector, national legislation in a number of countries, including the UK and the USA, may give the government the right to requisition ships in case of armed conflict. For example, in the UK, the Crown has by right of its prerogative, a *jus angariae*, that is to say, a right to appropriate the property of a neutral where necessary in time of war. This right of angary can only be exercised subject to the right of the neutral owner to receive compensation, which may be enforced by legal process. See *Halsbury's Law of England*, 49(1), 4th edn (LexisNexis 2005) at para. 410. I am grateful to Christopher Lau for helping with this point.

is Groupe Danone, the French food company. It originates from a glass company (BSN), which, after failing in its attempt in 1968 to merge with another French giant glassmaker Saint-Gobain, switched to food products and after a long string of mergers and takeovers became one of the world's biggest food companies. The French government's position was that, after efforts over many years to establish a food giant using France's position as an agricultural country, a takeover of Groupe Danone by a foreign company could not be tolerated. When rumours surfaced in the summer of 2005 that PepsiCo was weighing up a takeover bid, Prime Minister Dominique de Villepin pledged to defend Danone as one France's industrial "jewels" (DairyReporter, 2005).

The French position reflects its sentiment that some countries, for a variety of reasons, have a competitive advantage in selected areas and they cannot allow corporations to come under foreign control. It can be interpreted as a national security issue because those advancing this position regard it as necessary for the nation's pride and identity to develop their assets under national leadership. A more sophisticated interpretation points to the supply chain, as foreign ownership of some companies inevitably has negative consequences — in the case of Groupe Danone for French agriculture — and thus in the long term would undermine this sector's position as an integral part of the country's social fabric.

5. It is interesting to stop for a moment and ponder upon divergent views between governments and private companies in recipient countries. Governments may worry about inward FDI from SWFs and point to their national security concerns, but owners and management of many private companies may prefer capital injections from SWFs to capital from other companies or funds. They may see other companies or funds as predators in disguise looking for a bid to resell at a higher price or split the company into separate units to sell them one by one. The investing company may itself be a "victim" of analysts on the stock market, who may conclude that breaking up the recipient company or selling some of its knowledge will be good for the share price and force management into such policies. Inviting capital from outside, and especially in the form of SWFs looking for long-term development of the recipient company, may help to fend off pressure from the stock market as outlined above. For example, Daimler AG did not hesitate to welcome a capital injection from SWFs, but it might have been wary about a private investor having links to companies interested in Daimler's expertise.

SWF — Risk-Taking Profile

A great deal has been written about the risk-taking attitudes of SWFs, but there is little evidence that this is the case. The decisive question is, of course, whether the risk profile is such that they are ready to undertake investments, which could not find a "normal" investor or whether they seek safe investments.

Danmarks Nationalbank (Schrøder and Humle Slotsbjerg, 2008) has looked into risk management of SWFs compared with how central banks manage currency reserves, assuming that SWFs are an alternative to traditional management of currency reserves, and Danmarks Nationalbank draws the following conclusions:

> The primary difference between the investment strategies of central banks and SWFs is that central banks have to take monetary and foreign-exchange policy into account, whereas SWFs typically seek to achieve high returns and therefore have a greater risk appetite.
>
> From a risk-management perspective, it might be appropriate for a SWF to diversify in the same way as, for example, pension funds.
>
> SWFs with a long investment horizon have invested large sums in stocks and other, more risky assets in the expectation of achieving a higher return in the long run.

Turning to a comparison with other funds, the available evidence (Setser and Ziemba, 2007; IMF, 2008) reveals SWFs to be fairly prudent investors with a gradual rising share of equities in most portfolios.[16] The majority employ external fund managers and look to long-term and passive investment. In many cases, they diversify risks by investing according to a market index. If anything they seem to be more risk adverse and more prudent than many EU/OECD countries' private funds. An indication of the low willingness by SWFs to run risk is that their leverage seems to be low, separating them from hedge funds.

Most SWFs hold only minor stakes in companies and there are only a few cases of attempts to obtain control over companies. There is little evidence of SWFs seeking to take an active part in management of the company in which they invest (for example, by asking for a seat on a board or acquiring management responsibility). As minority stakeholders, they are less likely to influence management and the operation of the company they have invested in than many other funds without transparency and accountability.

Due to their ownership and origin, they are less transparent and less open to accountability than funds listed on Western stock exchanges. This is why critical observers point to the possibility that "secrecy" may lead them into investments

---

[16] The studies available all examine behaviour prior to the economic/financial crisis starting summer 2007. This means that known investment practice for the SWFs were developed when equities were rising in value and appearing to be a good and safe long-term investment.

not open to, or likely to be pursued by, "normal" funds. This argument, however, is flawed. Looking at the development of capital markets over the last decade it seems obvious that a number of funds domiciled in EU/OECD countries have been set up to avoid rules applicable for "normal" funds. For example, pension fund A and pension fund B can set up pension fund C that is not under the same supervision and thus is able to undertake operations not open to the other pension funds.

It is wrong to conclude that SWFs are without accountability. The fact that many are not listed on the stock exchange (although some of them are), and because the home country does not operate a Western-style political system, does not mean that the political system neglects the sentiment of the population, who for obvious reasons are interested in how the wealth of their nation is managed.

It is clear that ownership of SWFs, although less transparent and with less accountability, does not necessarily represent pursuing investment policies that are different from most "normal" funds. Unwanted repercussions in the recipient country are just as likely to occur from activities by "normal" funds as from SWFs, although they may be of a different character.

SWFs — Points of Concern and Answers

When a SWF obtains a controlling share in a company, there is a widely held concern that it could gradually transfer the "brain" of the acquired organisation (strategic planning, "high-tech", management knowhow and financial centre) into its own headquarters, and this could result in the recipient country being deprived of assets that are not only vital for the company being "robbed", but also for the economic development of the recipient country.

Several points arise from these fears. First, SWFs have up until now primarily taken small stakes in companies. While this makes the risk of transferring vital assets away from the recipient country remote, it does not prevent this scenario from materialising at a later stage when SWFs have grown larger. In addition, it still leaves open the question of corporate governance.

What would motivate an SWF to pursue such a policy? It would only be profitable if the "brain" produced a higher output in another country and although this cannot be ruled out (for example, if clusters of companies are created), it only seems feasible in a few cases.

The risk seems much more likely with inward FDI by a foreign company undertaking the investment on the basis of short-term calculations or for strategic reasons — for example, getting rid of competitors, or enlarging the research and development base.

It is not difficult to see why recipient countries react defensively to guard them-selves against this kind of FDI, but it is difficult to see why SWFs should be more likely to entertain these methods than other companies or why they would be set up in a predatory way to buy and later deconstruct a corporation.

SWFs — Perceived Impacts

Finally, we come to the question of the impact of SWFs on economic policy, the national capital market and the currency rate.

Recipient countries, many of which are running a deficit on their balance of pay-ment, would like the money controlled by SWFs to be invested with them. Without an orderly "recycling" of money accumulated by SWFs the global capital market would be in difficulties.

Recipient countries might like to impose constraints on inwards FDI, but are pre-vented from doing so by international rules that were written by them in an age when they were global investors. They cannot violate, at least not openly, rules set by themselves; if they try to do so, they will disrupt the global capital market that is necessary for them to finance their deficits and/or channel capital into research and development for their enterprises.

As the almost catastrophic development on the U.S. capital market, and to a certain extent the global capital market, illustrate that instability in financial markets comes from financial inventions initiated by institutions in the EU/OECD countries rather than by SWFs. The record of SWFs suggests that they are much more interested in keeping markets stable than in seeking short-term profits that would compromise the stability of the system.

The EU/OECD's negative reaction to SWFs in late 2007 and most of 2008 was replaced by a period of relief as a large number of Western financial institutions that had violated almost all the rules of good corporate governance were rescued by an injection of capital from SWFs.

An argument is sometimes promoted that an SWF may be used to destabilise another country's economic policy. There are many precedents where monetary policy in particular has been rocked by inward FDIs, but it is difficult to see how any destabilisation could have taken place because of an SWF in view of their lim-ited investment. This brings us back to one of the major observations of fears: that growing SWFs may be able to destabilise another country's economic policy in the future. As outlined above, the size of SWFs is still limited and an attempt to influence economic policy (for example, by trying to push the exchange rate up or down or force interest rate adjustments) will require a massive effort.

It is also postulated that SWFs, by non-economic motivated operations, can create a negative sentiment around a country's industries and/or selected industries. When a company sells shares to an SWF, it might set in motion a wave of uncertainty about the future prospect of a company, thus destabilising it. This argument is unfounded as it rests upon the assumption that other investors and rating agencies are unaware that the selling was initiated by an SWF and that they are unable to decide whether they should sell shares or not.

Investment by an SWF might, in some cases, interfere with competition. For example, suppose that an SWF from a country that is among the world's biggest steel producers undertakes a large investment in iron ore suppliers. In these circumstances, it is not unthinkable that price and delivery may be slanted in favour of steel mills in the home country of the SWF.

For the EU there is a special concern as the European capital market is evolving and consequently a number of capital market provisions, including supervision, are being transferred from national to European level. Fundamentally, it is a problem of discrimination/non-discrimination. The European capital market is built to favour, or at least to accord preferential treatment to, European companies *vis-à-vis* non-member countries. On the one hand, the Europeans need to make sure that rules are drafted in such away that foreigners do not reap benefits;[17] on the other hand, international commitments (for example, as undertaken in the OECD or World Trade Organisation) must be observed. At its core, the problem for the Europeans is to avoid a situation where SWFs unintentionally act as a spoiler in their endeavours to further European integration.

---

[17] The cornerstone of the EU as economic integration is often misunderstood or misrepresented. The main idea is non-discrimination between member counties, but not necessarily according foreigners the same treatment — often labelled "community preference". Foreigners sometimes criticise this, but neither politically nor economically is there anything wrong with "community preference", as long as it conforms with international commitments. There is no reason why the Europeans should accord preferential treatment to other countries without reciprocity. The basic idea of the WTO is to spread such *quid pro quo* arrangements, which explains why countries do not do it unilaterally. Several Free Trade Agreements enter into this area, but without exception they act in conformity with WTO commitments and normally the words "WTO plus" are used to inform that preferential treatment is accorded on top of what WTO delivers and usually it is stipulated that in case of subsequent WTO agreements the Free Trade Ageements will be swallowed up by what WTO may agree upon.

CONCLUSION

EU/OECD countries fear SWFs without explaining why they do so. These countries often put forward platitudes such as "national security problems" with little evidence as to what the threat of SWFs actually is, apart from "foreigners" owning domestic enterprises or having a stake in them. In practice, these countries find it difficult to come to terms with their declining role in the global economy as witnessed by a falling share of global GDP and the growing rate of outsourcing.

In addition, they fail to realise that a swing of global savings away from the EU/OECD countries to Asia and the Middle East necessarily and unavoidably means that ownership of a larger share of global economic activities will follow. Consequently, capital markets and the control over financial institutions move away from EU/OECD countries and are taken over by countries standing for the savings.[18]

In short, the problem is not about the power of SWFs, but the psychological barrier in acquiescing to the change of power in the global economy.

ACKNOWLEDGEMENTS

I am grateful to Ib Hansen and Frank Mols for a number of comments to the first draft. Klaus Regling and Ole Beier Sørensen helped me in my preparations.

REFERENCES

Cimilucca, Dana, Shai Oster and Amy Or (2009), 'Rio Tinto Scuttles its Deal with Chinalco', *Wall Street Journal*, 5 June.

Commission of the European Communities (2008a), 'Communication from the Commission to the European Parliament, the Council, the European Economic and Social Committee and the Committee of the Regions: A Common European Approach to Sovereign Wealth Funds, Brussels', available at http://ec.europa.eu/internal_market/finances/docs/sovereign_en.pdf.

---

[18]China and Japan have for several years competed for the number two slot for global value of stock markets and in July 2009 China moved into that position again after Japan had been number two for 18 months. See *Bloomberg Online*, "China's Market Value Overtakes Japan as World's No. 2", 16 July 2009, available at http://bloomberg.com/apps/news?pid=20601087&sid=a_84o9PPPGqk. There are those who think that China's stock market is soon going to be number one. See *Bloomberg Online*, "Mobius Says China Market Value to overtake U.S. in Three Years", 18 July 2009. available at http://www.bloom.berg.com/apps/news?pld=2060l080& sid=a4.VQEZdQ_M.

Conway, Edmund (2007), 'Darling Warns Over Politically Motivated Bids', *Telegraph*, 20 October, available at http://www.telegraph.co.uk/finance/markets/2818013/Darling-warns-over-poliltically-motivated-bids.html.

Council of the European Union (2008b), 'Presidency Conclusions', Document 7652/1/08, Rev.1, Brussels European Council, 13–14 March, available at http://www.consilium.europa.eu/ueDocs/cms_Data/docs/pressData/en/ec/99410.pdf.

Council of the European Union (2009a), 'Presidency Conclusions', Document 7880/1/09, Rev. 1, Brussels European Council, 19–20 March, available at http://www.consilium.europa.eu/uedocs/cms_data/docs/pressdata/en/ec/106809.pdf.

Council of the European Union (2009b), 'Presidency Conclusions', Document 11225/09, Brussels European Council, 18–19 June, available at http://www.consilium.europa.eu/uedocs/cms_data/docs/pressdata/en/ec/108622.pdf.

CRS (Congressional Research Service) (2009), *Sovereign Wealth Funds: Background and Policy issues for Congress*, Analyst Marin A. Weiss, Order Code RL34336, Updated 26 March 2009, available at http://assets.opencrs.com/rpts/ RL34336_20080326.pdf.

DailyReportet.com (2005), 'Water Charge Batters Danone Profits', 21 July, available at http://www.dairyreporter.com/Financial/Water-charge-batters-Danone-profits.

Dougherty, Carter (2007), 'Europe Looks at Controls on State-owned Investors', *New York Times*, 13 July, available at http://www.nytimes.com/2007/07/13/business/worldbusiness/13iht-protect.4.6652337.html.

Emmanuel, William and Tim Hepher (2008), 'Sarkozy Vows to Defend France Against Wealth Funds', Reuters, 9 January, available at http://uk.reuters.com/article/idUKNOA93430220080109?pageNumber=1&virtualBrandChannel=0.

Euobserver.com (2008), 'Sarkozy Launches €20 Billion 'Strategic' Industries Fund', 21 November, available at http://euobserve.com/9/27157.

European Commission (2009), *The So-called 'Sovereign Wealth Funds': Regulatory Issues, Financial Stability and Prudential Supervision*, Economic Papers 378, Brussels, April.

European Parliament (2008), 'Resolution on Sovereign Wealth Funds', RSP/2008/2589, available at http://www.europarl.europa.eu/sides/getDoc.do?pubRef=-//EP//TEXT+MOTION+B6-2008-0304+0+DOC+XML+V0//ENandhrtp://www.europarl.europa.eu/oeil/FindByProcnum.do?lang=en&procnum=RSP/2008/2589.

Eurostat Pocketbooks (2007), *European Union Foreign Direct Investment Yearbook 2007.* Luxembourg: Office for the Official Publications of the European Communities 2007, available at http://epp.eurostat.ec.europa.eu/cache/lTY_OFFPUB/KS-BK-07-001/EN/KS-BK-07-001-EN.PDF.

Eurostat Pocketbooks (2008), *European Union Foreign Direct Investment Yearbook 2008.* Luxembourg: Office for true Official Publications of the European Communities 2008, available at http://bookshop.europa.eu/eubookshop/download.action?fileName=KSBKO800IENC_002.pdf&eubphfUid=604157&catalogNbr=KS-BK-08-001-EN-C.

Fotka, Veljko and William Meggison (2009), 'Are SWFs Welcome Now?', *Columbia FDI Perspectives, 9*, 21 July, available at http://vcc.columbia.edu/documents/ FotakandMegginson-Final.pdf.

Gugler, Philippe and Julien Chaisse (2009), 'Sovereign Wealth Funds in the European Union, General Trust Despite Concerns, NCCR Trade Regulation', Swiss National Centre of Competence in Research, Working Paper No. 2009/4, January.

House of Commons Library (2008), *Sovereign Wealth Funds,* Ian Townsend, Standard note SN/EP/4767, 1 July.

IMF (2008), *Sovereign Wealth Funds.* IMF, Washington, DC.

IMF, COFER tables, available at http://www.imf.org/external/np/sta/cofer/eng/cofer.pdf.

International Monetary Fund (IMF), *Sovereign Wealth Funds — A Work Agenda,* 28 February, available at http://www.Imf.org/external/np/pp/eng/2008/022908.pdf.

Jen, Stephen (2007), 'Currencies: How Big Can Sovereign Wealth Funds Be By 2015', *Morgan Stanley Global Research,* 3 May, available at http://www.morganstanley.com/views/gef/archive/2007/20070504-Fri.html.

Laurance, Ben and Louise Armistead (2009), 'The Rising Powers of Sovereign Funds', *Sunday Times,* 28 October, available at http://business.timesonline.co.uk/tol/business/industry_sectors/banking_and_finance/article2752048.ece.

McCreevey, Charlie (2008), 'The Importance of Open Markets', Speech to Council of British Chambers of Commerce in Continental Europe (COBCOE), London, 10 January, available at http://europa.eu/rapid/pressReleasesAction.do?reference=SPEECH/08/4&format=HTML&aged=0&language=EN.

Monitor Group Assessing the Risks (2008), available at http://www.monitor.com/ Portals/0/MonitorContent/documents/Monitor_SWF_report_final.pdf.

OECD (2008a), 'Chair's Summary of the OECD Council at Ministerial Level: Outreach, Reform and the Economics of Climate Change', Paris, 4–5 June, available at http;//www.oecd.org/document/56/0,3343,en_2649_34487_40778872_1_1_1_1,00.html.

OECD (2008b), *Guidance on Sovereign Wealth Funds,* available at http://www.oecd.org/document/19/0,3343, en_2649_34887_41807059_1_1_1_1,00.html.

Regling, Klaus (2008), 'Sovereign Wealth Funds: Building Trust in a Changing Economic Environment', Speech given in Singapore to the 2nd meeting of the International Working Group of SWFs, 10 July 2008.

Reiter, Chris (2009), 'Daimler Sells Aabar a 9.1% Stake for $2.7 Billion', *Bloomberg Online,* 22 March, available at http://www.bloomberg.com/apps/news?pid=20601087&sid=a0eAzATgnNcU.

Reuters (2009a), 'Sarkozy Attacks Wealth Funds on Eve of Middle East Trip', Reuters, 12 January, available at http://www.reuters.com/article/oilRpt/idUSL1220023020080112.

Reuters (2009b), 'France in $19 Billion Strategic Fund Stake Transfer', Reuters, 6 July, available at http://www.reuters.com/articte/innovationNews/idUSTRE5651ZT20090706.

Setser, Brad and Rachel Ziemba (2007), 'Understanding the New Financial Super-power — The Management of GCC Official Foreign Assets', *RGE Monitor,* December, available at http://www.cfr.org/content/publications/attachments/SetserZiembaGCCfinal.pdf.

Schröder, Søren and Esben Humle Slotsbjerg (2008), 'Foreign-Exchange Reserves and Sovereign Wealth Funds', *Danmarks Nationalbank Monetary Review,* 2nd Quarter, available at http://www.nationalbanken.dk/C1256BE9004F6416/side/Monetary_Review_2008_2_Quarter/$file/kap05.html#_ftn3.

Twickel, Nikolaus von (2008), 'Barriers Going Up All Over Europe', *Moscow Times*, 13 March, available at https://www.usrbc.org/resources/russiannews/event/1366.

Walker, Marcus (2008), 'Germany Tinkers with Foreign-Takeovers Plan', *Wall Street Journal*, 14 January, available at http://online.wsj.com/article/SB120027192850787365.html.

Agonising Wait for U.S. Economy to Rebalance*

While the limelight is on the global economy, in reality it is about the state of the U.S. economy and repercussions on other economies of recent policy measures, in particular the policy of quantitative easing (QE) recently announced by the U.S. Federal Reserve.

Behind the curtain looms the future of the international monetary system, which has been, so far, based on the U.S. dollar.

The U.S. has boxed itself into a tight corner from where there is not much it can do to rescue its economy from the doldrums. After President Barack Obama's inauguration in January last year, there was a chance to make bold moves and push for new policies, blaming — rightly — former President George Bush and former chairman of the Federal Reserve, Alan Greenspan, but it was not taken. Now the crisis is owned by Mr Obama.

Fundamentally, the U.S. suffers from a toxic combination of insufficient savings and too low demand. If policies are implemented to increase savings, demand would fall further. If demand is stimulated, savings would fall, at least in the short run while rising debts would aggravate the already low confidence in both the economy and political system.

American policy makers face the difficult question of how to reconcile the drive for higher savings and higher demand simultaneously. Economic theory gives the answer: You cannot, at least not in the short term.

Quantitative easing, now in its second round, will do little to boost U.S. aggregate demand. The current problem is not a lack of liquidity or too high interest rates preventing consumption or investment, but stagnant — or at best slowly rising — consumption combined with sluggish investment. Monetary policy operates on the supply side of the economy making it cheaper to borrow. In principle, this should lift consumption and make investment more profitable. But that pre-supposes consumers and investors expect the U.S. to be on a strong growth curve. This assumption is not valid at present, which renders the stimulus via monetary policy ineffective.

* First appeared in *Business Times*, 11 November 2010.

There are no prospects that U.S. unemployment will start to fall visibly in the near future. Over the last six months, annual GDP growth has been 1.9 percent annualised, well below the 2.8 percent which the Fed says is necessary to keep employment stable. Almost all growth forecasts for next year, even by international institutions, come in well below 2.8 percent.

The U.S. also suffers from a structural mismatch between the supply and demand for skills. The conventional instrument to reduce unemployment is higher aggregate demand, but this presumes that the economy will recover without structural changes so that the new demand will produce a cyclical recovery in the same sectors that were hit by the recession. This is clearly not realistic. The global recession has led to heavy cost cutting in which many traditional jobs have been axed or have moved abroad.

Mr Obama is hoping for a doubling of exports in five years' time and on paper, that looks fine. The administration seems, however, to have overlooked that it is not exports, but the trade balance that determines growth, production, and employment. Doubling exports will not help much if imports also double. Then the impact on growth and employment will be muted.

This helps to explains why the U.S. will not only allow, but wish the U.S. dollar to fall. Treasury Secretary Timothy Geithner's repeated statement that the U.S. favours a strong dollar rings hollow.

The success of a deliberate policy to depreciate the U.S. dollar depends upon two things. First, that a lower U.S. dollar is accompanied by restrictive economic policies at home, which obviously is not happening. Second, the U.S. dollar must fall relative to other currencies. If other countries resist this, that will not happen, or at least not to the extent desired.

Here is the snag. The QE will not do much for the U.S. economy, but will make it harder for America's trade partners to resist a depreciation of the U.S. dollar. The influx of U.S. dollars into their economies will lead to increases in money supply.

Traditionally, this is countered by a hike in interest rates which would push their exchange rates upwards *vis-a-vis* the U.S. dollar.

Countries suspect that this is indeed America's main policy objective and the battle lines are drawn between those countries which are not ready to let it happen and the U.S. which is flexing its muscles in its capacity as the international reserve currency country.

The U.S. can use that role for its own purposes — but at a price. A growing chorus is emerging for taking away from the U.S. the privileges linked to be a reserve currency by switching to a global monetary system that is less dependent upon the U.S. dollar.

Those foreign countries which have the best chance to escape the U.S. dollar inflow are those which, like China, are resisting pressure to fully liberalise capital movements and are standing firm on their refusal to make their currencies convertible.

But this in turn prevents their currencies from taking on a bigger role as reserve currencies. The fact is that there are still only limited alternatives to the U.S. dollar in this respect. This permits the U.S. to go on enjoying its current advantages.

This brings us to the agonising conclusion that there does not seem to be an alternative to sitting and waiting for the rebalancing of the U.S. economy to work its way through the system. Meanwhile the international monetary system and in particular the role of the U.S. dollar as a reserve currency will come under closer scrutiny, and it may not escape unscathed.

But the unanswered question is whether that also goes for the system as a whole.

Get Out While You Can*
Why the U.S. Dollar is Doomed

A reserve currency grows out of the strongest, largest, and most dynamic national economy spreading its wings over the global financial market. This is how the British pound sterling worked before 1914 and it is how the U.S. dollar has worked since 1945.

Other countries were ready to accumulate pounds and later dollars because they constituted a claim on British or American production or opened the door to invest in their companies. These two countries were — in the respective periods — the biggest economies with products in demand, envied by the rest of the world. Until about 1960, the key term in international economics was "dollar shortage." There was no hesitation in accumulating dollars because they were not hanging suspended in free air, but anchored in the real U.S. economy.

What happened to the United States over the last two or three decades (and to Britain after 1918) was a decoupling from the real economy. The rest of the world no longer wanted to buy American production, resulting in a high, persistent, and growing deficit in the balance of payments, and the incentive to buy American production was over-shadowed by the drive of U.S. industry to invest abroad.

Even if the U.S. economy had lost its lure, foreigners might still be tempted to hold dollars if they were looked upon as some kind of global legal tender perceived in the sense of a generally accepted vehicle for settling payments.

For that to be the case, there needs to be confidence in a stable purchasing power. Nobody wants to accumulate a currency if they fear that some years down the road the purchasing power will deliver a smaller amount of goods and services than originally available.

U.S. economic policy has undermined that confidence. At the beginning of 2010, U.S. foreign debt is the same size as U.S. GDP. Even worse, total debt run up by U.S. private, business, and public sectors over the fat years amounts to almost 400 percent

---

* First appeared in *The International Economy*, Winter 2010.

of GDP. Net interest on public debt accounts for approximately 7 percent of GDP. Net interest on public debt accounts for approximately 7 percent of the federal budget, and according to optimistic forecasts will rise to approximately 20 percent in 2020. It seems almost inconceivable that a debt of that magnitude can be sustained. This leaves three options. The first is to service the debt by raising taxes, resulting in sluggish economic growth. The second is to introduce a levy on the yield flowing from Treasury bonds, introduce a levy on the yield flowing from Treasury bonds, hurting — deliberately — the creditors. The third is to print money, asking inflation to do the dirty job of making inroads into the real value of claims on the United States. None of these options appeals to the creditors. The signal is quite the contrary: get out while you can.

This spells doom for the U.S. dollar as the dominant reserve currency. How will the game unravel?

It will start with questioning of the role of the U.S. dollar as the unit of account for international trade in oil, gold, and commodities. Logically, these goods were denominated in dollars as long as the United States was the main buyer, but that now ceases to be the case. The first step to dismantling the U.S. dollar will be switching to an international unit of account composed of a number of currencies, a so-called basket of currencies like the Special Drawing Rights used by the International Monetary Fund. Currently, a group of oil-exporting countries contemplates just such a step.

For suppliers of commodities and purchasers except the United States, the effect of a shift away from the dollar will be price fluctuations less dependent upon the U.S. economy and more in tune with the global economy. For the United States, this will be one more straw on the back of the camel. The U.S. economy has been shielded from the effect on commodity prices of dollar fluctuations. A unit of account other than the U.S. dollar will remove that anomaly and allow fluctuations in commodity prices when the dollar moves on the currency markets to spill over into inflation, competitiveness, and wages. The United States is totally unaware of what that means, never having been exposed to it, and equally unprepared to deal with this further limitation of maneuvering room in economic policy.

Next will come a switch out of passive investments in the U.S. dollar such as Treasury bonds. Contrary to much discussion, the alternative to the dollar is not other currencies. There are no obvious candidates. Neither the European nor the Japanese economies radiate more strength and inspire more confidence than the U.S. economy, so why should creditors want to replace one currency of dubious value with another equally dubious? Instead, creditors increasingly will put their money into oil, gold, and commodities and stock markets, By so doing, they will cast off their dependence on U.S. economic policy. These assets will be classified as safe investments. Commodity prices will be presumed to be on an upward curve, and stocks, representing not debt but a claim on future production, will trump bonds.

The uncertainty of the U.S. dollar implies not so much a move away from dollar-denominated assets as a switch into assets not dependent upon the U.S. government, the Federal Reserve System, and the policies they implement. What matters is not the currency label, but the character of the asset. Recent price levels for the assets mentioned above disclose that many creditors are following such a course, which is a bad omen for future bond markets.

Another unit of account will gradually take over in international financial transactions, crowding out the U.S. dollar. Companies will loan and borrow in SDRs and publicize their annual statements in SDRs. This can easily be done without an actual SDR currency being used. It reflects that with a less-important U.S. economy, it is not worthwhile to own claims on U.S. production or investment opportunities, which are not in demand, but claims on global production and investment opportunities.

The ultimate step in the decline of the U.S. dollar will take place if or when creditors feel that another economy has grown sufficiently strong to offer what the British economy did before 1914 and the U.S. economy did after 1945: namely, incomparable goods, services, and investment opportunities. It appears likely, but is by no means certain, that the Chinese economy may get there by the middle of this century.

Meanwhile, we all have to muddle through as best we can.

U.S. Recession: Spend Now, Save Later*

The governments want their citizens to go shopping and reverse the economy's slide toward recession. But consumers, as the Bush administration found out, cling to their tax rebates and avoid the shopping malls.

Now the Obama administration gears up to provide massive stimulus to create jobs and get people spending again. The fate of the U.S. economy and that of the world hangs on the success of his effort. If history is any guide and people behave the way one school of economic thought predicts, the chances do not appear bright. Unless citizens are convinced that their future earning will be more than the total of their annualized income from job or business, they are more likely to save than spend. The health of the world economy depends on U.S. performance, which in recent years emerged as the principal engine of growth. In 2007, private consumption reached 71 percent of the U.S. gross domestic product, after standing steady at about 62 percent for more than 30 years, from 1950 to the early 1980s. American consumers turned their economy into an engine of growth at the expense of economic balance, as consumption far outran production, resulting in a debt race never seen before in peacetime.

Understanding how such a rapid change occurred is critical to understanding consumer behavior during this crisis. A clue is found in comparing asset prices with consumption as share of GDP. Stock-market prices were also basically stable from 1950 to the mid-1980s, moving slowly upwards during the second half of the 1980s to take a mighty jump from the early 1990s to 2008, with a brief interruption when the IT-bubble burst in 2000. Housing prices, adjusted for inflation, were basically unchanged from 1950 to 2000, thereafter expanding into the property bubble that started to burst in 2006. Exactly at the moment when share prices leveled off, their stimulatory impact was replaced by property prices; when both stopped going up, consumption was hit, no longer stimulating the economy but pushing it into contraction.

The theory about consumption coined by economist Franco Modigliani about 50 years ago reveals the effect of asset prices on consumption and offers insights for judging how effective proposed U.S. expansionary measures might be. Broadly

* First appeared in *YaleGlobal online*, 11 February 2009.

speaking, the theory suggests that expectations and stability are crucial, that people consume portions of their anticipated lifetime income steadily throughout their lives. Lifetime horizon means that temporary fluctuations in income do not influence consumption. Instead the consumer absorbs fluctuations by building up or running down wealth: young people borrow, anticipating higher incomes, the middle-aged save more and the elderly exhaust their savings.

This is precisely what happened in the U.S. during the last decade. With property prices soaring, individuals changed their perception of resource availability over the course of their lifespan. Expecting constantly growing resources in terms of asset price, consumers spent more money. When asset prices suddenly turned around, falling instead of rising, the individual was caught flatfooted, forced to reduce consumption and increase savings, re-establishing the consumption equation steered by lifetime income only: despite any federal government splash-out of funds, consumers cannot be expected to return to past behavior as happy spenders.

When the Great Depression started with the stock-market crash in 1929, conventional economic wisdom was to lower interest rates, making it more profitable to invest and triggering higher investment, thus stopping the economic downward spiral. Yet, that did not happen. Companies did not invest even if the money was almost free; instead, they hoarded cash. British economist John Maynard Keynes saw that monetary policy, with lower interest rates, would not work, because of the liquidity trap: faltering demand discouraged investment even when debt carried little cost. Consequently, he ordained demand stimulus via fiscal policy, even if contrary to conventional wisdom, it meant rising public deficits and higher public debt. The policy worked.

Now we're in a congruous position with regard to fiscal stimulus. With the lifetime consumption theory in mind, it's unlikely that money handed out will be spent. So we move into what Keynes might have labeled a "fiscal policy trap," meaning that regardless of money poured into the economy, spending will not go up. Spending will rise only when the individual concludes that future resources warrant increased spending. The brutal fact is that the U.S. cannot spend its way out of the crisis. On the contrary, the more the U.S. spends, the more likely individuals will deduct limits to future resources, because debt incurred must be repaid, meaning future higher taxes and less disposable income. This may well prove to be the revelation to the science of economics of the present crisis.

People may ask why fiscal stimulus helped in the 1930s, but is judged to be impotent now. The answer is, in 1929 when the Great Depression struck, the U.S. debt level was far lower than today's level. Broadly speaking, total debt amounts to almost 400 percent of GDP in 2009, compared with 170 percent in 1929.

Pump-priming, as proposed by government stimulus plans, will be hoarded by consumers to reduce their debt as money was hoarded in the 1930s. There's a clear parallel to Japanese companies in the 1990s, which used capital to rebuild balance sheets, not to invest. The lesson is clear: it's no use giving people money to spend if economic rationale tells them to save. The most noteworthy aspect of pump-priming will be redistributing savings between the private and the public sector with no visible effect on production, consumption and employment.

So what can be done to extricate the U.S. from "the fiscal policy trap"?

Consumption patterns cannot be rolled back to boost the economy. Demographics works against higher consumption with the increase of households primarily taking place in the age bracket 50 years and older, with its low propensity to consume. What's needed is a restructuring of the U.S. GDP — acquiescing to a lower share for consumption and welcoming a higher share for investment and net exports compared to the last decade or two. This calls for an orchestrated panoply of policy measures that require years to work through the system. Understandably, the loss of jobs calls for action. The American export engine is unlikely to be fired up again. But a combination of measures to enhance the skill of the workforce, allowing the U.S. to regain some of its competitiveness, and extended unemployment benefits as a temporary help until the economy grows again might prove effective and at the same time address fundamental problems behind the present calamities, including loss of competitiveness plus economic and social inequality.

The best way is to take the bull by the horns and stimulate savings to eliminate the oppressive debt burden, thus restoring balance between production and consumption and lay the foundation for future growth. The contraction or lower growth imposed by debt-reducing policies may be worth sustaining. The alternative now pursued, including massive tax cuts, is running up an even higher debt, jeopardizing confidence in re-balancing the economy and undermining long-term capability to restore sustainable growth spearheaded by investment and net exports.

A quick fix cannot redress a fundamental disequilibrium. The more frenetic attempts to deliver a policy solution here and now will most likely not address the fundamental disequilibrium underpinning the crisis. The stimulus should be for saving and enhanced competitiveness rather than spending.

Part IV
The Euro-zone

Introduction to Part IV

The Euro-zone is not the first attempt to shape a currency union. The Latin Monetary Union was formed in 1866 and encompassed France, Italy, Spain, and several other European nation-states. It lasted about 50 years. A Scandinavian Currency Union with Denmark, Sweden, and Norway was formed in 1873 and lasted until the economic stress brought along with the outbreak of World War One. In 1834 the German states — not yet united into one German nation-state — formed a kind of currency union that lasted until the German nation-state was declared in 1871 thereafter to be replaced by the currency of the new-born nation.

These experiences may not have weighed heavily on the Europeans when they decided in 1988 to draw up plans for an economic and monetary union to be agreed in 1991 and translated into reality with the Euro as the single currency in the hands of the citizens as per 1 January 2002.

The background was economic and political.

Economic in the sense that after four decades of integration, the prevailing view is that a single currency would solidify and strengthen the single market, the common agricultural policy, and the common external trade policy thereby enhancing Europe's competitiveness *vis-à-vis* the U.S. as it was seen in those days when the Asian countries had not yet changed global competitiveness through labour arbitrage and outsourcing. Several decades of currency adjustments to bring competitiveness of the member states of the EU into line with each other had proved to be ineffectual mainly because of the openness of the economies. Policy-makers came to reject that economic policy instrument; that being the case, there were very few arguments against taking the step to set up a single currency to reap the full benefits instead of a half-built house.

Politically, the initiative was taken before the fall of the Soviet and Russian Empire in 1991, but implemented in the light of these tumultuous and seminal events. Europe had to be stronger to shoulder the burden of integrating the Central- and Eastern European nation-states who formerly were inside the Soviet sphere, but now trying to find a place among other European nation-states. They looked to the European Union and to reject their ambitions of membership would have been a political and psychological betrayal that would have traumatized Europe for decades, maybe even centuries.

It was not because there were no voices pointing out the difficulties and challenges and after the treaty was known for its deficiencies. The member states, however, decided that it was now or never. If it was not done when the strong tailwind of change — even euphoria after the breakup of the Soviet and Russian Empire — the political support plus not the least popular understanding, it might never have been done. So the decision was to go ahead knowing that the work was not perfect and needed amendments along the road, but what proved necessary was what would be done to keep the single currency afloat. As the founding intellectual father of European integration, Jean Monnet, stated, *'L'Europe se fera dans les crises —* Europe is forged through crises'.

The prospect of a political union loomed in the background. It did not last long before observers pointed out that unless such a step was taken, the single currency was unlikely to survive. They referred to historical experiences to support this thesis. The truth is that those who drafted the treaty were fully aware of that. That explains that substantial progress was made at the same time for immigration, judicial co-operation, and similar items plus the launch of a common foreign and security policy. Behind this construction was the approach chosen by European integration since its inception to move forward step by step. A political union might be necessary for the single currency, but the sentiment was "let us see along the road and decide accordingly".

It is sometimes brought forward that Germany gave up the Deutschmark in return for French support of the reunification of Germany. It is highly doubtful whether this thesis survives closer scrutiny. Suffice to recall that the initiative to draft a treaty for the single currency was agreed more than one year (June 1988) before the upheaval in Central- and Eastern Europe started.

It is closer to the truth that German industry analysing the currency turmoil in the 1970s and first couple of years in the 1980s concluded that its competitiveness would be undercut by other European member states bringing back competitive depreciations *vis-à-vis* the Deutschmark. If so Germany would be caught between the devil and the deep sea. Either Germany stuck to its strict economic policy with low inflation and no-or low-deficits on public finances with the result that its industry would lose market shares or it relaxed its economic policy allowing a higher inflation to prevent loss of market shares. Neither of these options was palatable for politicians, voters, and industry. Germany found the way out of this dilemma. Instead of seeing itself pushed into an economic policy leading to higher inflation or job losses, why not turn around and convince, maybe even force on other member states the strict and stringent economic policy embedded in Germany's post war recovery and subsequent success as the world's biggest exporter. That happened. Germany convinced the other Euro members of the virtue and advantages of this economic policy; it became the Euro-zone policy. It was not too difficult as its scoreboard recommended it. It is wrong to label it "German economic policy"; there is nothing "German" about it and similar policies have successfully been adopted by many other countries with analogous success.

Several member states of the EU chose not to join. Britain had always been sceptical about the depth of integration and except for a couple of years around 1990, stayed outside the mechanism for fixed but adjustable currency rates (ERM). While those member states joining did not fear a political union even if some of them may have had their reservations, Britain was not disposed to embark on a voyage with this destination. Furthermore, Britain's economy was fundamentally different from the economies of the continental European nations. It was dependent on oil production and the financial sector together accounting for as much as 15–20 percent of GDP. A currency union requires the structure of the member state's economy to react similarly to outside economic events, which is only the case with a congruous economic structure. The main idea that the most competitive producer takes the market from the less competitive one also requires congruous economies. On top of that, a large number of British and American economists were convinced that the Euro would not work. They saw a single currency (economic and monetary union) in the prism of how the American economy worked and concluded that as the Euro-zone looked different it could not work. They did not incorporate neither the political will among the Euro-zone countries to make it work nor the possibility that other accompanying policy instrument might compensate for the higher mobility and flexibility found in the American economy.

Until the global financial crisis, the Euro-zone worked well; it looked solid and the markets behaved like there was no doubt about its future. The markets worked too well. The weak member states like Greece did borrow to the same interest rate — almost — as the stronger countries like Germany. They used the money to fuel an unsustainable asset boom coming back to haunt them a few years later. Why this happened is difficult to answer. The financial markets should have known better. When the treaties were drafted, no one expected Greece to borrow at the same interest rate as Germany and banks in France and Germany to lend just because the bonds were nominated in Euro instead of Drachma. The expectation was that, of course, the financial markets would distinguish between a Greek bond guaranteed by Greece, not the Euro-zone, and a German bond — like no-one expects the financial market to think that the U.S. guarantees a foreign bond just because it is issued in U.S. Dollars. The financial markets did not.

When the global financial crisis struck the weakness of the Euro, the flaws, and shortcomings of the treaties surfaced.

First of all the dichotomy between the Southern European countries and the Northern European ones were exposed. The first group had for years been running a much less competitive economy, but managed to do it by depreciation of their currencies until the early 1980s and later by borrowing. Now the birds came home to roost. This was neither a monetary nor fiscal problem. It was two economic systems inside the same currency area.

Secondly, although some progress had been made through free right of establishment, the Euro-zone did not have a genuine banking system with banking services, regulations, and supervision still mainly national. The large banks did not operate all over Europe. Branches of *inter alia* Deutscshe Bank or BNP Paribas in Saloniki was few if there at all. The adjustment mechanism seen in currency zones with banks transferring funds around according to needs were simply not there, closing the door for interbank lending (the money market), instead opening it for a credit crunch, deepening the crisis.

Thirdly, although the treaty and subsequent agreements had introduced rules for debt and deficits on public budget, they were not binding and not respected as member states saw fiscal deficits run out of control.

The banking crisis called for public funds. The member states duly stepped in. Unfortunately their funds were insufficient to solve the banking crisis, but large enough to cast their already fragile public finances into disarray. They acted to solve one crisis, but brought upon themselves another one ending up with two crises plus a credibility gap. The main culprit was the imperfect integration due to gaps in the treaties. It was not the Euro-zone who stepped in, but the member states calling upon other Euro-zone countries to support them — in vain. The signals followed by actions from the European Central Bank apparently with German consent changed the course of 2012. Not for the first time and certainly not for the last one, the lesson that the markets look at actions and not declarations had to be swallowed by monetary institutions.

This diagnosis took some time to digest. For a couple of years, it is not too much to say that the Euro-zone's answers were too little and too late. Policy-makers were behind the curve. They managed to get through by sheer political will although from time to time the situation looked precarious. It turned into a contest about "who is in charge here". Is it the Euro-zone politicians elected by the people, or financial markets gambling against them, aiming at a profit for themselves? The Euro-zone politicians won because they wanted the Euro to survive. The prospect of a break up was so frightening with such disastrous economic consequences that the costs of keeping the single currency might have looked high but was much lower than the alternative in form of a break-up. In August 2012, it was estimated that the cost for Germany of a break-up could go as high as 10 percent of GDP. Even an isolated Greek exit could bear substantial risks to business.

Not surprisingly, the key was the attitude of Germany. The message coming out may from time to time have been messy (clumsy?), but when the roll call came, Germany was willing to do what was necessary to do and support ECB to do the same and even more importantly, to provide the funds in question. There was a caveat, however. The weak countries undertook commitments to restructure and reform their economies and policies preventing them from running up deficits of similar nature in the future. Germany was willing to keep the Euro-zone provided that future crises like the one harassing the single currency from 2008 to 2012 would not appear again. Not to forget: On the condition that the weak countries helped themselves by restructuring and reforming what for them was painful, but necessary. Germany was not altruistic. Its action reflected what guided it to the single currency in the first place: Access to the markets, a level-playing field for competition, and a European economic policy analogous to the one Germany had pursued over half a century.

At the end of 2012, the situation was that all the major problems have been addressed. The weak Southern European countries have all introduced steps to "restructure & reform" and a turnaround of their balance of payments and sharply falling unit labour costs show that they are on their way albeit the fact that much still needs to be done. A banking union has been agreed to prevent banks to repeat reckless lending similar to what was seen before 2007. A fiscal union forcing member states to respect rules for debt and deficits has also passed. Both have to be written into treaty text to be ratified. Taken together, these measures constitute a layout for getting the single currency back on track.

It remains to be seen when and in what form this will be implemented, but it seems to be enough to tie the Euro over current difficulties and then we will see how it fares in the future.

The true lesson to be drawn is confirmation of the plinth of European integration.

First: The integration goes on despite difficulties and temporary setbacks.

Second: There is no alternative; the point of no return has been passed. Those not willing or interested can no longer stop the integration, not even temporarily, but only choose between joining what the core around the Euro agrees or ask for an exception or quit the EU altogether.

Third: If in the future problems arise, they will be dealt with.

Will this lead to a European Union with much stronger integration and pooling of sovereignty to be exercised in common, with adjacent nation-states pursuing analogous political goals? Yes it will, but there is no blueprint for where the European Integration end. Time will show.

Lessons Asia Can Learn from Europe*

The European Union was born more than 60 years ago. From integrating coal and steel industries it has gone on to pool sovereignty[1] for most economic activities and a large number of other crucial policies such as immigration and domestic security. It has grown from six to 27 member states, which next year will be 28 when Croatia joins. Iceland, Serbia, and Turkey are all negotiating membership.

This is by any standard impressive. No observer watching the embryonic integration sixty years ago would have dared to predict such achievements. Recently the EU was awarded the Nobel Peace Prize and the following three reasons were mentioned: promoting peace, democracy, and human rights over six decades.

Some sceptical Europeans and some overseas observers disputed this award, but it is in fact true that the EU has delivered these priceless assets to Europe. The climax came in 2002 when the original Western European EU welcomed ten Central- and Eastern European countries who from 1945 to 1990 were under the heel of the Soviet and Russian empire.

And yet, it is difficult today to open a newspaper, access the web or tune into a news channel without hearing about crises threatening the EU. First of all, there is the debt crisis hitting the weak member states of the Euro-zone hard. Disagreement about the future budget for the Union comes next, with Britain insisting on its rebate and many other member states disputing it. Indeed there is a growing feeling in Britain and in particular among members of the Conservative party that the time has come to loosen Britain's ties with the Union, yes even go so far as taking Britain out of the Union. Foreign and security policy decisions about Iraq and Libya even if they go back some years still remind observers that the Union failed to reach agreement on a common position. Institutionally the European Parliament has never developed into a genuine parliament and frequently voices its frustration, casting doubt on the strength and validity of the institutional set up and the decision-making process.

---

* First appeared in *ISEAS Perspective*, 29 November 2012.

[1] Many observers talk about the surrendering or abandoning of sovereignty by members states. This is not correct. Economic integration means that a member state pools or transfers sovereignty to exercise it in common with adjacent nation-states pursuing analogous political goals.

From an Asian perspective the time may be right to look at the European Union and analyse its strengths and weaknesses, and ask what went right and what went wrong, what the lessons are, and what works and what does not.

Economic integration is happening in one way or another in Asia. While the European Union is the only genuine example of such a development, it does not mean and should not mean that other regional integrations including what we are going to see in Asia should follow the European model. European integration is *European* while integration among Asian countries cannot but be *Asian*. The European model may provide a toolbox, from which one can borrow what one will, but any other model must be designed to handle the unique problems, challenges, and opportunities involved.

The starting point is to understand that economic integration is the strategy of domestic political systems to maintain or regain control over economic activity in the era of economic globalization. During the industrial age most economic activity was national — taking place inside a national framework. With economic globalization, trade increased and investment flows grew to an unprecedented size, pulling economic activities from the national to the international level. As the global financial crisis showed, they became so big, so powerful, and moved so fast that no nation-state — not even the U.S.   can shield itself against the impact. The total value of the world's financial assets is estimated to Euro 160 trillion — about 3 1/2 times bigger than world GDP. Most of these funds are in the hands of financial institutions operating globally and many of them make transfers at the speed of light to take advantage of differences in interest rates, growth rates, and inflationary trends. Phenomena like hedge funds or offshore financial centres are well known — and not for helping national policy makers in their endeavours to pursue domestic political goals either. They seek short-term profits and are not disposed to grant time to nation-states going through an adjustment process.

National/domestic political control over international economic activities has become ineffective, but voters still expect politicians to be in the driver's seat and prevent abuses and violations. Politicians thus respond by moving policy making above the national level, so that economic activities and political control are now both found at the international level.

Looking at the legislation found within the EU, the European experience points to a high degree of success in this respect.

Voters may not see it exactly that way, though. Economic globalization in the form of trade, investment, disruptive capital flows, and mergers & acquisitions are not always visible to the citizen. When mortgage borrowing costs go up, they may not associate it with hedge funds moving money out. What they see and feel in their daily life is legislation coming out of the EU institutions — from Brussels as it is called in the jargon — often disturbing their daily life and are seen as unnecessary bureaucracy. Often the outburst is heard "why do Brussels have to do this or that".

The EU institutions and indeed national politicians have not fully managed to get the message across that their aim is to maintain political control over economic activities influencing the citizen's daily lives. The alternative would be an unwanted degree of power in the hands of huge international or global corporations or financial institutions. European nations could not do their job individually because their power measured against the large conglomerations is too small.

Nor has the message filtered through that very little of EU legislation is unnecessary or bureaucratic. Seldom is it heard that many EU legislative acts replace national/domestic legislation, which means that 27 national rules are replaced by one single European rule or regulation. The most famous example of this was seen in the early 1990s when rules for the degree of curvatures for cucumbers were introduced. It is frequently brought forward as a symbol of waste, even madness — Eurocrats being paid to sit there measuring cucumber curvatures! But it is in fact a very sensible rule allowing cucumbers to be packed in boxes, transported across borders, lowering the price consumers pay while at the same time giving producers a better price. Everyone benefits. The regulation was a sensible one that followed what most member states had already done domestically, and the EU regulation was a simplification exercise meant to facilitate cross-border trade!

Lesson number one drawn from these experiences is to bring across to the public why the integration is there, and how it is solving problems faced by the ordinary citizen, and make sure that perception matches reality.

The ordinary citizen is not much interested in the Euro currency rate *vis-à-vis* the USD or Libya or Iraq, but sees the integration in the prisms of whether it improves the daily life. The former Speaker of the House of Representatives in the U.S. Tip O'Neill once said "all politics are local". And so it is with economic integration. If integration cannot connect to the daily life of the citizen, it starts to lose traction because anti-integration arguments tend to attract voters who only see strange rules or regulations adopted far away from where they live.

Contrary to the domestic political system, citizens do not see EU decision-making as "their" political system; it is much more "them and us". There are many reasons for that, such as history, geographical distance, and languages. The counterweight against criticism being a citizen's personal contact with the system does not exist, opening the door for all kinds of myths and unfounded criticism. The large number of Eurocrats is often mentioned despite the fact that all EU institutions employ around 50,000 persons whereof 1/3 is due to the use of national languages; necessary for the citizen to communicate with the EU institutions and to read the legislation passed and applicable for them. As comparison, suffice it to state that the City of Birmingham and H.M. Treasury & Customs in Britain each employ 50,000 persons.

This leads to the next observation namely that an economic integration is not a free standing enterprise, but linked to the current state of global economics and the role the member states want to play.

The EU was launched precisely at the moment in the late 1950s when the global economy was moving into higher growth. Under such conditions, dismantling trade barriers was not so difficult. When the oil price chock hit Europe in the 1970s, integration came to an abrupt stop and only got going again when the economy picked up. Judging from the example of the U.S. the benefits of a single huge market, in particular for high technology production, were too obvious to miss.

The next logical step was to agree on a single currency. In the early 1990s when a global currency crisis struck, the plan for an economic and monetary union (single currency) was torpedoed. But it stayed afloat. The common foreign and security policy was born when the fall of the Soviet Empire signalled that the NATO alliance could no longer be counted upon considering America's limited commitment to Europe's defence in the new situation it now found itself in, and America's growing commitment in other parts of the world. Immigration and domestic security followed the influx of foreign workers and the rising threat of terrorism.

At present, it is not difficult to appreciate the level of integration at its current stage, but it is less easy to argue the need for deeper integration. When the proposed constitution was put before voters in several European countries (France, The Netherlands, and Ireland) in 2005, politicians found it hard to explain why it was necessary to enact a constitution — and why now? A very simple question was: What is it we can do with the proposed constitution that cannot be done with the existing treaties? This question had been easy to answer with the Single Act of 1984 and the Treaty of The European Union of 1992. In 2005 the voters drew the conclusion that it was not obvious why the treaties should be amended; so why support the change?

Lesson number two is therefore first that integration is much easier to forge under benevolent global economic conditions blessed with high growth than otherwise. Second that the integration must respond to a challenge or put forward solutions to problems that member states cannot solve on their own or where solutions defined in common are clearly better than if each member state had tried on its own.

Voters understand that participation in economic integration improve material living standard, but also feel that it exposes them to political decision making by institutions not close to them. In short: Voters sense that they trade in a part of their cultural identity and links to the well-known national political framework, for the prospect of a higher living standard. They are willing to do so as long as an unequivocal answer is arrived at where increasing living standard outweighs the pressure on cultural identity — which is more the case under high growth. They are far more sceptical when that is not the case.

My own personal experience as State-Secretary in Denmark where the majority of the population are for the European Union, is that ordinary people are basically steered by emotions, while policy makers follow logic and reason. That sours a dialogue even if both sides are interested, because they tend to speak different, even conflicting languages.

Lesson number three is to bring economic integration close to the citizen and avoid making it a remote academic or business-biased exercise. The EU has tried to square the circle by introducing subsidiarity, which stands for taking decisions as close to the citizens as possible — an admirable ambition. But even then, even when acknowledged as the right way, for many citizens it is just one more "bureaucratic manoeuvre".

This leads to the dilemma: Shall we start with and a focus on institutions and expect them to come up with relevant answers to the challenges or is it better to begin with the substance — what can integration do for member states, business, and citizens — and thereafter define the necessary institutional framework?

The role of institutions can be defined in many ways, but to my mind they can do very little on their own. They transform political will, political preferences, and political objectives into legislations, rules, and regulations applicable for business, citizens, and society. At the same time they function as a channel for feedback from those affected by political decisions to those who make these decisions. A clutch pedal!

The European public, like people anywhere, is not interested in the institutional set-up. The public wants economic integration to focus on the substance — the deliverables! Under current circumstances, these are an improved economy, reduced unemployment, and better daily living conditions. They do not care very much if at all who it is who are behind the decisions that bring those benefits.

It is actually detrimental to the image of the integration process if institutions, once Europe and its citizens face a wide crisis, fall back on institutional infighting. The public does not feel compelled to understand such a situation, and it eats away confidence.

A couple of years ago, the EU agreed on changes to its Common Foreign- and Security Policy, appointing Catherine Ashton as High Representative of the Union for Foreign Affairs and Security Policy. This sounds good, but only makes sense if the EU has a common policy and even If some progress has been made to that effect in particular concerning soft policies such as climate change, the EU is still far away from a genuine foreign and security policy. A gap opens up between perception and reality. Ordinary citizens fail to see why institutional set-ups that encroach on limited financial and staff resources are necessary when the substance — a common policy — is not agreed upon.

In October 2012 the European Parliament rejected the nomination of Luxembourg's Yves Mersch to the European Central Bank (ECB) executive board on the grounds that insufficient effort had been made to find a suitable woman for the post. Gender equality is certainly a commendable objective, but it is a fair assumption that the 25 percent of the population who are unemployed in several member states take the view that the European Parliament should concentrate on helping and supporting the ECB to fight the economic crisis.

Lesson number four is: First, to put substance ahead of institutions, we need to understand what has to be accomplished, and design institutions to do that. Second, to bring across to the institutions that the more serious the problems are, the stronger is the need to close ranks and work together. Third, to ensure that perceptions match realities in the sense that institutions are doing what they are supposed to do — making decisions.

The fifth observation is that public opinion does not always — far from it — move with the same speed as is the case for the political and technocratic elite plus business leaders. People find it difficult to adapt and adjust. They tend to see the world and economic surroundings as they used to be.

The elite may be tempted to move fast and far and there are many reasons for doing so, but if the public is not on board, growing scepticism may be the result. Under benevolent economic conditions, this scepticism may not surface, but if or when global conditions change, it will. People will vent their frustration — "we were left behind"!

This has been felt by the European Union when, for good reasons from 1990 to 2010, it introduced the single currency and a number of other steps. When global growth was high and the global financial crisis was not haunting Europe, a large majority was on board. But when global growth turned to what has been termed the great recession in the slipstream of a global financial crisis, the support for these steps became less solid and robust.

Lesson number five is that the public must be on board, and must support and understand why integration is being pushed, what necessitates the steps, and what results are expected. The European Union has over the last five years managed to stick together to prevent a break-up of the single currency, but it has been tough and sometimes it has looked as if the integration was on the brink of failure. Reading the European mass media, the feeling one gets is that politicians are not really conveying to the public why it is of paramount importance to bring the single currency through the financial crisis, what kind of policies are being implemented, why they have been selected, and the results they are to produce. Otherwise, one should not wonder why opinion polls show such high scepticism among Europeans.

The main lessons for politicians, business leaders, and the intellectual elite are:

- to communicate constantly to the public why economic integration is better than the alternative — standing alone;
- why economic globalization demands international institutions and why such institutions are the best way to safeguard domestic policies even if the instinct may be to look for domestic institutions;
- why domestic policy measures are not fully effective under economic globalization,
- explain the paradox that participation in international binding agreements increases instead of reduces the room of manoeuvre for domestic policy goals;
- and what may be most important of all, that economic integration is not an end in itself, but an instrument to pursue domestic political goals — 'all politics are local'.

It would indeed be a serious set-back if economic integration, in itself a demonstration of how to reach consensus and compromises by co-operation, seeking solutions in common, and reflecting political maturity; is stopped in its tracks just because communication of these fundamental and simple messages failed.

Europe, Not Euro, May Break Apart*

The fear about the euro's collapse has receded, but Europe as forged after the industrial revolution is fracturing, reverting to traditional regional entities with cultural traditions, languages and animosity against nation-states that swallowed them without their consent.

There's Scotland in Britain, Catalonia and Basque Country in Spain, Flanders in Belgium, Lombardy or Padania in Italy. Soon maybe Wales in Britain, Bavaria in Germany, Brittany and Occitania in France. On top of this litany, there's also growing concern about Britain exiting from the European Union.

The Holy Roman Empire dominating Central Europe before industrialization counted 1800 states ruled by kings, knights and bishops. The states were too small to reap the fruits of industrialization. Fragmented markets prevented transnational supply chains and were incapable of shaping the logistics; transport infrastructure; and, most important of all, the political system necessary for transition from feudal and agricultural states to manufacturing. So the European nation-state emerged. Admittedly Britain, France and Spain could trace their roots back 100 or 200 years earlier, but were not solidly secure until around 1800. Italy and Germany were born between 1860 and 1871.

The nation-states masterminded regional economic integration, but never completely succeeded in shaping a national culture. Yes, a national language gradually took over, but the regions preserved distinct cultural identities. They acquiesced with the nation-state and obeyed respective capitals in London, Paris, Berlin, Rome or Madrid because force compelled them to do so and the economic advantages were evident. The standard of living rose as industrialization conquered the regions, and prosperity followed. The end result: the increasing standard of living was sufficiently higher to compensate for attacks on cultural identity to ensure the nation-state's prerogative. The people in the regions traded in some but not all cultural identity.

This became even more manifest as industrialization went into the next phase: Economic globalization. International treaties strengthened the capitals' hold over regions. The regions could not access global markets without the capitals' consent

---

* First appeared *YaleGlobal online*, 2 November 2012.

as laid out in international rules negotiated among nation-states. Scotland could not on its own strike a deal with the United States or Argentina for export of ships from the shipyards at the Clyde. Only London could. And over the first half of the 20th century, Europe showed little support for regionalism or cultural identity. Few Scots genuinely felt as Scots or saw Scotland in any other way than as part of the United Kingdom.

The role of the nation-states as imperial powers solidified this view. For the Scots, being part of the United Kingdom provided a platform for a central role in running the empire and profiting by doing so.

Conditions favoring the nation-state are disappearing — and rapidly. The empires are gone. Industrialization is giving way to an economic age shaped by information and communication technology, ICT, opening access to the world outside the nation-state framework. Manufacturing used to be the cornerstone of European economic activity, but except for Germany, no longer. The burden of transition has been unevenly distributed aggravating the skepticism among regions about the virtue of the nation-state. Over the last four years national political systems have lost legitimacy because of impotence in dealing with the crisis. A feeling of unfair distribution of hardship and burdens when capitals cut welfare and increased taxes fuels the idea among regions that more fairness may be found if they handled these questions on their own while relying on the EU despite its shortcomings for economic policy.

Most important of all, the EU has taken away from the nation-state and its capitals the key to participate in economic globalization. Regions no longer need to go through the capital to request changes in rules of the game or help in accessing foreign markets. Regions have set up embassies and lobbying associations to promote export and attract investment abroad. For example, in Washington, a Scottish Affairs Office implements Scotland's plan for engaging with the U.S. To drive home the point, the office flags its Gaelic name, Riaghaltas na h-Alba. Or the Scots work via the European Union with Scotland's European Union Office implementing an action plan for engagement. If Scotland, Catalonia or Lombardy want to safeguard their interests in global negotiations, the negotiators are no longer found in London, Madrid or Rome, but in Brussels. Sure enough, politicians and civil servants in the capitals still want, indeed crave, serving as the channel to the EU for all regional preferences, but this posture increasingly falls on deaf ears. The view in London that Scotland's interests should be weighed against interests put forward by other parts of Britain doesn't matter much north of the border.

The wave of austerity rolling through all of Europe reinforces the separatist sentiment. During the industrial age, in particular when the welfare state was introduced, the center or capital was shuffling large sums of money around via taxes and welfare payments to and from the regions. Then, it seemed quite the gamble to cut this lifeline. Now such fiscal transfers are falling by the wayside as the state pulls back from the super welfare state. Regions increasingly view themselves as capable, perhaps even better equipped, of competing without the support of the nation-state, and find it less attractive to be part of an acrimonious redistribution struggle.

The European Union is on the radar screen. Not only do the nation-states shave fiscal transfers, but current plans for a fiscal union augur a stronger role for the EU. Plans are being drafted to give the EU some kind of veto over national budgets, further transferring power from the capitals of the nation-states to the EU, stimulating regions to strike their own deals with the supranational political leadership. The proposed banking union works the same way. The regions do not see why their interests and the negotiating about a European supervisory body should be controlled by the nation-state. They may or may not have common interests with banks in other parts of the nation-state, but it cannot be taken for granted, and in some cases they may fear being held hostage to nation-state policies disregarding their interests.

It's no coincidence that Scotland stands first in the queue to have a go at secession. Britain's conservative party, the leading coalition partner in the British government, toys with the idea of a referendum about continued membership of the EU. Polls indicate that in the UK as a whole 51 percent of the voters favor leaving the EU with only 34 percent preferring to stay. Inside the conservative party 83 percent want a referendum, and 70 percent would vote to leave. But Scotland has always voted overwhelmingly with the Labour Party and abhors the risk of being forced out of the EU by a political party that enjoys limited support among the Scots. The prospect of the conservative party taking Britain out of the EU combined with Scotland leaving Britain to join the EU might have once seemed like pure fantasy, but no more. Breakup may be the most realistic scenario.

The Scots will vote yes or no to stay in the UK in 2014. The next general election of the British parliament is set for 2015. But if Scotland decides to leave the UK, all dates and plans are up in the air. The vote in Scotland may advance the parliamentary election, giving the EU referendum a dominating role.

Now Comes the Hard Part for the Euro-zone*

Over the last few weeks, the Euro-zone has been blessed with a stream of good news — for once. In the past five years, the group of 17 countries using the single currency had been tested with a cascade of bad news and criticism.

Last Wednesday, the German constitutional court gave the green light for ratification of the European Stability Mechanism (ESM); the strings attached do not seem onerous. The Dutch — who for some time seemed to question not only the single currency, but the whole European construction, which they contributed to as one of the founding fathers — voted in a parliamentary election the same day overwhelmingly for political parties supporting the European Union and the euro.

The long-awaited plan for a banking union to repair flaws in the original design of the single currency was tabled by the European Commission. It supplements a fiscal union or fiscal compact, which was agreed to in March 2012 to enforce much stricter fiscal discipline on member states.

Not to be taken hostage by one or two recalcitrant countries, the fiscal compact enters into force when ratified by the 12th of the 17 countries using the euro.

Germany will be the sixth euro-country to ratify. It is also open for EU member states not part of the single currency, three of whom have ratified so far.

Growth figures are depressing, but not alarming. Over the last six months, the Euro-zone has contracted by 0.1–0.2 percent and the forecast for the fourth quarter is a modest growth of 0.1 percent. This is certainly not good enough, but offers a glimmer of hope that slowly but steadily, the Euro-zone is working its way out of the crisis.

The positive side of these figures is that they come in at the same time as all member states stick to a rigorous austerity programme. Expectations pointed to a more severe contraction.

That this is not taking place must be due to a stronger than anticipated private demand (consumption plus investment) holding up despite falling public demand

* First appeared in *Business Times*, 19 September 2012.

and higher taxes. Once the austerity programmes have run their course, this offers hope of stronger growth. The global financial markets have been slow to recognise this development for various reasons, but now seem to detect the swing around.

First quarter of 2012 saw an outflow (stocks and bonds) of 80 billion euros (S$128 billion). Over May and June 2012, this was more than compensated for by an inflow of 86 billion euros. According to a Bloomberg poll, more than one in five international investors picked EU markets as among those that will offer the best returns over the next year. That is the highest reading for the region since the poll began in 2009 and the Euro-zone came in as No. 2 after the U.S.

Italy and Spain have been harassed by high interest rates at times above or close to the magic ceiling of 7 percent signalling the need for a bailout. In July 2012, 10-year Spanish government bonds showed a yield of 7.62 percent, but are now at 5.65 percent. Italian 10-year government bonds showed a yield of 7.26 percent in November 2011, but are now at 5.05 percent.

For these two countries, and indeed for the Euro-zone, the hope is that neither the "take what it needs" scheme to buy treasury bonds announced recently by the European Central Bank (ECB) nor the soon-to-be-activated ESM will be needed.

If international investors start to believe in the future economic prospect they will buy bonds, supplying liquidity to these two countries, thereby further reducing the interest rate and borrowing costs, making official intervention by the Euro-zone mechanisms superfluous.

We are not there yet, but it is possible. The hard-won experience from financial crises reveals that confidence is the crucial factor, making or breaking efforts to steady the ship. No amount of money can compensate for loss of confidence. No money is needed if/when international investors have been won over.

Then why were the ECB bond buy scheme announced and the ESM put in place? To signal to the weak countries that support can be called upon, but only if they stick to the reform cause and convince the financial market that reforms and structural changes will take place.

All this is good, indeed splendid. But now comes the hard part.

When the weak countries stood with their backs to the wall, they had no other choice than to pursue austerity, however much it hurt. And it has worked.

According to the International Monetary Fund (IMF), they are now half-way through the structural changes that will make them competitive. Two more years and with a bit of luck, they will be there.

Recent economic development means, however, that have got some breathing space. Things look brighter. Politicians who have braved the storm and forced through agonising, stressful, and extremely unpopular measures feel better. The hard-pressed populations being confronted with package after package may think that the situation does not warrant continuation of strict austerity and reform policies. And yet, if they give in and ease the pressure, it won't be long before international investors will see through the veil.

Financial flows will not only dry up, but start to flow out again. They will be back to square one. All the sufferings and everything achieved will be lost. Attempts to restart the reform process will prove impossible. The willingness of the stronger Euro-zone member states to help will have been lost. Neither the ECB nor the ESM will come to the rescue because their help was conditioned upon fiscal stringency, reforms, and structural changes implemented by the countries.

The temptation to relax will be enormous, but for the sake of the euro and indeed the EU, political leaders in the weak Euro-zone countries must stay the course. It is a lose-all or gain-all situation. If they stay the course they will be doubly rewarded by the financial markets.

Why the Euro will Survive*

The Euro-zone's economy is stronger, more robust and sounder than the U.S., the Japanese and the British economies. This has escaped headlines, but is nevertheless true.

Public debt and deficit measured against gross domestic product (GDP) is lower. Contrary to the United States and Britain, the Euro-zone is not running a deficit on its current account *vis-à-vis* other countries making it hostage to foreign creditors.

Unemployment is high (11 percent), but a realistic comparison shows that despite lower official figures due to omitting workers no longer looking for a job, American unemployment is at least as bad.

Growth is clearly higher in the U.S. (2 percent) but achieved through splashing several trillions of dollars, eroding whatever confidence was left, pushing the private sector towards deleveraging debt, thereby keeping demand low.

The Euro-zone faces many challenges that must be dealt with at the same time. But even taken together, they do not constitute an insurmountable obstacle.

The first is public debt and/or deficits. The Euro-zone as a whole is doing well. The public debt is 91.8 percent of GDP compared to more than 100 percent for the U.S., 91.2 percent for Britain and 230 percent for Japan. The budget deficit is forecast at 3.2 percent for 2012 with the corresponding figures being 7.6 percent for the U.S. 6.7 percent for Britain and 8.1 percent for Japan.

Furthermore, both the debt and deficit are expected to be on a falling trajectory. In fact, the Euro-zone is close to a surplus on the primary balance — defined as the budget balance excluding net interest payments, a luxury none of the other three economies enjoy.

The fiscal problem is confined to three to four countries: mainly Greece and Italy and to a lesser extent Spain and Portugal. The problems are smaller than the picture given by many financial newspapers. Italy's debt is 123 percent of GDP, but its deficit only 2 percent forecast to fall to 1.1 percent in 2013. Moreover, Italy has a surplus on its primary balance.

---

* First appeared in *Business Times*, 13 June 2012.

Spain's debt is 80.9 percent and its deficit 6.4 percent and expected to be marginally lower in 2013. We read a lot of bad news from Greece. But the good news is that its debt ratio is stabilising around 165 percent of GDP and its primary balance is in surplus.

Looking at fiscal consolidation among industrialised countries over 2011–2013, the top three come from the Euro-zone (Spain, Portugal, and Greece) all improving by more than 5 percent of GDP with Italy just below 5 percent — the fifth on the list. The U.S. is eighth with around an improvement of around 2.5 percent followed by Britain with just above 2 percent and Japan about nil.

This reveals a gigantic effort is underway in the Euro-zone, under political and economic stress rarely seen in modern economic history.

To prevent future fiscal problems by individual member states, the Euro-zone has agreed on a fiscal stability treaty introducing fiscal discipline. A litmus test of how the Europeans judge it came when Ireland submitted its ratification to a referendum. Some 60 percent of voters voted "yes".

The Europeans realise the gravity of fiscal discipline, but as the new French President Francois Hollande has made clear, they also want to strike a balance between growth and austerity.

There are rumours about a fiscal union preventing member states from lending above a specified ceiling through the establishment of a central institution to which member states have transferred sovereignty.

The second big problem is a banking crisis. Hardest hit were Ireland that seems to be working itself out of the woods, and Spain which has received support to prop up its banks. The 100 billion euro (S$160 billion) provided to Spain is manageable for the Euro-zone's rescue funds. A number of Italian banks were recently downgraded by Moody's, but generally its banking system appears to be in better shape, being less exposed to soured property loans.

When the crisis started a couple of years ago, it was obvious that a number of banks, in particular German and French banks, would be hit hard if the Southern European countries faltered.

That was indeed one of the explanations for the tactic that was followed — buying time for the creditor banks to improve their balance sheets and thus enabling them to withstand losses when forced to write off some of their claims.

This tactic looks to have achieved its purpose. Europe's major banks remain afloat despite their reckless lending to Southern European countries that was partly responsible for the crisis in the first place.

The way ahead is to build some kind of banking union with a centralised regulator, a bailout fund, and a European Union (EU) deposit insurance backstop — measures that should have been introduced long ago.

COMPETITIVENESS GAP

The third problem is the gap in competitiveness between Northern Europe and Southern Europe. The hard truth is that Greece, Italy, Spain, and Portugal suffer from archaic economic structures with licences, regulations and monopolies imposing heavy transaction costs on the economy.

There is no easy way around it, but to reform the economy and go through a couple of years of protests from those being deprived of their privileges.

Some observers advocate quitting the Euro-zone and depreciating national currencies. That will keep these countries going for a limited number of years, and then they will be back to square one, only poorer through the deterioration of their terms of trade — that is, paying more for imports and getting less for exports.

This is difficult to swallow and some observers refuse to admit it, but their membership of the Euro-zone will force these countries to embark upon reforms which actually should have been undertaken many years ago. Without such reforms, they will continue on a downward spiral whether they are within or outside the Euro-zone.

Based on this analysis and the policy responses implemented or in the pipeline, the scoreboard for fulfilling the four conditions to form an optimal currency union looks like this:

- Converging economies responding broadly similar to outside economic shocks. Compared to the U.S. economy, the Euro-zone does not seem to be far off this mark. Its economic and industrial structure may not be perfectly congruous, but is good enough to warrant a satisfactory score.

- Labour mobility. Conventional wisdom says that the European scoreboard is bad, but comparisons with the U.S. shows that the difference is not so large after all. One study a couple of years ago finds that in the U.S., 2.8 percent of working age residents move from one region to another. The corresponding figure for the EU is 1.21 percent. Even in the U.S. with high unemployment only one out of 35 workers move. This does not support the thesis of labour mobility as a major factor for adjustment inside an economic and monetary union. In fact, a study a couple of years later showed that from 2007 to 2010 when labour mobility should have played a role in adjustment, it came to an almost abrupt halt with the lowest figure since 1945.

- Capital market. The Euro-zone lacks a banking union, but as outlined above, it is on its way. And with free capital movements and rights of establishment, the scoreboard may not be bad.

- Fiscal transfers. Many observers point to the small size of intra-Euro-zone fiscal transfers combined with absence of rules for fiscal discipline as a major culprit for the calamities — and they are correct. This was well known when the treaties were drafted, but the sentiment was that member states would adhere to the limits set for public deficits and public debt inscribed in the treaty; alas, they did not do so. With the new fiscal pact probably followed by a genuine fiscal union transferring sovereignty to a central institution, this bridge may be crossed.

When the treaties were drafted and the single currency was introduced the global economy was very strong. That coloured the outlook, luring experts and politicians into a complacent attitude. Had they known that a full blown financial crisis would hit the world in 2007–2008, they would surely have chosen another road.

Observing the Euro-zone facing the crisis — part of it due to the U.S. sub-prime bomb, part of it due to its own failures and shortcomings — some observers may ask too much of the Euro-zone compared to other economic and monetary unions. The idea that a member state can leave and subsequently depreciate its own currency is in the back of their minds.

They overlook the fact that depreciation is not an end in itself. It is a policy instrument to achieve economic goals. There is nothing depreciation can bring about that cannot be achieved through fiscal and monetary policies.

The plain fact is, however, that even if crisis management could have been better, the Euro-zone has not done so badly. It is turning its economy around under agonising conditions. Debt and deficits are being brought under control; something the U.S., Britain, and Japan have been unable to do.

The member states are supporting each other. The political will to stay together and weather the storm is visible for all who want to see it.

In Europe, North Battles South*

As Greece struggles with its debt crisis, a growing chorus favors leaving the euro and devaluing the drachma. This focus on a single currency masks the real problem for the Euro-zone: Pressures of globalization have exposed two economic models within the zone — one embraced by Europe's north and the other in the south.

Reluctant to embrace painful reforms, some in Greece regard devaluing the currency an easier solution. Devaluation may bring immediate relief, but would sap the country's economic strength. Economic reform proposed by northern European countries promises higher growth in the longer term, but pain and sacrifices now.

The clash between the northern and southern models is shaping up in the forthcoming presidential election in France. In many ways France is a microcosm of the Euro-zone with an economy and a societal structure reflecting both the efficient northern economies and the southern non-competitive ones. Underlying the programs presented by President Nicolas Sarkozy and Socialist challenger François Hollande is the contest between an old-fashioned, less malleable structure found in the southern tier of the European Union and the model successfully used by Germany.

The election's outcome may indicate which way European citizens want to go. German Chancellor Angela Merkel senses this, which explains why she has openly, strongly supported Sarkozy. He's trying to change course, get into the German lane and pull southern Europe along by example. Merkel fears that Hollande, if elected, will spread uncertainty about France's pledge to reform and in the process roil the entire Euro-zone.

The vast gulf within the Euro-zone, apparent in recent years, has long been plagued by this dichotomy between northern Europe's competitive economies, in particular Germany, plus the Netherlands and Denmark, Sweden, Norway, Finland and the southern nation-states epitomized by Greece, but also Italy, Spain and Portugal.

As the rigid, debt-ridden economies of the Mediterranean seaboard have undergone economic shock from the debt crisis, many economists jump to the textbook answer — a hefty devaluation.

---

* First appeared in *YaleGlobal online*, 16 March 2012.

Devaluation makes exports cheaper thus boosting volume. Imports fall because import prices go up. Increased exports and falling import stimulate production and employment. Income is redistributed to the advantage of the business sector promoting investment. The trade balance improves. The main disadvantage is that higher import prices reduce real income, making the devaluing country poorer, but it shouldn't be a surprise. Devaluation is often chosen after a country has lived beyond its means.

Devaluation only delivers if market conditions prevail. Price and wage changes must be allowed to work their way through the economy. And this is precisely not the case for the southern countries. The competitive advantage they gain would be neutralized by rigid rules and license systems designed to prevent changes.

Regulations approved by legislatures make it almost impossible to cut a company's workforce, so companies hold back on hiring until absolutely sure that future economic growth supports a higher workforce. They resist repeating mistakes — hiring in good times, then forced to soldier on during bad times, with a high wage bill eating into profits and investment.

Large parts of the economy — trucking, legal services and pharmacies, just to mention a few examples — are shielded from market forces by license systems, particularly damaging when distributed in corrupt ways, including favors or kickbacks. Limiting licenses allow owners to charge high prices for the services and pass some revenue on to government agencies. Greece's freight-transport industry is dominated by 33,000 trucking licenses, with the newest dating back to 1970. The licenses trade for as high as $400,000. Such a system penalizes the competitive part of the economy and rewards the non-competitive, creating a market barrier and slowing growth. Prohibitively high transport costs hike food prices leading to wage demands in urban areas, thus hollowing out competitiveness. So tomatoes grown in Dutch greenhouses and shipped from Rotterdam compete with home-grown tomatoes on the shelves of Greek supermarkets. And when organizing an event on the Greek island of Corfu, the Greek International Chamber of Commerce saved costs by renting tables and chairs from Brindisi in Italy than bringing them from Athens.

The Southern European countries have run such economic systems far too long. Greek citizens can retire with pensions at age 53. And on the World Bank ranking for ease of doing business, Italy is 87, just after Zambia, the Bahamas and Mongolia; Greece is number 100; Germany, Denmark, Sweden, Finland and Norway are ranked among the top 20.

Leaving the Euro-zone could bring only temporary relief for Greece. Its best chance is to stay in the Euro-zone and tackle structural changes now with financial support and advice of other member states and the International Monetary Fund. If Greece and other southern states quit the euro or procrastinate, they could slide into an abyss with no one willing to offer rescue.

The northern tier runs more flexible, competitive economies with higher mobility. Northern Europe invented flexicurity, a pro-active labor market policy, with flexibility emphasized through retraining, lifelong education and systematic efforts to develop new employment opportunities. Security in the form of allowances is linked to schemes for re-employment.

But the northern countries, too, must bring welfare expenditures under control. For a number of Euro-zone members, including France and Germany, welfare expenditures are well above 30 percent of gross domestic product — as compared to 19.4 percent in the U.S. and 25.9 percent in Britain. Such expenditures are not sustainable with a low growth decade ahead, even more so as some of the money flowing into schemes blocks flexibility and mobility in the labor market.

Europe's attempt to trim its welfare state to sustainable levels may be the biggest and most daring socio-engineering enterprise over the last 50 years. The Europeans must make health and pension benefits fit what they can actually finance instead of amassing claims on future generations. Rather than borrow to pay for such welfare programs, governments must withdraw privileges that were given to citizens during an era with a better economic outlook.

The goal is not to demolish the welfare state, but to trim it, eliminating excesses, exaggerations and aberrations, ensuring a chance at benefits for future generations.

It's imperative for the northern tier to return to a growth pattern to generate funds necessary for financing policies and help the weaker parts of the Euro-zone. This is the way an economic and monetary union should work.

The alternative is much worse, actually quite dangerous for social and political stability:

The first effect would be for rich northern European countries to abandon the southern nations, opening the doors for political and economic experiments or extremism. History gives ample warnings on the dangers of this path.

The second effect would be, not mere trimming of the welfare state and safeguarding its basic principles, but a near dismantling of a socioeconomic system built over nearly 80 decades, putting its stamp on almost every aspect of daily life in Europe.

Geographically, yes, there would still be something called Europe, but the continent would have a new, unwanted character politically, economically, and socially. And the rest of the world might soon regret the loss of the European welfare state, a model demonstrating concern for every human being.

Europe After the Debt Crisis*

Abstract: The Euro-zone was caught unprepared by the financial crisis originating in the USA followed by the recession. Severe flaws in the designs hidden by the "good" years surfaced calling for action. After a good deal of fumbling, the Euro-zone moves towards a fiscal union anchored in acceptance of a "German" economic model — low inflation, low deficits, and debts. The Euro will survive with two major changes. The integration will be stronger and the core countries in the Euro-zone will exercise stronger leadership raising awkward policy decision for the skeptical members of the EU, but outside the Euro.

The Greek debt problem and the broader debt crisis in the Euro-zone is part of the global debt problem. A brief historical look into the debt issue would provide some perspective on the scale of problems we are facing right now.

After World War I, global sovereign debt was 70 percent of Global Gross Domestic Product (GDP). After World War II, it was 100 percent. In both cases, war devastated economic activity while at the same time calling for a colossal financial effort. There was no other way than resort to running up debts to rebuild the devastated economies. Realizing such high debt ratio was abnormal, nation-states managed to bring global debt down to 30 percent of GDP in the early 1970s to see it rising again with the first oil crisis. However, two decades of unusually good economic growth from the late 1980s to the first few year of the twenty-first century which should have made it possible to bring debts down and save for rainy days did not so happen. Instead debts in many developed countries kept rising and exploded over the first decade of the twenty-first century to reach again 100 percent of global GDP in 2010. Primarily, this was because developed countries put the foot on the speeder with disastrous results. Politically, it was almost criminal; economically, it stoked the emerging financial crisis with no easy solution in sight.

The question that need to be asked and answered are: what does it mean to run up high sovereign debt, what to do about it, and how to convince all those caught in the debt trap to move towards an acceptable level of burden sharing — between debtor (Greece) and creditors (mainly Germany and France), burden sharing inside Greece, and among creditors (financial institutions versus taxpayers).

---

* First appeared in *Asia Europe Journal*, Volume 9, No. 1, November 2011.

Running up a high debt means that the current generation has overconsumed and encroached into the consumption of the next generation. Debt does not disappear, least of all by waving the magic wand. The slate must be wiped clean by reducing consumption and that usually means a corresponding drop in standard of living.

There is no easy way to solve a debt crisis. Many American economists have advocated the reintroduction of the drachma in Greece to allow the drachma to float downwards on the currency market. But this would not remove the debt. It is one of many ways to bring about the necessary adjustment. A depreciation of the currency hike inflation that erodes real income, thereby reducing consumption with the end result of a lower standard of living. The same can also be achieved by lowering domestic wages and income. A third way is fiscal tightening (lower expenditure and higher taxes) combined with a tighter monetary policy. Whatever policy is applied, previous overconsumption has to be rolled back. The debt is repaid not with money, but with lower consumption.

The difference between these three policies is the issue of burden sharing — who should bear the brunt of the adjustments and how.

It does not matter so much whether the culprit is the Greek government that allowed an untenable situation to develop or European banks that earned good money by facilitating the process through reckless lending knowing very well — or should have done so — that it was not sustainable. But it matters when looking at the political and psychological arguments for demanding strong action from the Greek government and parliament.

Inside Greece, a societal structure allowing a large number of rich people to maintain privileges or accruing benefits from avoiding taxes increases the feeling of social injustice of those people who are unable to do so. Outside Greece, taxpayers in other European countries feel aggrieved by being presented with a bill that should have been divided between Greece and European banks profiting from financing the Greeks' overspending, but now refusing to register the losses.

Amidst all this tumult, European policymakers have tried not to fall between two chairs, one of which would be to act too fast in a semistate of panic and the other one to sit and wait for too long hoping that the problem would just go away. In due course, we will know whether they were successful, but so far the scoreboard does not seem as bad as it is often represented in the international financial press.

Very few, if any, believed that Greece could pay bank in full its debt inside the existing time frame and with the current interest rate. Something has to give — the size, the length, or the interest rate. The game plan has from the outset been to buy time to digest burden sharing — in its size, distribution, and timeframe.

The first objective was to get the Greek budget back to balance or near balance. History clearly shows that default under a budget deficit is synonymous with a meltdown of the state as it cannot pay for the continuing function of services. When balance is achieved in the budget where revenue is sufficient to pay for running expenditures, and then a default, if that is the wish, can be managed in an orderly and controlled way. It is difficult to predict but with some luck, Greece may get near to budget balance in 2013–2014 depending upon a number of assumptions whose validity, admittedly, remains doubtful.

The second objective was to build a wall preventing the Greek problem from spilling over and hitting Ireland, Portugal, and maybe Spain and/or Italy. These countries were in various stages of difficult and vulnerable deficits and debts and a Greek collapse would almost certainly have pulled one or several of them down.

The third objective was to give banks primarily in Germany and France time to improve their balance sheets and so allowing some room of maneuver to write off or roll over a part of their claims. As economic growth picked up in the Euro-zone in the course of the first half of 2011, this looked manageable. French banks held USD 56.7 billion in claims on Greece with Germany second holding USD 34 billion. There is, however, a significant difference in composition; the private sector accounted for the majority of the claims by the French banks and only USD 15 billion were in Greek government bonds compared to USD 22.7 billion for German banks. Total outstanding Greek government bonds amounts to USD 54.2 billion — 96 percent is held by European creditors, and of this 69 percent is held by German and French banks.

The status for these three elements during summer 2011 looks like this: Greece is moving into a critical phase of rebalancing its budget. It is too early to say whether it will be done or not although a large array of policy measures have been put in place by the government. The game is neither lost nor won. The anticontagion element looks more than halfway won even if the game is still going on. The two large countries, Spain and Italy, have both put massive restructuring and reform plans through their respective parliaments. Ireland and Portugal do not seem near default. The best part of the operation has taken place for German and French banks being able to reduce their exposure to the weaker European countries by 30–40 percent since the problems started taking them a long way from, but not definitively, the abyss of a banking crisis.

It is relevant to ask why it has been so difficult for the Europeans to solve the Greek "problem". There are several reasons for that.

In the beginning, the scale of the problem was probably underestimated. Even if it was known that there was something "wrong", the size and depth was not fully appreciated. Among the other Euro-zone countries, there was an under-standable unwillingness to be drawn into what was initially regarded as a Greek phenomenon. Neither fiscal nor institutional mechanisms were available in the Euro-zone or the European Central Bank. It took quite some time before the European Financial Stability Fund was established armed with the financial means to address some of the issues. There were some dithering as member states and the European Central Bank tried to grasp the scale of the problems, which hardly inspired confidence.

Another reason more difficult to pinpoint is that — as we know from the financial crisis in 2007/2008 starting in the USA — some financial institutions actually earn money by forcing other institutions or nation-states into default. In the Greek case, there can be little doubt even if it is hard to prove with figures and statements, that some, primarily American, financial institutions would earn money by forc-ing Greece followed by Ireland, Portugal, Spain, and Italy into default. An invest-ment policy based on the assumption that this would happen is surely applicable. As German and French banks would be hit hard, it goes without saying that American banks would benefit. This is not a conspiracy theory guessing that some bankers in the USA got together behind closed doors and decided to topple the Euro. It is a simple analysis of how the financial market watches out for profit, try to guess what will happen, and invest accordingly. And if you guess that Greece will default and place your money to make profits if it happens, the cost for Greece to bor-row goes up — the prophesy becomes self-fulfilling. There may also be an element of diversion in the sense that as long as Greece is in the limelight, the USA with catastrophic forecasts for debt and deficits escapes relatively unnoticed; the U.S. banks are not exposed to Greece but will be hit by an alarmist development in the USA. Coinciding with a general strike in Greece flashed on the first page of financial newspaper in the USA and Britain, Minnesota's government shut down and officially laid off 20,000 state workers without drawing much interest from the same media.

In today's world, there unfortunately is very little, if any, recognition especially in the financial sector of what a corporation owes society. One of several flaws in the current economic model is the growing dichotomy between business interests, pure and simple, and consequences of business decisions on the societies in which they are part of. The growing concentration of assets allows the financial sector to reap the profits of activities even hazardous ones in good times and to be bailed out by the public sector when facing losses in bad times. In the USA, the top three banks' share of total bank assets was stable around 10 percent from 1935 to 1995. This has seen gone up to 40 percent in 2010. Of the 1,000 largest global banks, the five larg-est ones have, over the last decade, gone up from 8 percent to 16 percent of total assets. No wonder that Greece is small, and a potentially lucrative, prey for them.

The resilience of the EU and the Euro-zone has been underestimated time and again. The crisis is not a textbook exercise searching for the "correct" answer according to prevailing economic theory; this is real life where the sum of economic plus political losses and benefits goes miles beyond pure economics.

Leaving the Euro-zone will lead to a collapse of the Greek economy combined with social unrests and even more important: Greece may stay in the EU, but it will be a sleeping or passive partner as it will carry no weight and have no good will. Greek politicians know that very well. Situated in a traditionally unstable corner of Europe with strong interest in adjacent countries to the North and a rivalry and mistrust towards its Eastern neighbor, Turkey, the consequences would be dire indeed. Such a step would be close to suicide for Greece. It has gone almost unnoticed that simultaneously with the Greek case, Croatia to the North probably followed by Serbia are on their way in, auguring potential power shifts in the region running against Greece.

The other member states may be reluctant to pay the price, but even more reluctant to see Greece slide into chaos or leave the Euro-zone. Irrespective of the pros and cons debated within university classrooms, this would be looked upon as a severe defeat for the European integration project. It may well be that sometime in the future, member states may choose to leave the EU — there are voices inside the British Conservative party advocating such a course — but deliberate policy decisions to that effect carried out through negotiations would differ from a member state grudgingly being pushed over the brink.

Germany has attracted considerable interest and many commentators question the willingness of the Germans to "pay" for what is going on. It may well be that many Germans are critical, but leading politicians and, more importantly, Germany industry players support wholeheartedly the Euro. They do not want a return to the 1970s and early 1980s when German economic stability was threatened by other member countries' competitive devaluations. Without the Euro, Germany's European competitors could and very likely would devalue their currencies introducing an inflationary trend in Europe making it almost impossible for Germany to maintain sound public finances and a low inflation. One of the main arguments for the introduction of the Euro was precisely that getting the other European countries onboard was the only way for Germany to hold on to its preferred economic policy. Outsiders may have forgotten this, but German industry has not.

It is starting to dawn upon the Europeans that the USA is withdrawing from the "old" continent. If any doubt, it was removed when the outgoing US Secretary of Defense Rebort Gates told them so in early summer 2011 revealing that much more than pure economics is at stake. The EU may need Greece and Greece may need the EU to maintain stability in this corner of the continent where history reveals numerous examples of the need for "presence", politically or militarily of powers stronger than the local ones.

There are many uncertainties and many scenarios for what may happen over the coming years looking forward to 2020. Here is what the author thinks is the most likely, with the caveat that it may turn out quite differently.

Greece will come through and after a couple of years some kind of restructuring or write offs or roll over or postponement of part of its debt — as actually played out in the Euro-zone meeting on 22 July 2011 — will have taken place. Relieved of the debt burden, the Greek economy will settle down for a reasonable growth pattern influenced by the reforms forced upon it — indeed long overdue. It may not turn into a high growth economy, but less will do.

The other weak Euro-zone members — Ireland, Portugal, Spain and Italy — will follow the same pattern albeit reflecting that none of these debt problems are exactly the same.

The periphery of the Euro-zone will gradually come along although they will not be able to get on the same growth pattern as the strongest countries, Germany and France. But other economic and monetary unions see these phenomena as well. Growth is not the same across all sectors or in all states of the USA. The Euro-zone adjustment mechanism — factor mobility and transfer of public funds — is not as bad as presented and will be sufficient to keep the ship afloat giving the Euro-zone time to take two further steps without which the construction is unlikely to survive.

Sooner or later, some kind of Euro bonds will have to be introduced meaning that the Euro-zone as a whole stand by the debt of individual member states. Technically, it does not pose problems, but politically it requires that each member state follows a sound fiscal policy keeping debt and deficits inside established thresholds. That requires some kind of a fiscal union imposing stronger and binding obligations on their fiscal policies giving the EU the right to step to step in if these obligations are not met.

When the treaty was written, few people denied this logic. There were uncertainties about how it would work in practice and politically the time was not ripe then to take what was regarded as a quantum leap forward. To borrow a phrase from history, it was regarded as "a step too far". The treaty might not have passed, so the policy-makers decided to give it a try, assuming that if time showed a need for a genuine fiscal union appropriate steps to that effect would be taken. That time has come.

Much of the criticism of the construction pointing to the need for a fiscal union comes from the very people who 20 years ago fought against the Maastricht Treaty with tooth and nails. They crow now that they were right, but one of the reasons that the imperfect treaty was adopted was the genuflection to them, hoping that a treaty with a lower degree of integration would get their support — in vain it turned out.

It is unlikely that such a mistake will be repeated. Over the next years, some kind of fiscal union introducing strict rules for public budgets and putting real and compulsory guidelines on the member states will be passed. It is difficult to see exactly in what form and how far they will go. The European construction chooses its own path and domestic political constraints will play a role. The lesson has been learned, however, and the leading countries, Germany and France, are adamant that the Euro must survive and will take whatever steps necessary to that effect.

The almost unavoidable political consequence is a two-speed Europe with the core of the Euro-zone in the driving seat taking policy decisions also outside the sphere of the Euro leaving it to the other member states to follow or be left behind.

It may come as a surprise to the more skeptical countries, but the answer to their grievances will be that they got their chance to step into the core of Europe, shape the integration, and shoulder responsibility for the future. They did not take it, but chose instead to stay outside core common policies, often trying to block or delay new policies. They have only themselves to blame.

For those interested in history, it may be worthwhile to cast a glance on what happened in the USA in 1790 when some states were close to bankruptcy and those in a better financial situation refused to bail them out. Many observers believed the young union faced a civil war or risked falling apart. A plan was drawn up and after some political maneuvering carried through based upon the technically simple, but politically difficult operation of letting the union take over the debt of the states. The phrase "after having done their duty, to contribute to those states who have not equally done their duty" may well have been spoken by many Germans over the last 1.5 year, but was in fact said for the first time in 1790 by James Madison on the floor of the U.S. Congress.

Painful Euro Crisis and Lessons for the World*

The Euro-zone crisis has not only raised questions about the viability of the common currency, but could also jeopardize an economic model that has so far reigned supreme. The course taken to resolve the crisis in Europe will have long-term impact on the most vibrant parts of the world — from Asia to Latin America.

In developed countries of the West, debtors have run up a high debt ratio to gross domestic product, even while economic growth was high — overspending when they should have saved. They borrowed to spend more, demonstrating a disastrous failure to grasp basic economic principles as well as flaws in moral behavior and ethical judgment. Among these borrowers are established heavyweights — the United States, most European nations and Japan. The United States, one of the wealthiest countries, became an importer of capital instead of exporting capital, registering its last balance *vis-à-vis* the rest of the world in 1991.

After accumulating savings over several decades through prudent and cautious policies, the creditors sit on a large pile of reserves with low domestic debt and government deficits. These reserves are largely held by emerging countries with China at the forefront. As a paradox, the emerging economies have taken it upon themselves to lend to the richer countries — exporting capital almost as vendor's credit. Indeed, this reversal of roles is one explanation for the global financial crisis. The global monetary system is not geared to function under such circumstances.

This development was framed by the so-called Washington Consensus of the 1980s — a neoliberal formula that spurred globalization by promoting liberalization of trade, interest rates and foreign direct investment; privatization and deregulation; as well as competitive exchange rates and fiscal discipline. Fundamental flaws were exposed, raising the question about which economic model might replace it.

There are two possibilities in this competition: one strategy is from the United States and a group of Democrats who suggest that more short-term borrowing and spending could lead to growth, tax revenues and exit from recession — even if the debt grows and deficits become permanent. A breakthrough by the U.S.

---

* First appeared in *YaleGlobal online*, 18 November 2011.

Congressional super-committee to make substantial cuts over the next 10 years won't fundamentally change this stance, merely reducing rather than eliminating the deficit. The Europeans have taken the opposite view: They advocate starting the recovery by reducing deficits and debt even if that seems counterproductive for economic growth in the short run. The Europeans are also raising taxes across the board, regarded as indispensable for restoring balance in government budgets.

The results of either plan won't be known for a few years. Chances are, however, that the European policy will carry the day for the simple reason that creditors call the tune. It's highly unlikely that creditors favor continued reliance on deficits as the inevitable consequence will be inflation, eroding the purchasing power of their reserves. Indeed, the Chinese rating agency Dagong has announced that it may cut the U.S. sovereign rating for the second time since August if the U.S. conducts a third round of quantitative easing.

Early in the crisis, as Europe set up a stabilizing bailout fund, there were rumors in the market that China, Russia and Japan might rescue of the euro, either by buying European bonds or going through the International Monetary Fund. It's unclear how China wants to proceed with such an undertaking, but Russia and Japan have allegedly acted to do that through the International Monetary Fund or by buying European bonds.

Countries with surpluses do not dream of rescuing the euro; they act in their own interest. Economically they prefer the European fiscal discipline, reasoning that American prodigality will shift much burden of adjustment onto them. They may dread being left with the U.S. dollar as the only major international currency, forcing them to endure, at times, whimsical policy decisions by the Federal Reserve System, the U.S. Treasury Department or U.S. Congress. The euro and the European Union are seen, and indeed needed, as a counterweight. The EU may look weak, but it's a respectable global partner, offering the euro as an alternative to the dollar and serving as a major player in trade negotiations and the debate about global warming, just to mention a few examples.

It can be expected that other nations will step forward to support the euro. But at what price? What conditions, if any, will be put on the table and will the Europeans consent? A case can be made that, as creditors undertake investments to help the euro, they actually help themselves, and there are no reasons why the Euro-zone should pay any price. We can expect a game of hardball, in which nerves matters, and who gives what to whom may not be clear at all.

Another question has arisen about who decides and who is in charge. The G20 meeting in Cannes revealed a growing consensus to stop the financial houses amassing and subsequently abusing power. If the global financial system is big enough to force Italy into a default-like situation, many countries are surely asking whether they'll be next. The big financial houses are viewed by many as irresponsible stakeholders, if stakeholders at all. Consider, the U.S. government is suing 18 banks for selling US$200 billion in toxic mortgage-backed securities to government-sponsored firms, the Federal National Mortgage Association and the Federal Home Mortgage Corporation, known as Fannie Mae and Freddie Mac. In April 2011 the European Commission initiated investigations into activities of 16 banks suspected of collusion or abuse of possible collective dominance in a segment of the market for financial derivatives.

The market has muscled its way in as judge about whether a country's political system or economic policy are good enough. But the market is neither a single institution nor a broad, balanced mix of diverse players. It's become a small group of large financial institutions, the power of which overwhelm what even big countries can muster: 147 institutions directly or indirectly control 40 percent of global revenue among private corporations. A sore point is that they pursue profits without concern over implications for countries and societies. Rather than let measures work, these financiers force the issue here and now, even as they speculate against efforts, many admittedly delayed and inadequate, to resolve debt crises. Financial institutions holding sovereign bonds that could default insure themselves by buying credit default swaps. What seems like prudent corporate governance becomes a shell game as these obligations are traded among financial institutions, some of which don't hold sovereign bonds in their portfolios — all of which heightens interest in forcing default.

The temptation to roll back economic globalization *inter alia* by breaking up the Euro-zone or restricting capital movements has been resisted. Economic globalization is holding firm.

Creditor countries can set the course on future economic policies — likely highlighting fiscal discipline. While the West had vested interest in the big financial houses, the incoming paymasters do not, and they can be expected to increase their control over investment patterns. This can be done either by setting up own financial houses or buying into Western financial institutions as was the case in the slipstream of the 2008 global debt crisis.

The global financial market is changing course, away from looking after Western interests and acting in accordance with corporate governance as defined by the West toward a more global outlook guided by the interests of new group of creditors.

The Euro-zone Fights for Survival*

With the Euro-zone shaken by debt crisis, the question is being raised: how did it happen. In retrospect, it's clear that the fault was not in the terms of the European Union Treaty, the Treaty of Maastricht, itself but lack of political courage to supervise the implementation and reform flawed measures. Focus was on fiscal policy with well-known guidelines for deficits and debts. What wasn't foreseen was the anomaly of capital markets over the first 10 years. That weak countries could continue to borrow at interest rates determined by the strongest country — Germany — fueling an irresponsible monetary policy escaped notice.

The countries exploiting this opportunity cannot in any way be exonerated from guilt. But they were not the only ones missing the looming disaster. A large number of European banks, the rating agencies, and the cohort of primarily U.S. and British economists and columnists now somewhat belatedly queuing to criticize the EU overlooked it.

The financial markets delivered a prime illustration of overshooting: warnings went ignored and lending continued even if the highly paid experts should have seen the writing on the wall. When it went wrong, the markets abruptly stopped lending thereby aggravating a crisis partly of their own making.

The crisis is comparable to the 2007/2008 U.S. financial crisis, highlighting an increasingly agonizing swing of corporate governance. Is it acceptable that financial institutions can pursue a course boosting profits from a purely egotistic policy, ignoring an implicit contractual obligation to incorporate societal repercussions in their policies? Is it so that governments can neglect the effects of such policies, referring to free enterprise and the market? The answer: yes, that is so, but the results in the form of a global recession, the U.S. economy heading full speed into a debt trap, and severe difficulties for the euro gives rise to second thoughts.

This leads to one of the main questions placed squarely on the European agenda: burden sharing. Weak countries like Greece have acted irresponsibly, without doubt, but what about the banks allowing them to do so in their own quest for profits? How to distribute the burden among countries, taxpayers in debtor versus creditor

---

* First appeared in *YaleGlobal online,* 18 August 2011.

countries, and the private sector, including banks inside debtor countries and creditor countries?

The future of the euro depends upon policymakers' abilities to find economically workable and politically acceptable solutions to this problem. Until a couple of weeks ago, the fumbling and hesitation did not inspire confidence, irrespective of the fact that the euro was doing well — it has risen *vis-à-vis* the U.S. dollar over the last 12 months although that may say more about the dollar's weakness than the euro's strength.

The Euro-zone took a decisive step at the July 21–22 meeting, trying to move ahead the curve by putting in place a respectable package designed to revive Greece and establish a fence around Ireland, Portugal, possibly Spain and Italy, asking the banks to write off a bit more than 20 percent of their claims — low compared to other cases over the last 20 years — beefing up the European Financial Stability Fund plus other measures to ensure the euro's survival.

The package looks reasonable, but is it good enough? That depends upon three points:

First, the rating agencies have become a bit erratic. They were far too lenient prior to the global financial crisis, and now they adopt the opposite attitude, crying wolf at the slightest movement in the forest. Granted, time is needed to allow rating agencies evaluate policy measures and find their own feet after having been so wide off the mark, but too many players in the market seek short-term profits for themselves in forcing one or several member states into default and possible breakup of the euro. A test of willpower between the Euro-zone governments and the financial markets is playing out. The Euro-zone will win this contest because it's a question of survival while the markets can and will switch their search for profits to other victims, like the U.S. and probably also the U.S. states, many of which will be severely hit by spending cuts in the federal budget.

The second test is success or failure of the weak countries to appear more solid and competitive over the next few years. The jury will be out for some time, but the answer seems positive provided the markets give these countries a chance. All have adopted and implemented serious austerity measures. Compared to the inactivity of the United States, the measures look gigantic. According to Goldman Sachs, the Euro-zone budget balance in percent of gross domestic product was −6 in 2010, estimated to fall to −4.4 in 2011 and further to −3.6 in 2012. Greece will go from −9.2 in 2010 to −5.6 in 2012. Italy and Spain anticipate a similar trajectory. The public generally seems willing to go along despite some protests. Indeed, widespread predictions of street riots and governments tumbling have not materialized. The reward is that economic growth in the Euro-zone is neither falling nor flat. It is going up.

The third point is a revision of the terms in the 1993 Treaty of Maastricht. Not fundamental changes, but steps towards a stronger fiscal union not only in words, but in deeds to prevent a repeat of the challenges during the euro's first decade. This will be accompanied by euro bonds, or bonds guaranteed by all Euro-zone member states. Reading between the lines, the message is emerging from the leading countries that they recognize the need for revisions and are prepared to act accordingly, but as so often seen with the European integration, time is required, not just a snag of a year or two, but more during which political will be tested.

The crisis will break or make the future of European integration. The overwhelming odds are that the current debt crisis will usher in a new phase of integration. The crisis has hammered home: No European country can survive alone. Without the euro, the global financial crisis would surely have led to a currency war among the European countries with disastrous results for the global economy.

Some people flirt with the idea of Germany leaving the euro, standing alone as a knight in shining armor with a strong currency, low inflation and fiscal responsibility. It was seen during the 1970s and 1980s that this cannot be done and was the prime motivation for the single currency. It would be odd if Germany left precisely when the Euro-zone slowly, steadily is coming round to adopt fiscal responsibility and low inflation, not because it is the German model, but because it's been tested and viewed as best.

Nor is it realistic to see other member states leave the euro, choosing to face economic and social meltdown brought along by failure to control fiscal imbalances and manage the economy. The markets would avoid such players. Their voices in other EU matters would carry little or no weight.

There are no viable alternatives. If for no other reason then, the Euro is here to stay.

Part V
Asia in the Global Economy

Introduction to Part V

Asia is in many ways blessed with high growth, having eluded the global financial crisis, and in possession of the ingredients for a self-sustaining economic development. There is, however, no guarantee that Asia "will make it" into such a magnificent era. Much depends on decisions by policy-makers. There are many elements pointing to and supporting a robust future economy, but it is overlooked that Asia and Asian countries also have their problems and some of them look pretty scary. Problems like inequality, pollution, distortion of production factors, and weak political regimes often accompanied by corruption, nepotism, and kickbacks undermining the economy, erodes trust among people and confidence in the political system.

By far, chances are still, that Asia will maintain a healthy trend growth underpinning the rise of Asia, making the twenty-first century Asia's century, but wait for the second half before things really start to look that way. Many observers lean backwards with admiration, looking at charts showing how magnificent Asia has been doing — and in a way they are right — but they may have overlooked that so far, Asia has caught up with the West. There was an economic blueprint to take from the shelf and use. Technology was available. The trading system was there for Asian countries to use.

The world may congratulate itself that the big Asian nations decided some decades ago to join the existing global system formed by the U.S. and Europe since 1945 instead of setting up an alternative system or work for fundamental changes that would have rattled the global economy.

Now when Asia is approaching the stage where the catch-up phase is going to end, the question remains: what now? Will Asia be able to forge a new global economic model or at least retool the current one making it better able and suitable to frame what the future has in store for us? Will Asia be able and willing to switch from applied research to basic research using its savings to long-term scientific research where the reward may come after many years of waiting or maybe not at all? How will Asia use its large savings that positions it as the world's biggest and most important investor?

Leadership is a question of political maturity reflecting willingness to enter into or shape agreements and use power to forge global solutions even if agreements are not the most profitable solution for the country shaping solutions. Despite criticisms, the U.S. and Europe have been doing that over the last 50 years. Grinding their teeth and sometimes through tergiversation, they managed to get there. It may sometimes be a hard sell to the public because the economic benefits of leadership may not be visible in the short run. History shows that it takes time for countries to grow into that role. The burden of leadership does not easily appear attractive.

In an economic context, Asia falls in four groups. Japan is in many ways "different" influenced by its island history — as is Britain in Europe — and in many ways a country that has adopted many of the West's economic paradigms and by so doing built an economy that cannot be compared with its Asian neighbours except Korea. Adding to this is the trauma after World War II followed by American troops that still exists. China has now surpassed Japan as the second largest global economy and operates with USD 8,000 in income per capita (calculated by purchasing power parities) compared to the U.S. with about USD 50,000. South Asia in particular India operates at USD 2,500, and Southeast Asia ranging from almost USD 50,000 for Singapore to USD 1,300 for Myanmar and with the largest country, Indonesia, at USD 4,700.

It is interesting and promising for Asia's future that over the last decade or two a much stronger and deeper Asian supply chain has emerged linking Asian countries much closer to each other. With the rise of megacities/megaregions as centres for economic growth and a more compact supply chain, the picture looks quite good. Asia is in fact better placed economically than both the U.S. and Europe for sustained growth over the next half century.

To turn the potential into reality Asia needs to avoid military conflicts, which, evidently, tap the nations for resources and block trade and investment. The good thing is that no Asian country threatens vital interests of adjacent countries. They compete with each other to exploit resources. There are unresolved quarrels about borders. Minorities inside countries may give rise to animosities. Vital interest with outcomes upon which the survival of the nation, depends upon and can only be found in one place, such as the water flowing from the Tibetan plateau into India may tempt China and if it is diverted, would constitutes a lethal threat. Both nations realize the importance of this matter and apparently that makes conflict about water supply a remote possibility.

The resources in disputed areas and to a certain extent also border problems can be solved if the will is there. It is surely hard to see Asian leaders letting these problems escalate into war, although a growing nationalism getting out of control or even worse, fuelled by politicians may do precisely that, unless the lid is kept on.

The way ahead seems to be a stronger drive for the Asian integration. Looking at the issues about islands, reefs or shoals in the sea from Japan-Korea to the Malaccan Strait, it is clear that it is not sovereignty but the access and the right to exploit the resources that drives these disputes and in some cases confrontations. Politically it may pose problems, but the conclusion is not that far away as to forget the issue of sovereignty and work out some kind of sharing of resources inside a mechanism for integration, bringing to Asia the benefits flowing from such a step in the form of division of labour and access to markets. There are already purely economic arguments speaking in favour of forging Asian integration and initiatives to that effect have been taken albeit the tangible results in the form of higher growth clearly traced back to these endeavours remain to be seen.

Compared to the European integration, which by the way should serve as an inspiration, but not a blueprint, the grand design captivating the mind sets, promoted by strong political leaders do not yet seem to be forthcoming. As long as this is the case, Asian integration will progress slowly and steadily and this will be good, but still without the major design convincing the Asian countries that they are in the same boat and share the same destiny — which they do!

Southeast Asia is the only example of an integration process worth mentioning in this context displaying significant progress and a crucial role in stabilizing the region, but still in the early stages of a genuine integration. The Southeast Asian nations enjoy the prospect of a promising economic future, being one of few regions in the world with a good mix of agriculture, commodities, manufacturing, and technology plus services. ASEAN (Association of Southeast Asian Nations) may play a role in shaping an Asian integration. The region is sufficiently strong to influence the two giants, China and India, and important for them as partners in the Asian manufacturing circuit and supply of resources while not really strong enough to do well in the longer run on its own. In a geopolitical context it also offers the advantage that while China and India may have their own ambitions in the global or maybe more relevant regional power game, ASEAN does not harbour such ambitions — like Cesar's wife beyond suspicion.

In a way, Southeast Asia is the contrast to South Asia, which has a large and growing population, an economy that requires mostly imported resources for growth, and the prospect of falling food production in the coming years plus water shortage either economically or physically. There is only one other area in the world with a convergence of such similar ominous elements — the southern part of the U.S. plus

Mexico. If analysed in the prism of domestic instability and social upheavals, South Asia may harbour the biggest threat to the peaceful rise of Asia, especially when incorporating the drain on decision-making required by restructuring the economy to provide jobs through labour-intensive, low-cost manufacturing.

It is for Asia to shape its own future. But the outside world can and should play a role.

The European Union offers experiences and knowledge about integration and Asia is by far its biggest trading partner — China alone almost account for the same level of trade as the U.S. does. The EU can offer a good deal of soft power, which is useful in shaping Asia's future, solutions in many areas where the Europeans have know-how — education, social welfare, pollution, and global warming. All this is good, but not enough; Asia asks for more and only the U.S. has in its power to do or undo Asia's rise.

Basically, the U.S. confronts two choices: support an Asian integration as it did with the European integration, which also means seeing China in an increasingly dominating regional role or try to pull the handbrake to stop or at least make China's rise slower through drawing the rest of Asia away from China by offering lucrative opportunities through an American-led integration. The snag is the waning U.S. economic clout makes the second alternative less attractive for the rest of Asia now more dependent on the Asian supply chain albeit still benefitting from the huge American consumer market. The advantage for the U.S. of choosing the first option is that as a Pacific nation it has a legitimate right to take part, underpinned by its still strong economy; if handled in the right way, it could help the U.S. to stay on a higher growth pattern. So far it seems that the U.S. has not made up its mind and as long as that is the case, Asian integration will not really take off or alternatively be put on the backburner.

The U.S. economic problems of rising debt and persistent deficits on the federal budget plus balance of payments may push it toward favouring Asian integration conditioned on a major role for the U.S. However, with less money maintaining a large military presence in Asia, it may be beyond its financial reach.

Maybe, just maybe, China and the U.S. could find a way to agree on curbing military spending and use their funds for something more interesting for their populations. China is still a weak nation with an acute and high need for addressing problems inside the nation. The U.S. has for many years downgraded, even neglected its own nation building leaving a big gap for public investment.

It may be too much to ask for or hope for, but these two nation-states should by their own domestic problems be pushed toward a mutual accommodation not necessarily because they want to or like each other, but because they find it increasingly hard to find the money for a greedy military machine for which there does not seem to be much use.

Economic Integration — The Future for Asia*

Over the last half century economic transactions have jumped out of the nation-state box and take place globally, while the political systems put in place to control economic activities are still mainly national and domestic. This schism between international economic transactions and national political systems exposes the impotence of policy-making and thereby undermines the legitimacy of the political system in the eyes of the citizens. This spills over into scepticism about the advantages of economic globalisation. The choice for politicians is to share decision-making with other nation-states or to lose influence, which is difficult to explain as it looks as giving away powers while in fact it is the only way to preserve power.

Nowadays, a sovereignty's prime objective is to ensure that international rules are sufficiently wide to allow the nation-state to pursue domestic political goals i.e. avoid a clash between national political goals and international rules. Sovereignty shifts from defending the nation-state against the outside world (a defensive posture) to participation in international decision-making (offensive actions). A concerted effort with adjacent nation-states is sought to that effect under the label of economic integration, which becomes the vehicle for this transformation lifting politics from the national to the international level. It is not an end in itself, but an instrument to achieve political goals beyond reach if nation-states tried on their own, alternatively do better than if nation-states wanted to do it alone.

If in doubt recall the number of international meetings in the slipstream of the financil crisis starting inside one nation-state, the U.S., but spreading like a prairie fire. The U.S. fought almost desperately to keep the repercussion on the domestic economy under control, but in vain. It was also unable to prevent it from turning into an international — global — financial crisis. International economic flows dwarf the nation-state confining it to empty gestures if acting alone.

Economic integration imposes discipline on nation-states forming a barrier for transferring burdens of adjustment to neighbours — beggar thy neighbour policies. It is rarely mentioned, but without the Euro a currency war would probably have erupted with everybody scrambling to depreciate against the Deutsch Mark, which would have been pushed up destroying Germany's competitiveness bringing along a

---

* First appeared in *Diplomatist, Special Report*, 2012.

genuine recession. Britain is sometimes named as having done better than the Euro-zone, but few observers note that it has depreciated 20 percent *vis-à-vis* the Euro since the beginning of 2009. Sweden, another "success story" has depreciated over the same period with about 25 percent. Just imagine that all European countries had tried this ball game and the disastrous effect on the global monetary system is unraveling before our eyes.

The headlines are full of stories about the Euro crisis, but in fact the world faces a global debt crisis with the U.S., Britain, Japan, and the Euro-zone all mired in histori-cally high debt (private & public) combined with high deficits on the public budgets.

Debt does not go away. Repayment takes form of lower future consumption to the same extent as past consumption was higher — both measured against Gross Domestic Product (DGP). The discussion is not about this, but about over how many years and who is going to shoulder the burden. Austerity points to the debtor and inflation to the creditor.

The Euro-zone is going through an acrimonious adjustment process bringing spend-ing into line with production — you spend what you earn. It hurts, but in the long run makes the economies more robust opening up for growth anchored in confi-dence among domestic consumers & business sector and international creditors. The U.S. seems firmly on the path to kick the can down the road continuing to run up debt and deficits until its creditors do not want to lend anymore — you spend what other people will lend you. Currently the real interest rate for lenders to the U.S. is negative. That won't continue. For how long will creditors see the purchasing power of their investment eroded? No one knows, but definitely not indefinitely!

For Asia the challenge is that the main lenders to the U.S. are found here. Sooner or later the U.S. debt crisis will threaten to undermine the Asian economies in one way or another — losing part of the investment, lower U.S. demand, or semi-protectionist policies. So far American and British financial institutions have shuffled around Asia's savings, but as seen after the outbreak of the financial crisis in 2007/2008, this is coming to an end. The Asian confidence in the still predominantly Western — American — financial system is waning and fast.

The challenge then becomes how to shape and establish an Asian capital market, making room for Asian financial institutions, and find a place for Asian currencies as international currencies. This is a tall order especially as the timeframe is not open-ended in view of the apparent flaws in the existing system.

History tells that economic power in the form of manufacturing comes first to be followed by financial power. Asia is now getting a foothold in economic power even in China, India, and Southeast Asia still have some way to go — currently China accounts for 10.45 percent of global GDP, Japan 8.4 percent, India 2.6 percent, Southeast Asia three percent, and Korea 1.6 percent. Looking at the contribution to global growth in 2000–2010, these countries score more than 35 percent as an indication of their growing clout.

Predicting future trends is not a precise science — in fact not a science at all — but it seems a fair guess that Asian economic growth and subsequent managing of its own wealth will not be easy without some kind of economic growth and subsequent managing of its own wealth will not be easy without some kind of economic integration. Enterprises will hesitate to commit to an Asian and invest in other Asian countries without guarantees of continued free flows of trade and capital movements. Binding commitments through economic integration is in practice the only way to deliver such guarantees. Business leaders watch what policy makers are doing and pay much less attention to what they are saying. Add to that, the political imperative of distributing benefits among Asian countries ruling out that a few countries monopolise the benefits — a supply chain and economic integration also serve that purpose.

Demographics point to a seminal change in economic structure among China and India over the next decade or two. China's labor force starts to fall in 2015; India's continue to rise until around 2050.

Inevitably labor intensive, low cost manufacturing moves out of China. Some of it will go to Southeast Asian countries, but South Asia is well placed to be the main beneficiary — already seen for Bangladesh. India's growth over the preceding two decades is partly due to technology. While still important it is unlikely that this comparatively small sector can sustain growth and in particular provide job openings over a longer period.

To maintain competitiveness, China and India can be expected to move in opposite directions. China up the value added ladder into technology, quality, and service as competitive parameters. India to be the place for labor-intensive, low cost manufacturing. China needs to invest more in supporting sectors like R&D, which is already visible. India must look at transport, logistics, and basic skills for the labour force.

It is by no means an insurmountable task to manage such adjustment processes, but it poses a number of obstacles and challenges. Some analysts point to a shortage of highly-skilled workers in China and medium skilled workers in India forcing the two countries to operate with bottle necks posing economic and social problems unless they take the jump to open up for movement of labour across borders and the population is willing to move.

So far the two Asian giants have reached a trade figure of approximately $70 billion, expected to be $100 billion in 2015. But it is lopsided with a large Chinese surplus ($40 billion) underlining the need for economic relations to work as mutually beneficial to be durable.

The two countries also shy away from investing in each other's industries with investment flows negligible compared to trade flows.

Confronted with low growth among the G3 countries. (U.S. EU, and Japan) Asia must rely on its own demand in the future. As the figures for the Asian supply chain show this is taking shape, but still a large part of the Asian economies are geared to export of final products. China and India must step up to replace faltering demand from G3 with domestic demand and by far the best way to do so is economic integration.

Not any kind of growth will do the trick however. The world is moving from the era of plenty with ample and cheap supply of food, commodities, energy, and water to an era of scarcity where resources will be physically or economically scarce. This is borne out by rising prices and the plain fact that export restrictions for food and commodities are seen around the world.

In this context the challenge is to switch the growth pattern from well-known growth to more sustainable growth saving resources by introducing a new kind of production processes incorporating resource savings and gradually nudge the people towards a less materialistic consumption pattern.

Recycling and remanufacturing, even three-dimensional design (additive manufacturing) and the next step, three dimensional assembling are gaining ground pointing to a production system without waste — for the simple reason that waste rules a company out of the competitive game as it becomes too costly. Recently a global survey including 28,000 people in Asia-Pacific showed support for brands that 'give back to society' and number one cause to support was environmental sustainability.

China published a white paper in October 2012 where the bar for sustainable and nuclear energy to be reached in 2015 was lifted significantly. This not only reflected strategic reasons, technology, and security of supply, but also response to a growing call from the Chinese public to political leaders for decisive action in the fight against pollution.

Asia may use the current turmoil in the global economy to switch to another and more sustainable growth model. That requires investment, technology, and innovation — all elements that will support growth and the kind of growth that globally will replace the industrial age.

If done through economic integration the benefits will spread to all Asian countries and thus not only serve economic purposes, but solidify mutual confidence among Asian countries reducing risks of confrontation and conflicts so unwelcome and so dangerous for the prospect of prosperity encompassing all Asian citizens.

From Asian Financial Crisis to the Western Debt Crisis
An Emerging Southeast Asia*

My arrival as the Ambassador of the Kingdom of Denmark coincided with the start of the Asian financial crisis: September 1st 1997. In the eighties and first half of the 1990s, Asia had seen marvellous economic growth and received praise for its economic policy from such illustrious organizations as the International Monetary Fund (IMF) and the World Bank (WB). Suddenly everything started to go awfully wrong. Almost all countries in East and Southeast Asia saw economic contraction up to fifteen percent; exchange rates fell through the floor.

It looked like the Asian "miracle" had come to an abrupt stand still. The drive towards a market economy and liberalizing domestic economies seemed to have failed, indeed the countries faring best in those calamitous times were those who had either been reluctant to liberalize such as China or had put on the handbrake when the storm broke, as Prime Minister Mahathir did in Malaysia.

And yet, after a few years of hard work, most of the East Asian countries were back on the growth track even if for some countries such as Indonesia took a little longer. Since then the world has seen Southeast Asia, Northeast Asia and South Asia on a firm growth pattern.

The effect of this was in the first place a regained confidence that "Asia could do it". After the global financial crisis in the U.S. and Europe, Asia sailed on more or less out of harm's way, and the world saw a growing self-confidence among Asian nations.

The "West," as it is often called even if in doing so I would also caution against these sweeping generalizations (a caution which extends to the comparable use of the word "Asia"), had played its cards. When 1997/98 financial crisis hit countries in Asia, American economists travelled around the region telling everybody why it had gone wrong, spelling out in no uncertain terms using clear vocabulary that if only the American way of managing the economy and control the financial

---

*First appeared in *Changing Tides and Changing Ties — Anchoring Asia–Europe Relations in Challenging Times*, edited by Yeo Lay Hwee and Barnard Turner (Singapore, EU Centre: 2012.)

system had been applied everything would have been fine. It was like *My Fair Lady* in which Professor Higgins sings "why can't a woman be more like a man". The U.S. market model showed the way! The Washington consensus underpinning the work of the IMF and the WB was in fact a carbon copy of the American edition of economics. On top of that, democracy as practised in the U.S. — despite the fact that only half of the population casts their votes — was put forward as the ultimate political model. The combination of the American economic model and the American political system would do the trick. A few years before Francis Fukuyama had published his thesis about the end of history conveying the message that the Western model had won, it was here to stay. America preached, Asia listened — until 2007/2008.

Then the global financial crisis struck with the speed of lightning and strength of a thunderstorm. It began in the U.S. revealing that the U.S. had acted against all the advice and prescriptions that they had given to the Asian audience in 1997/98. Europe followed. Japan as a member of the G-3 had been in the doldrums since 1990 and showed little promise of getting out of semi-stagnation. The West found it difficult to find an answer. The U.S. political system put forward as a model soon started to be labelled dysfunctional even by the Americans themselves. It was unable to produce solutions. The Europeans managed barely to keep together in the Euro-zone haunted by difficulties.

Under these circumstances it is not surprising that Asia started to grow in self-confidence and belief in what we may term "the Asian way of doing things" even if again these generalizations are dangerous as they do not fully reflect the various nuances and differences. But the Asian concept of finding solutions, of doing things, of probing to see what works and what does not work looked like a clever way, out-competing the American much more ideological stance.

Around the world many countries in particular among emerging countries or developing nations noted that the Washington consensus did not any longer lead to the Promised Land. Instead the Asian way — or maybe we should call it the Chinese way — seemed a better bet. It worked, the Western model did not.

The U.S. led a military operation to bring democracy to Iraq with a grander aim at changing the political architecture of the Middle East and perhaps open the door to a solution of the perennial, insurmountable problem of the complex tangle between Israel–the Palestinians–the Arab World. This, however, did not seem to succeed. Iraq's president Saddam Hussein was ousted — yes executed — and a regime change implemented, but many people around the world asked the rather simple, but basic question whether the Iraqi citizen was better off and whether the political situation in the Middle East had become more stable. The jury is still out, but close to a decade after the regime change doubts persists about the effectiveness of this course and its ability to achieve the laudable, but evasive and difficult objectives: peace, democracy, and stability.

Seminal changes are easy to describe after they happen, but difficult to detect when they take place. However it seems to me that the fifteen years from 1997 to 2012 has brought along doubts among Western countries about their own model raising intellectual and psychological barriers for geopolitical leadership. The U.S. is still — by far — the strongest nation and will continue to be so. But the American themselves are baffled when seeing what has happened around them. They do not any longer believe it is the obvious thing to offer their model to other countries with the consequence that U.S. foreign policy does not any longer have a firm hand on the tiller with a steady course towards a clear goal. The Europeans are fighting to preserve their economic integration and have little appetite for leading the way except for a number of soft policy questions such as climate change.

Asia on the other hand is brimming with confidence and belief in its way of doing things and its model whatever its characteristics may be. Polls show that a minority of Americans believe their children will have a better life than themselves. In Asia it is the other way around; a large majority thinks that the children will have a better life than they have enjoyed.

Interpretation of history is not an exact science. There is no ready-made answer. I draw the lesson, however, that in the longer run it is not so much absolute and measurable power that counts as belief in yourself and your abilities. And on that score Asia wins hands down. The game is not over and things may still change, but the trends we spot cannot be ignored.

Inside Asia itself, Southeast Asia's perception of its role has undergone interesting changes. Until the early 1990s — yes may be until 1997 — Southeast Asia was looked upon as the "best" place to invest. China was still a comparatively newcomer with some uncertainty about the sincerity of its reforms. The leadership was dominated by Soviet trained technical people. India did not start reforms until the early 1990s, and Japan was caught in stagnation. So the door was open for Southeast Asia to attract international investment — and it did with tremendous success.

After the Asian financial crisis in 1997 doubts grew both among Southeast Asian countries and in the circle of international investors. China was surging ahead, promising a large domestic market, outsourcing, and a stable economy. India was entering the game. Together these two countries had more than 2.5 billion people, much more than Southeast Asia, which was not a common and even less a single market.

This forced some soul-searching among Southeast Asian countries about how to get back on the playing field to offer an alternative and a serious one to the Chinese and Indian markets.

The answer was found in the virtues of economic integration. By moving towards a common market, whatever label it was given,[1] Southeast Asia could bring into play some of its advantages *vis-à-vis* the two Asian giants — educated labour force, infrastructure, and in some cases legal systems and corporate governance. A stronger integration among the Southeast Asian countries could serve as a catalyst for a broader Asian economic integration in the first place and subsequently linking up to the Northeast Asian countries moving ahead, and in a longer term perspective reaching out to South Asia.

If this was successful, Southeast Asia would not only benefit from access to the larger Asian markets, but regain some of its role as an attractive place — a hub — for international investments. The basic idea was simple enough namely to make it just as good to be placed in Southeast Asia as in China or India. This strategy has not yet been fully implemented, but Southeast Asia has moved some of the way, most observers would say sufficiently long, to demonstrate that it works.

For Southeast Asia itself the policy and the economic development since 1997 and after 2007 has solidified the belief in the region and its abilities. Even if ASEAN is sometimes classified as an organization that has not really managed to deliver economic integration, it has certainly helped to deepen the economic interdependence inside East Asia and enhanced mutual confidence which has served Southeast Asia well under difficult economic conditions. Despite some turmoil, it has also helped to search for common views on political questions confronting Southeast Asian countries such as the South China Sea and Myanmar.

So Southeast Asia has turned around from doubts and uncertainty to belief in its future. It is a serious partner in the on-going game about designing the future of Asia and how Asian countries will tackle the unavoidable problems in the slipstream of economic globalization. China and India increasingly look at Southeast Asia as a group of countries instead of individual nations even if the age old game of divide and rule still goes on.

The changing conditions for trade in commodities have played into the hand of Southeast Asia. We are moving from the era of plenty to era of scarcities. That benefits Southeast Asia with commodities in many countries ensuring a steady income from export.

---

[1] AFTA (ASEAN Free Trade Area), AEC (ASEAN Economic Community).

Indeed one of the factors benefitting Southeast Asia is its diversified economy. This is one of the not too many places in the world where we have commodities, manufacturing, technology, and services in a good mix auguring a good growth pattern even if the region is not immune to global problems.

The feeling of self-confidence and belief in its own way of doing things is clearly good for Asia. It is equally good that the playing field is not the monopoly of China and India, but that Southeast Asia in its own and sometimes timid or reluctant way stages a claim of being at the table when the future of Asia is decided.

The Asian Supply Chain Becomes More Compact*

Singapore as a transport hub will benefit hugely from a massive change in the Asian supply chain. It is going to be more "compact". Goods will increasingly be transported inside Asia and to a nearer customer rather than long distance/globally.

This is due to several factors.

Container transport, which used to be trivial part of the final product costs, will still be cheap, yes, but not that cheap anymore. The main culprit is the hike in oil prices that not only seems to be permanent, but to continue.

Obviously this strengthens efforts by companies to seek a nearer source for their purchases of components. And they do. British retailer Marks & Spencer plans to overhaul its supply chain i.e. by stopping the purchase of supplies from one hemisphere to another, which may save the company GBP 175 million annually.

Several European companies are gradually discovering that transport costs erode the competitive advantages of outsourcing to China.

Insourcing is a new catchword. To a certain extent production is going back, but the much more interesting phenomenon is that other Asian countries step into China's shoes even serving as recipient as China starts to outsource.

Financial reports show that almost all container transporters suffer when moving goods from one continent to another, but container transport inside Asia is still profitable.

What we see here is the impact of the coming era of scarcities. Commodities go up in price. Oil likewise. The significance of labor costs as a competitive parameter declines relative to costs incurred by commodities and transport.

Even looking at it without incorporating scarcities and rising commodity prices, it seems clear that the share of world trade shifts from Asia to and fro the established industrial countries (G-3 i.e. the U.S., the EU, and Japan) to take place inside Asia. The figures show that intercontinental trade is losing to intra-Asian trade.

---

* First appeared in *Singapore Business Review*, 10 August 2012.

Asia is already the place for global manufacturing, but where in the past Asian trade in components and semi-manufactured goods went to China to be turned into export to G-3 requiring global transport, we now detect a rising share of Asian production to domestic demand, diminishing the demand for global transport, but asking for more local/regional transport.

It may well be that demography combined with several other factors reduces China's position as the manufacturing hub, but its place will be taken by other Asian countries with a high and growing labor force like Vietnam, Indonesia, Bangladesh and India solidifying the intra-Asian trade and consequently the changing supply chain.

What Makes S'pore Different*
It's a Quality City that has Harnessed the Hub Concept to its Advantage

As a Dane who has lived in Singapore for more than 14 years, I naturally find similarities between Singapore's and Denmark's endeavours to carve out a niche for themselves in the harsh climate of economic globalisation.

Both countries try as best they can to use their geographical position to their advantage. The basic idea of the hub strategy comes naturally to the fore.

Countries like the United States and China use their domestic markets as a platform for economic strength. That is even feasible for middle-sized countries well-established in certain segments of the global market. For example, in Europe, France in luxury products (fashion, haute couture, wine) and Germany in engineering. In Asia, Thailand in agricultural products and Vietnam in seafood.

These countries brand themselves via a strong position in industrial segments, producing first for the domestic market before subsequently being turned into an export industry.

Neither Singapore nor Denmark can do likewise. They need to find something else to brand them — to be different. And they need branding because high-cost countries — and Singapore has, for some years, been in that category — find it agonising to compete on wages and prices.

For such a strategy to be successful at all, it requires a tremendous effort, as the competition is with a whole string of countries with a much larger pool of labour, thus benefiting from lower wage cost. Singapore must do something else, something better to lift itself out of this box, and branding is an obvious way.

A brand offers something more than just the user value. The consumer enjoys something special by using a branded product and is ready to pay a higher price for that special "something else".

---

*This article appears in the Singapore International Foundation's new publication, *Singapore Insights From The Inside*, a collaboration with the international community to share unique insights and personal experiences.

Singapore's brand pertains to efficiency, reliability, good corporate governance, good government and rule of law — which attract multinational companies.

For years, Singapore's harbour and shipping sector have been an important element in the country's economy and they employ a large number of Singaporeans. These days, few people realise that it was by no means certain that Singapore would be the busiest harbour in Southeast Asia and among the largest container harbours in the world.

It was achieved by realising that efficiency and the ability to deliver high-quality services every time a ship docks matters most, which in turn conveys to shipping lines that Singapore can be relied upon. This brought about a virtuous circle: the larger the number of shipping lines using Singapore's harbour to their satisfaction, the more likely new shipping lines *inter alia* serving the Chinese market and/or established in China would also use it.

Having acquired the knowledge of running a harbour competently, Singapore's next step was to use that as a competitive parameter in offering this knowledge to harbours in other countries, supplemented by investing in harbour facilities in some of these markets.

THE GLOBAL COMPETITION

Building an airline and an airport which, year after year, are ranked among the best in the world illustrates how a country using the hub concept can overcome the disadvantage of a small domestic market and establish itself as an important player in the global competitive game.

Now, Changi Airport seems a natural place for an air travel hub in Asia, but a look at the map shows that this fruit could have been plucked by many countries. Thailand, Vietnam and Malaysia are all as well-positioned as Singapore, maybe even better, and might have supplemented that with a larger domestic market.

They have done so, yes, but Singapore grasped better than its competitors one of the essential things in global competition: you move in with both feet and wholehearted commitment, or you stay away. As the famed American general George S. Patton said: get there firstest with the mostest.

There is a good deal of risk associated with the hub concept in areas such as shipping and air transport. The investment required is enormous and cannot be changed with a snap of the finger.

Therefore, good planning and strategic foresight are indispensable to ensure the success of the hub concept.

In these areas, Singapore can also be described as a hub. There are not many cities around the world that welcome the global intellectual elite for lecture tours, seminars, conferences and brain-picking as consistently as Singapore. These people come to Singapore to share their knowledge and ideas about future trends, and by doing so, they enhance Singapore's knowledge, which explains why Singapore enters the high-risk investment game with so much confidence.

The picture is the same when looking at the fields of information and communication technology and biotechnology. Likewise, for education and health care. A country choosing the hub concept and branding itself as a hub prospers by cultivating a stimulating intellectual climate and making itself an attractive place for talent.

MEGA-CITIES, MEGA-REGIONS

There is much talk about mega-cities and mega-regions as drivers of global growth in the years ahead. These economic powerhouse possess sufficient weight to forge ahead on their own, as is the case for, *inter alia*, Shanghai and several other Chinese cities. They show us that columnist Thomas Friedman's message that the world is flat conveyed a basically correct analysis — in the global economy, everybody competes with everybody else. But there is another aspect to this, which is the notion that the world is also spiky, meaning that economic activities tend to be concentrated in large cities, hence mega-cities and/or mega-regions.

The gist of this dawned upon me in 1994 when I visited Seattle. I was shown an analysis pinpointing the key advantages of being in Washington state for biotech and medtech industries. The absolute top scorer was quality of life with 35 percent, followed by high quality of workforce accounting for 21 percent. Academic institutions came in at No. 3 with 19 percent. Income tax and cost of living scored a meager 6 percent. This is what started me thinking about quality cities.

I later talked with the head of research of Novo Nordisk (a world leader in diabetes), and he told me that the company encouraged researchers to take an interest in cultural life because it would enhance their powers of observation — a vital ingredient when judging whether a research project was worth pumping money into.

I have often thought about this lesson: it is not so much the research as its applicability and the interdisciplinary, intersectoral approach to get there. That leads to quality cities.

What has not attracted so much attention, but unquestionably will in the future, is the notion of quality cities offering an economic and intellectual climate that attracts multinational companies and the intellectual elite to place some of their activities there. These global players do not put all their eggs in one basket; they spread them around, thus opening the door for quality cities to get a share of these lucrative activities taking place at a high — and in some cases the highest — level on the value-added ladder.

This is what the hub concept offers, and looking at SIngapore over the past 14 years, what strikes me most is seeing how this concept has sunk deep roots in Singapore.

Lessons for Asia from the Global Financial Crisis*

The global financial crisis exacerbates the ongoing shift in global economic and financial power from the West to Asia. It does not change the prediction that the Asian economies will gradually take over from the West, but tells another and perhaps more fundamental story. The economic model invented and refined by the West and used by the rest of the world does not function anymore. The so-called Washington Consensus, the plinth of economic globalisation, has effectively gone with the wind.

Asia has one trump card: it sits on the world's savings and will continue to do so for some time. This is likely to trigger a shift in policymaking, and concomitantly, global investment flows to serve Asia's interests over that of the West. On the flip side, there is a lack of sufficiently strong financial institutions in Asia. The world's financial powerhouses are still to be found in Europe and the United States. Asian banks also need to build up strong reserves and reduce their exposure to the contagion from the West.

The global financial crisis is an opportune moment for Asia to start thinking ahead about the kind of international monetary system it would like to lead and fashion. Asia needs to step up and assume more responsibility in the global system, but it is not enough just to seek influence in international institutions. More fundamentally, Asia needs to decide what it wants to do with its growing influence. To do this, Asia needs to distil the correct lessons from the current economic crisis.

First, any durable financial system must be part of the productive. Its function is basically simple: to channel savings into investment. To serve the economy properly, the system needs to be able to screen investment projects to determine which ones are profitable and which ones to skip. The more complicated and sophisticated the financial system becomes, the more likely it is that the basic function fades away to be replaced by self-serving operations that shuffle savings around financial instruments instead of channeling them into investments.

---

*This article was first published in Issue 12 (Oct–Dec 2011) of *Global-is-Asian,* the flagship magazine of the Lee Kuan Yew School of Public Policy, National University of Singapore. It is reprinted with the permission of the school.

The Asian financial crisis of 1997/98, the IT bubble of 2000 and the global financial crisis of 2008 have in common one shortcoming: the financial system did not do its homework. These could all be foreseen but were not, because the lure of short-term profit overshadowed long-term prudence. What were the highly paid rating agencies doing?

Research and development is vital for the dynamism of an economy, but it is also risky. As seen in the United States, venture capital is necessary, but a right balance has to be struck. It is not a good idea to jump into whatever R&D project is put on the table. A good financial system rewards bold entrepreneurs and punishes fool-hardy ones. Asia is going to be the home of the major capital-seeking multinational companies (MNCs) of the future. The financial system must therefore provide the capital needed for investment and overseas expansion, which calls for an ability to judge overseas operations and understand what is going on in the world.

Second, corporate governance is defined by the strongest economies, so in due course it will be up to Asia, Asian MNCs and Asian banks to sketch a new model for corporate governance. Thought must be given to this now, and if Asia acts wisely, it will achieve a win-win situation whereby governments, corporations and society interact — contributing to the wider development of society — instead of the quest for short-term profit which has only encouraged irresponsible behaviour.

Politically, Asia must play its cards right to maximise its influence. Many observers ponder over the likelihood of China coming to the rescue of the Euro-zone. China will decide whether to do so according to its own interests, not to save the Euro-zone *per se*. From a Chinese perspective, this may be the price worth paying to avoid U.S. dollar being the only major international currency and to stop China from being boxed in to acquire U.S. treasury bonds as the only financial instrument available.

The three global institutions — the International Monetary Fund, World Bank and World Trade Organisation — are all controlled by the West, with an American at the helm of the World Bank and Frenchmen sitting atop the two other institutions. Many view this as an anomaly, but it should be remembered that Europe and the United States still account for almost half of the global economy. The financial expertise, regardless of the flaws demonstrated when the global financial crisis broke, is still predominantly found there. Over many decades they have amassed tremendous experience in fielding candidates, getting them elected and thereafter running these organizations.

Eventually this will change. How fast it does rests on two issues. First, how good Asia will be in finding and putting qualified candidates on the table to garner global support. Europe and the United States did not just put their people into the director's chair, their candidates were elected. Second, will Asia be able to formulate a coherent policy about what it wants to do with these institutions? If Asia is content to be a bit player, it is insignificant whether the top person is Asian, European, or American. But Asia is now at an important crossroad: if it wants to transform the global system, it needs political will and courage to come up with a new paradigm and set of rules to organize the world financial system.

How Will Southeast Asia Position Itself in Asia's Future in an Age of Scarcities?*

Southeast Asia's economic prospects will be framed by four major trends: lower global growth, demography, urbanization, and, most crucial of the four, the coming age of scarcities. Together they weave a new tapestry for Southeast Asia's future.

GLOBAL GROWTH

Over recent decades the world has enjoyed exceptionally high economic growth rates. There have been examples of high growth (like Britain at the beginning of industrialization, Germany around 1900, and the United States at the same time), but that was never global growth. Now millions all over the globe have been lifted out of poverty and Gross Domestic Product (GDP) per capita has reached approximately US$4,000 for China — the most populous country in the world.

With this background it seems surprising, even astonishing, that lower growth looms ahead. The reason is that this high growth was fuelled by borrowing, which basically means that the present encroached into future consumption — this was especially seen in the United States with saving rates at around zero for the household sector over several years. In 2005 United States households were actually dissaving compared to a historically high savings rate of 14.6 percent in 1975. At the end of 2011 the household savings rate was around 4 percent. (The much maligned Euro-zone managed a household savings rate of 13.9 percent for the second quarter of 2011.)

The figures tell a disquieting story. After World War I global sovereign debt rose to 70 percent as the major countries borrowed to finance the war. It fell during the interwar period when debt was at least partially paid back. After World War II it rose again and this time approached 100 percent of GDP. Again it was paid back and in 1970 it was only 30 percent of global GDP. Waters seemed calm, but over

* "How will southeast Asia Position Itself in Asia's Future in an Age of Scarcities?" by Jørgen Ørstrøm Møller first appeared in *Southeast Asian Affairs 2012* (2012), pp 73–86. Reproduced here with the kind permission of the publisher, Institute of Southeast Asian Studies (http://bookshop.iseas.edu.sg).

the recent decades when high growth opened opportunities for savings, countries should have saved to prepare for rainy days, but they actually did the opposite and borrowed to increase spending. It was like an automobile racing downhill despite warning signals, with the driver putting his foot on the throttle just for the fun of it.

The result was what could be expected — disastrous. Global sovereign debt is now 100 percent of global GDP. More worrying is that the debt is concentrated among the rich countries that should have saved and lent to the developing and emerging economies to sponsor their economic development. Now it is the other way around; the poorer countries lend to the richer countries — a task the global financial system is not geared to handle.

Adding household, corporate, and financial sector debt, the astonishing figure of 300 percent of GDP among the OECD (Organisation for Economic Co-operation and Development) countries emerges. The biggest economy, the United States, is leading the pack with a combined total of debt in all sectors of approximately 400 percent of GDP.

Debt has to be repaid. That puts a lid on economic growth as consumption must be reduced to provide the savings to repay the debt. There is no other way. The current debate is not about the repayment, even if politicians try to skirt the issue, but about how to do it, especially how to exercise burden sharing among countries and various groups inside the debt-laden countries.

Southeast Asia is reasonably well positioned, with most countries running what look like sustainable budget deficits provided that economic growth can be maintained. Figures from the Asian Development Bank (ADB) show that the fiscal balance of central governments as a percentage of GDP in 2010 was between –0.1 percent and –8 percent for the ten countries compared to somewhat worse figures for South Asia, comparable figures for Central Asia, and East Asia showing better results albeit not displaying surpluses.[1] Public debt is manageable with figures not much above 50 percent for the major economies.

DEMOGRAPHY

The global population is seven billion people and will continue to rise, reaching at least nine billion around 2050 — barring unforeseen calamities like a major war, man-made catastrophes, or nature taking its revenge on mankind for exploiting

---

[1] Asian Development Bank, *Asian Development Outlook 2011* <http://www.adb.org/documents/books/ado/2011/ado2011.pdf>.

resources. The population growth, however, will be unevenly spread. In 2050 Africa may be the only continent with a rising population.

Demographically Asia Faces Several Challenges

The Asian countries fall into three groups. Those with a falling population: Japan and Korea; those with a stable population: mainly China, whose population will start to decline between 2025 and 2030; and those with a rising population, like South Asia, Vietnam, the Philippines, Indonesia, Myanmar.

Such a divergence does not necessarily augur conflicts, but neither is it a recipe for stability. It will certainly have an impact on economic growth and probably give rise to debate about immigration, including that of skilled labour.

The demographic composition is going to change with a larger share of the population in the age bracket above 65 years. Table 1 illustrates this for some of the major countries.

This will require financial support to the elderly and, perhaps even more important, building health care and support services, which currently are not available in Asia.

The ethnic and religious distribution of Asia's population is also going to change, with the share of Muslims going up. Asia is used to many ethnic and religious groups and over its history their share has certainly changed so this is not a new phenomenon, but nevertheless it calls for political attention especially in India where it is

TABLE 1   Share of People over 65 Years Measured against 15–64 Years of Age (%)

	2005	2020	2050
European Union	22	29	48
United States	18	24	34
China	11	17	39
India	8	10	21
Japan	30	47	74
Africa	6	7	11

Source: http://ec.europa.eu/regional_policy/ sources/docoffic/working/regions2020/pdf/ region2020_demographic.pdf likely that at least one of the states will see a Muslim majority sometime during the 2030–50 decades.

Most of Southeast Asia will in the coming years benefit from a favourable composition of the population pushing the problems of caring for the elderly into the future.

URBANIZATION

In 1975 17.5 percent of China's population lived in cities, in 2005 it was 40.4 percent, in 2015 it will be 49.2 percent — almost half — and in 2020 it will be 60 percent. In India the corresponding figures are 21.3 percent in 1975, 28.7 percent in 2005, 32 percent in 2015, and 41.5 percent in 2020.[2]

China and India have reversed roles, with China surpassing India as the most urbanized of these two giants.

Many potential problems as well as opportunities are embedded in such a high degree of urbanization achieved over a relatively short time span. Socially many people have moved from the countryside where they enjoyed close neighbourhoods and mutual support to the cities without these assets. The composition of GDP has shifted from mainly agricultural to mainly industry and services. Infrastructure including housing has emerged as a major contributing factor driving the economy.

Southeast Asia is going to see growing cities but, except possibly for a few cases, the region will not have the sort of large conglomerations that threaten stability. With some luck urbanization can be managed even if the challenges are obvious and need to be addressed.

THE ERA OF SCARCITIES

The world is transiting from the era of plenty deriving from the industrial epoch over the last 200 years to the era of scarcities. Such predictions have been made before and proven wrong mainly because of the opening up of new geographical areas and technological progress. Many observers take the view that the present cry of "the wolf is coming" will suffer the same fate as before. But they overlook the warning signals from which there is no escape. The index for commodity prices rose approximately 100 percent from 1945 to year 2000 and has since tripled despite

---

[2] UNDP, *Human Development Report 2007/2008* (UNDP: New York, 2007).

the global recession. It is in fact quite worrying that the levelling off of growth rates has not had a much bigger impact on resource prices.

The current situation also seems to differ from similar past discussions in the sense that we face across-the-board shortages. It is not some resources such as oil that see rising prices, it is in fact all them.

The shortage is seen in five main elements, all vital for the future of economic development: food, commodities, energy/oil, water, and clean environment connected to global warming and change of climate.

Food problems are visible. The UN Food and Agricultural Organisation has announced that forty countries suffer from a kind of malnourishment suggesting that a large number of people (maybe around one billion) do not get the food they need for a decent life, with obvious negative repercussions on their health and ability to contribute to economic activities. Just to maintain this unsatisfactory status quo the world needs a 40 percent increase in food production to 2030 and as much as 70 percent to 2070.[3]

These are frightening figures. Admittedly there are possibilities for bringing new land under the plough, but if so, harmful effects on the environment may follow. Analyses looking at potential for future increases of food production are sombre to say the least, pointing to falling instead of increasing agricultural production in areas with more than two thirds of the global population.

Commodities are going up in price. The world is starting to see export restrictions by the commodity exporting countries instead of import duties and import restrictions on industrial goods and services which in the past have been at the centre of trade policy.

It has dawned on the commodity exporting countries that they really have an asset to be husbanded carefully, but also a useful tool in the global power game. The commodity importing countries are beginning to fear interruption of access to raw materials — indispensable for their future economic growth. Those having the money to do so, step in to buy a large number of raw material sources, mines, mining companies, and similar economic assets. This economic "offensive" spreads fear

---

[3] *OECD-FAO Agricultural Outlook 2009–2018*, OECD and FAO 2009 <http://books.google.com.sg/books?id=VoQjj2MNgJ8C&pg=PA96&lpg=PA96&dq=fao+agricultura l+production+asia&source=bl&ots=EYitOsWDB8&sig=NCudvfHI8hWxL29UXzCQstQvXtE&hl=en&ei=IO-ZSsjROsefkQW_mIysAg&sa=X&oi=book_result&ct=result&resnum=6#v=onepage&q=fao%20agricultural%20production%20asia&f=false>.

among the commodity countries that they will not be able to maintain economic, and possibly political, independence.

Energy and oil has been the subject of so many analyses and studies that there really is not much to say that is new. So a few remarks will suffice. Much attention is devoted to sustainable energy sources and they certainly will become more important in the future, but it looks like coal will become even more crucial than it is today. In 2008 Asia accounted for 60 percent of global coal consumption, with China number one (39.1 percent), the United States number two, and India number three (8.8 percent). The International Energy Agency (IEA) estimates that in 2030 the share of coal in electricity generation will be 75 percent for China and 46 percent for India.[4] The reason is that coal is there — it is a domestic energy source to be exploited instead of pushing China and India into even deeper dependence on outside sources. Oil on the other hand, is in the Middle East, with the risk that in a crisis the U.S. navy could close vital sea routes.

Water may be even more important. It is possible, though difficult and costly, to substitute some commodities with others, but this cannot be done for water. Analyses show that half of China and the whole of South Asia plus part of Southeast Asia suffer from either a physical or economic shortage of water.

Water demand is estimated to grow 40 percent to 2030 — 40 percent greater than sustainable supply. In 2010 agriculture accounted for 70 percent of water use globally and industry 16 percent, of which half was used for energy production for industry. The 2030 prognosis is that Industry usage will rise to 30 percent, with China accounting for 40 percent of the additional demand.[5]

To this has to be added that the Western Hemisphere and Africa are net exporters of water while Asia is a net importer — Europe is more or less in balance. Products requiring water for production tend to move towards production where water is plentiful and that is the Western Hemisphere and Africa.

Southeast Asia fares reasonably well in terms of the outlook on food and water shortages. The real hotspot in coming years, suffering from high and a growing population but still having high economic growth that requires more resources, is South Asia, where food production is falling and water shortages are present.

---

[4] *ESI Bulletin* 3, no. 2 (2010) <http://www.esi.nus.edu.sg/docs/esi-bulletins/esi-bulletin-vol-3-issue-2-nov-2010084D65E6EEC2.pdf?Status=Master>.

[5] 2030 Water Resources Group <http://www.2030waterresourcesgroup.com/water_full/Charting_Our_Water_Future_Final.pdf>.

This combination of factors will push the subcontinent into a fragile and vulnerable position.

A clean environment was regarded as some kind of luxury; now it is an imperative. People no longer accept exposure to the negative health effects of a poor environment because they know that it happens because of failure on the part of the governments to implement stricter environmental standards. It is becoming increasingly difficult to export goods and services if globally acknowledged standards are not adhered to. The consumer, be it in the industrialized or emerging economies, is becoming more and more conscious of environmental standards, health risks, and ethical standards.

Disregarding environmental concerns also weighs heavily on the economy. The World Bank has calculated that the health costs of air and water pollution in China amount to about 4.3 percent of its GDP. By adding the non-health impacts of pollution, which are estimated to be about 1.5 percent of GDP, the total cost of air and water pollution is about 5.8 percent.[6]

IMPACT OF SCARCITIES

Scarcities have solidified the upward trend seen in commodity prices since the turn of the century, albeit with some blips caused by the global business cycle. With the exception of Singapore, Southeast Asian countries are commodity exporting countries and stand to benefit from this development. For the largest country, Indonesia, the International Monetary Fund (IMF) has calculated that commodity exports grew 180 percent compared to 75 percent for manufacturing in the period 2003–9.[7]

Table 2 shows exports of fuel and mining and agricultural products for the whole of ASEAN and selected Southeast Asian countries as a share of their total merchandise exports in 1992 and 2009.

Irrespective of industrialization and the benefits from outsourcing fuel, mining products and agricultural products in 2009 accounted for almost 30 percent of total merchandise exports, which certainly indicates the enormous potential in coming

---

[6] The World Bank, "Costs of Pollution in China", 2007 <http://siteresources.worldbank.org/INTEAPREGTOPENVIRONMENT/Resources/China_Cost_of_Pollution.pdf>.
[7] L. Lipscomb, U. Ramakrishnan, G. Adler, N. Budina, and X. Li, "Indonesia: Selected Issues", 2 August 2010 <http://www.imf.org/external/pubs/ft/scr/2010/cr10285.pdf>.

TABLE 2   Southeast Asia Exports of Agriculture, Fuel, and Mining Products (%)

	Fuel & Mining		Agricultural Products		Fuel & Mining + Agricultural Products	
	1992	2009	1992	2009	1992	2009
Indonesia	37.4	37.3	14.7	21.7	52.1	59.0
Vietnam	34.6	16.1	38.5	18.7	73.1	34.8
Malaysia	8.1	5.8	18.3	8.3	26.4	14.1
Thailand	1.5	6.2	30.5	18.3	32.0	24.5
Total ASEAN	16.4	16.8	17.0	11.9	33.4	28.7

Source: Appendix Table 2A, World Trade Report 2011, World Trade Organization http://www.wto.org/english/res_e/booksp_e/anrep_e/world_trade_report11_e.pdf.

years, bearing in mind how imports of commodities will rise in China and India while still being strong in the United States, Japan, and Europe.

This is not to suggest that Southeast Asia will regress to commodity exports instead of continuing the trend towards industrialization and preparing for the next step in the region's rise. It is just a factual observation of the strong asset Southeast Asia possesses in its commodity sector. In fact the continued development of the region's economies and indeed societies may find their financing from the commodity sector in the years to come. Southeast Asia may be one of the few regions in the world with the opportunity to build a diversified economy with commodities, manufacturing, high tech, and services. The challenge is how to get the right mix among countries and inside countries. If successful, Southeast Asia may possess an economic structure that is less prone to suffer from outside shocks than many other regions in the world that are heavily reliant on one or two sectors.

When many other regions and countries around the world will suffer from the scarcity and rising prices of commodities, Southeast Asia will benefit, possibly being one of few regions in the world in such a comfortable position. It will give the region more clout in forthcoming negotiations about Asian integration and indeed enhance its room to manoeuvre for safeguarding its own interests.

WINNERS AND LOSERS

Much will depend upon Southeast Asia's ability to grasp how the scarcities will change global competition and to focus upon new competitive parameters.

The *first* change is the switch in the definition of productivity. In the industrial era, for 200 years, labour was regarded as scarce. All research, technology, and innovation was geared to save labour, and productivity as defined by economic theory was a question of how to increase output per man-hour in the production process. Higher productivity meant that one person actually produced more, and, to do that, technology and learning was required. The world has been tremendously successful in doing this — so successful that unemployment is threatening the stability of our societies.

In the future the scarcity factor will be commodities, which means that first we need to change the definition of how much output we can squeeze out of one unit of resources, and second, reorient research, technology, and innovation to focus on the new balance between production factors.

The winners of tomorrow's competitive game will be those — countries and corporations — who master the skill of squeezing the most output out of one unit of resources supplemented by an understanding of the swing in technology from focusing on labour to saving resources.

The opportunity and challenge for Southeast Asia is to use its diversified economy and the financial resources available to do exactly this. The danger is that possession of resources and strong exports of commodities will divert attention from this new technological trend, making it seemingly unnecessary to introduce resource-saving technology and opening the door for doing this to other countries.

A deeper understanding of the side effect of using resources, such as external diseconomies (pollution) and climate change plus impact on health and safety, may help Southeast Asia to avoid that potential trap. Recognition of more qualitative growth instead of just growth for growth's own sake will play an important role.

The *second* change is about economic geography. Over the last half-century, economic globalization has been fuelled by a revolution in transport and logistics that made transport costs a negligible share of total price for the end product. That was the result of cheap energy combined with technological progress. This almost certainly will not last.

Energy prices are following an upward trend and, while cost efficiency is still achieved in the transport system, it is highly unlikely that something like the container will happen again. The consequences are that transport costs will have to be taken into account in the changing supply chain.

It looks likely that the supply chain will become more compact in the sense that goods and services increasingly will be sought nearer to production and marketing centres. Already the British retailer Marks & Spencer plans to overhaul its supply chain by stopping the purchase of supplies from one hemisphere for use in another, which may save the company £175 million annually.[8]

Another aspect is sea transport versus land transport. So far sea transport has been far more competitive than land transport, thus facilitating the concentration of most economic activity in coastal areas. Forty percent of the population of Asia lives within forty-five miles of the coast. A quick glance at the map confirms that Southeast Asia may be the region in the world benefitting most from this situation.

There is no guarantee that this will continue to be the case as scarcities of resources will lead to new methods of transportation of goods. On top of cost-effectiveness comes a crucial factor: greenhouse emissions. With current technology, large container ships emit less than railroads, but for smaller container ships it is about the same — road transport emits far more than both small container ships and railroads.

In the future it may well be the case that the combination of costs and emission of greenhouse gasses determines competitive parameters and railroads may emerge as more overall competitive than sea transport. If so, Southeast Asia's economic geography may be less advantageous than is the case today and call for investments in beefing up the railroad system.

Indeed a whole string of ambitious plans on the drawing board in China for high-speed railroads (HSR)[9] show how the western part of China plus Central Asia will be linked to the rest of Asia — coastal Asia — plus India, the Middle East, and ultimately Europe. Most observers focus upon transport of passengers, but the much more interesting question is what it will mean for freight and consequently sea transport and the advantage that coastal cities have so far enjoyed over landlocked cities. There is no guarantee that these plans will be carried out in the face of many constraints of a fiscal, technical, and administrative/foreign policy character, but given the scarcity factor and Central Asia's richness in resources it is likely that they will be.

For Southeast Asia this suggests a potential development in which the geographical distinction between mainland Southeast Asia and maritime Southeast Asia risks being turned into an economic and, perhaps also, a political split. Hitherto, maritime

---

[8] Michael E. Porter and Mark R. Kramer, "Creating Shared Value", *Harvard Business Review*, January–February 2011.

[9] "High-speed Rail in China", 12 January 2009 <http://www.thetransportpolitic.com/2009/01/12/high-speed-rail-in-china/>.

Southeast Asia has reaped the highest economic growth, but the potential changes enumerated above could produce a new situation over the coming decades.

The *third* change is about outsourcing, offshoring, and insourcing.

Outsourcing from established industrialized countries to Asian countries — including, but not particularly, Southeast Asian countries — has been driven by labour arbitrage, making it profitable to shift labour-intensive low-cost manufacturing production to areas with an ample labour force. The arrival of China as a production centre meant that the phenomenon of using cheap labour to start a development process, which had been seen earlier in Japan and some other Asian countries, acquired a totally new dimension. China emerged as the global place for manufacturing. Cost-effective transport systems stepped in to help this process get under way on a global basis. Even if productivity and quality was markedly lower, at least in the first phases of outsourcing, the cost difference far outweighed what was lost in these two segments. One of the interesting side effects was the diminishing relevance of currency rate changes. Differences in labour costs could run into such remarkable figures as to make currency rate changes of 10 or 20 percent look trivial. Outsourcing thus contributed to a higher degree of stability in the currency market (price sensitive production was outsourced, making remaining tradable production less likely to respond to currency rate changes).

Conventional — cost driven — outsourcing or offshoring was thus determined by wage costs, which again were determined by a high and growing labour force underpinned by a political system guaranteeing that the system would work by keeping a lid on potential social unrest and managing the wage rate.

Outsourcing and offshoring seem to have delivered most of the potential benefits to the global economy. Most manufacturing and services competing on costs are probably already outsourced, and the trend in most industrialized countries is that outsourcing may still take place, but not, far from it, to the same extent as before. There is a growing feeling that in many cases outsourcing went too far by allowing control over production of semi-manufactured goods, including inputs for the production process, away from the parent company, and raising questions about the quality of goods delivered from plants in countries benefiting from outsourcing.

One reason explaining this trend is the growing tendency for consumers to shift their preferences somewhat away from prices and costs to focus more on ethics and values. The implication is that it is not only the parent company's respect for ethics and values that is judged by consumers, but also how the same ethics and values are applied by subcontractors.

Another and perhaps more interesting trend for Southeast Asia in the context of outsourcing is that around 2015 the labour force in China will start to fall, which means that, assuming the driving forces behind outsourcing remain unchanged, labour-intensive low-cost manufacturing will move out of China to countries with a high and growing labour force. This will be South Asia, but also a number of countries in Southeast Asia, including Indonesia, Vietnam, the Philippines, and Myanmar.

Some of the Southeast Asian countries, e.g., Malaysia, may have found themselves in the so-called middle-income trap, with an income per capita too high to embody low wages, but not high enough to fund R&D plus quality to shift competitive parameters to other elements than price. China is moving into that bracket now, which explains why the Chinese Government is accelerating funds for R&D and has expressed a strong interest in qualitative growth instead of just growth. Economic theory tells us that countries entering the middle-income trap will find it difficult to maintain the high pace of economic growth that took them there. It does not necessarily signify that the same will be the case for China, but it does mean that new windows of opportunity will be opened for Southeast Asia, in particular Indonesia and Vietnam, which have high and growing populations.

Indeed, some years ago statistics certainly indicated that Indonesia was deindustrializing.[10] The overall share of manufacturing in GDP was 27–28 percent in the decade after the financial crisis of 1997, but subsectors of manufacturing showed decline. The main reason for this development was the competition from China making manufacturing in Indonesia, especially small-scale manufacturing, non-competitive. Over the last couple of years manufacturing in Indonesia has been on an upward trend, though figures and analyses are not clear enough to show exactly why and whether this trend has trickled down to small-scale producers or whether it only can be seen for a limited number of large corporations.[11]

The same factors may have contributed to difficulties for the Vietnamese economy in recent years.

It may be too early to know for sure and even earlier to conclude, but working on the assumption of rising wages in China triggered by a smaller working labour force, it seems possible that Indonesia may reverse the trend of deindustrialization and Vietnam hold on to industrializing.

---

[10] There are many papers and studies about "Indonesia and deindustrialization". See *inter alia* Ahmed Mansur, "Is Indonesia Undergoing a Process of De-industrialization? ISS, The Hague, 2008 <http://oaithesis.eur.nl/ir/repub/asset/6708/Ahmad%20Mansur%20ECD.pdf>.
[11] I am grateful to my colleague at ISEAS, Aris Ananta, for having discussed this question with me.

If so, a unique combination of industrialization with a strong foothold in manufacturing combined with possession of raw materials may boost the economic development for Southeast Asia's two largest countries, indeed turning them into powerhouses for strong economic growth that may benefit the rest of the region.

Add to this the strong position of Thailand and the Philippines in agricultural production, Malaysia's place as an established country in a number of medium high-tech sectors, and Singapore as a hub — global, not only regional — and a positive outlook for Southeast Asia's economic future emerges, even if the global environment is uncertain at best.

CONCLUSION

This will, however, not come by itself. It requires good state governance and good corporate governance. It will be up to Southeast Asia and its political leaders to create the conditions for these promising perspectives to frame economic growth.

- Taking into account the debt situation in the United States, Europe, and Japan, it can be taken for granted that investors will be more risk-averse in coming years, so prudent economic policies are called for. Deficits on the balance of payments and the trends in sovereign debt will be watched closely and must not get out of hand.
- There must be full confidence in the supply chain for the whole of East Asia and probably also Asia as a whole including South Asia. That requires steps towards some kind of economic integration guaranteeing that markets remain open and accessible, ruling out restrictions and any other form of discrimination to protect domestic production. Likewise, restrictions imposed on capital movements and foreign direct investment must be removed. Otherwise private investors will be wary about relying too heavily on an Asian supply chain. And without plugging into the larger economic powerhouses in the continent, Southeast Asia may not stand to gain.
- When discussing economic integration it is often overlooked that investors are not going to invest unless they are fairly confident about getting their money back, including a fair profit. Operating in an international environment it is imperative that investors are confident that money can flow freely. This is why economic integration with rules for trade and investment is so important for Asia's future. A strong integration that embodies rules for trade and investment gives investors this guarantee. This results in the supply chain blossoming. Weak or no integration has the opposite effect.

- The changing nature of the supply chain influenced by the era of scarcities with implications for the transport system needs to be digested. The whole idea of a more compact supply chain may change much of the region's economic geography.
- The role of cities taking over more and more of the economic activity thus giving credence to the theory that economically the world is spiky will benefit Southeast Asia only if preparations and plans have been put in place.
- Likewise, a correct reading of demography and its accompanying benefits and burdens would need preparations.
- The impact of the era of scarcities may be the most important of all. Southeast Asia needs to adjust. The production processes change as does the consumption function. There will be a strong effect on the social fabric. Benefits and burdens may not continue to be distributed in the same way as hitherto.

How Can ASEAN Stay Relevant?*

There are seven essential points to recall when building economic integration.

The first is that integration is not an end in itself, but an instrument to achieve political goals. Many ideas about the European integration have met with opposition because this fundamental observation has not been respected. Integration can be compared with fiscal policy or housing policy or similar domestic policies that all are designed to do something for the people. If this vital distinction between goals and means is not observed, confusion starts to reign and popular support for integration withers away, making it difficult to rally votes in parliament and among the public.

Economic interdependence among countries makes it impossible to pursue policy goals different from or contrary to what neighbours are doing. Pursuing analogous political goals with adjacent nation-states enhances room to manoeuvre for each nation-state. In today's world, sovereignty is not a safeguard against influence from the outside, but a mechanism to avoid international rules that are obstacles to implementing one's own domestic objectives. The defence of domestic policies takes place abroad as attempts to escape the trap of being caught by international institutions proclaiming that this or that is not permissible, or you have to do this or that to comply with commitments undertaken.

The second point is a strict observance that — again like domestic policies — the objective of building economic integration is to improve the daily conditions for the population. Much discussion about the direction of the European integration has focused on lofty goals such as Europe's role in the world. This is necessary, at least to a certain extent and when the integration has reached a certain level, but it is imperative to start with the basic and that is living conditions such as employment, higher real wage and lower consumer prices. It is useless to tell the population that the advantage of joining the single currency is to "sit at the table" when decisions are taken. For ordinary persons this is abstract and does not relate to their daily lives. It is important to stress lower consumer prices and more jobs. In the long

*First appeared in Chapter 37 in *ASEAN Matters: Reflecting on Southeast Asian Nations*, edited by Lee Yoong Yoong, (Singapore, Lee Kuan Yew School of Public Policy, Institute of Policy Studies and World Scientific: 2012).

term the integration will be judged by its ability to do something for the people that could not have been done without integration or by doing something better than if the nation-states in question had tried to do it in isolation.

The European integration has been quite good at that, even if not always successful. In its first stage, trade barriers were dismantled and a common agricultural policy established; taken together it markedly improved the living standards for a vast majority of the population. People felt in their own daily lives that the integration did something for them and consequently supported the integration. In its next stage, a single currency and a single market were implemented, again with better living standards as a result. Conditions were a bit more difficult for the second stage because these policies were overall beneficial for all member states, but the benefits were distributed unevenly within and among nation-states, which gave rise to misgivings. The integration process had to be adjusted to bridge the gaps between those who benefited largely, those who benefited marginally, and those who suffered a loss member states must be partners in all common policies, showing solidarity across the board even in areas of no interest, and ruling out an à la carte solution. Luxembourg, for example, is a full participant in the Common Fisheries Policy even though it is a landlocked country.

On paper, the benefits and losses weigh evenly, but in reality the losses are "heavier" for people than gains. It is of no use to elucidate the virtues of the integration by pointing out that the overall benefits are larger than losses, because those who benefit are less vocal in their support than the losers in their criticism. This poses an awkward dilemma for an economic integration as it normally works to ensure there are more winners than losers. The way ahead to solve this problem is to talk openly about the potential losses before the policy in question is implemented, adding what will be done to channel some of the benefits into policies designed to help those who will lose out.

It may be too early to judge whether the Europeans have been successful at that, but they have clearly tried hard with the Social Fund, the Regional Fund and a whole string of supportive policies brought in to redress imbalances created by new steps towards integration. Such policies only work as long as the benefits clearly outweigh the losses and one of the lessons from Europe is only to implement steps where this is the case.

When the Europeans tried to go one more step by creating a more competitive economic structure through focusing on technology and similar measures, the limits were all too visible. These policies, known as the Lisbon Strategy, may have been and probably still are beneficial for Europe as a whole, but the distribution of benefits among peoples and nation-states was not accompanied by an outline of what to do for the losers and that proves an almost insurmountable obstacle.

The third point is the necessity of relating to people. Any political system rests on the shoulders of the people in the sense that they must feel it is theirs. Looking at nation-states around the globe, it dawns on the observer how difficult it is to achieve this. In the United States barely half of the electorate bothers to vote in the presidential elections. In Europe votes cast reach 70 percent or even more for national elections, but fall below 50 percent for European elections.

Having worked with the European integration for decades, I am convinced that Europe's political system is fully democratic and offers the European population the same guarantees for transparency, accountability and legitimacy as the national political systems. The problem is that this is not how a large majority of the Europeans feel.

There may be many explanations for this: the distance between voters and political institutions or language barriers. The fact remains, however, that as long as we have not reached a level where the political system has been adopted by the populations, the integration remains fragile no matter what arguments can be advanced to sing its virtues. In a way it is the fault of the Europeans themselves for trying to build a strong integration while at the same time rejecting a move towards some kind of federation or confederation, which would have solved these problems, but the explanation for this "half-backed" solution is that this is what the Europeans so far want. Then the challenge becomes to achieve it inside this box.

The fourth point is about institutions. Institutions are necessary and irrespective of all good intentions there are fairly low barriers for how much can be achieved without an institutional framework.

There is, however, a misunderstanding to be dealt with. Institutions are instruments to channel decisions the member states wish to take to deepen the integration. If such a will is present, institutions can facilitate the process and serve as vehicle not only for creating a process but also ensuring compliance with commitments undertaken. If the political will is not present, even the best institutions are powerless and impotent.

The initial step in the institutional build-up is therefore not to look at decision-making mechanisms and institutional frameworks, etc., but to sketch very early on what the political objectives are, what the member states want to achieve, why they want to do it and then add what role the institutions are expected to play in this setting.

The Europeans have from time to time been hypnotized by institutions. At the end of the 1970s the catchword was to create a European Union by institutional improvements. Nothing came of that because the substance — what the union was supposed to do — was absent. The proposed constitution was rejected in 2005 by a majority of the voters in France and the Netherlands because in the eyes of the population it was merely institutional tinkering, offering little relevance to their daily lives. Except for the European political elite, not many Europeans bother whether the chairman of the European Council — the highest political body in the Union — is nominated for a number of years or rotated among the member states. The question was asked: what can be done with these changes that could not be done with the existing machinery? There was and is no convincing answer to this question. Consequently the people drew the conclusion that these changes were not worth making.

This is the heart of the matter for institutions. People seem to be willing to accept institutional changes if they are linked to new policies of substance and relevant to them. No one disputed a European System of Central Banks when the single currency and the economic and monetary union were set up. No one disputed that when a single market was to be implemented, qualified majority voting would promote the process towards this objective. Institutional changes were clearly necessary to implement political goals adopted.

Right now the Europeans have implemented changes in the institutional machinery for foreign and security policies. The question remains, however, what new policies such changes are going to facilitate. If only institutional changes not linked to new policies occur, no policy improvements will be visible and the step risks backfiring. Many people will ask why it was made and there will be widespread disappointment over institutional changes that did not lead to better policies. That will make it more difficult to deepen the integration the next time.

Fundamentally, institutions rest upon trust among the member states, which means that they and their citizens are convinced that decisions are not influenced by other nation-states or individuals appointed by nation-states occupying high posts. There is an European saying that "Caesar's wife must be above suspicion". The same goes for institutions.

A question often asked is why member states respect decisions taken by the European Court of Justice even if the Court and the other European institutions do not have real powers to enforce their decisions. The answer is that the Europeans comply because they wish to comply. They realize that the European Union is a kind of European judicial system operating in principle as the domestic judicial system, which means that if a member state does not comply neither will other member states. It is not because they are forced to do so or fear "punitive" action if they do not, but do so of their own free will. They trust in the institutions and the Court of Justice; this trust is the ultimate "enforcer".

No measures to give institutions teeth to enforce decisions can be more effective than such a political will; if the political will is not present, no powers, however strong they may seem, can do the trick.

The fifth point is to structure the integration in such a way that it is perceived as a win-win game, with every member state feeling that it is better off inside than outside. To a certain extent, this is an interpretation of the first observation (integration is not an end in itself). No member state can be expected to join and feel at ease unless the advantages are tangible, visible and understood. Why should they?

In the European context there have been at least two episodes where this was questioned by member states: in the 1960s by France about qualified majority voting for certain elements of the integration of specific interest to agriculture; and by Britain around 1980 taking the stance that economically the integration was not advantageous or at least less advantageous for Britain than for most other Member States.

In such cases a legal approach does not lead to success. It does not matter whether it can be argued that it is right or wrong as long as the country in question is convinced of the opposite. The problem must be addressed to hammer out a solution, squaring the circle between maintaining the structure and tilting it a bit towards changes asked for by the "dissatisfied" member state. The problem of course is that this must not be allowed to snowball into a situation where everybody asks for more benefits.

The sixth point is the ability to adapt and adjust. Challenges facing the member states change over the years and what was needed some years ago may be out of tune today. The Europeans have been good at adjusting albeit not without flaws and errors, but basically they have done it. Over the last few years a whole new chapter has been set up to deal with human security, fight against terrorism and common policies *vis-à-vis* immigration issues, dominating a larger part of the European political agenda. Only 15 years ago this was an embryonic part of the integration and 20 years ago it barely existed in the treaties. It shows an understanding of the shift in political priorities from economic issues to more value-based criteria for policy making and political choices in Europe. It is an illustration of continuing efforts to make it relevant to the citizens.

There is a seventh point of a more general nature Integration is normally presented as economic integration, as is indeed the case for this chapter. We must, however, be clear about three things. First, integration formed on a regional basis in anchored in globalisation. The idea is not to establish a group of nations separated from globalisation or deviating from the predominant global policies, but to deliver an input to the further development of globalisation. It is part of globalisation, not a measure to protect against globalisation. Second, fundamentally it is inscribed in the policy of cementing peace by entering into close contact with adjacent nation-states, trying to dispose of animosities and misunderstandings and adopting instead mutual good will, confidence and trust. Economic integration is an instrument to achieve peace and prosperity. Third, it serves as a disciplinary banister, forcing member states to observe rules and follow responsible policies.

These are some of the points that came to my mind when trying to answer the question of how to be relevant. There may be others and some of those chosen by me may be less important in the eyes of other observers. The main lesson from Europe is therefore to look at what has been done and draw your own lessons. The Europeans have gained experience and lessons and in some cases paid heavily for mistakes. ASEAN can use this experience by studying it and select what is found useful to guide its own integration suited to the circumstances and challenges in Southeast Asia.

Euclid, having opened a school of mathematics in Alexandria, was asked by King Ptolemy whether he could not explain his art to him in a more compendious manner. "Sir", said the geometrician, "there is no royal road to learning".

So it is with economic integration. Every group of nation-states chooses their own road to integration. There is no royal road, no easy way and no short cut.

Asia Faces U.S. Default on its Sovereign Debt*

Very few people believe it. The Americans totally discard it. Financial observers do not write about it. Rating agencies turn up their noses at it.

And yet, it is likely, almost certain that before 2020, the U.S. will default on its sovereign debt. What form default will take and how it will play out is difficult to say, but a restructuring to effectively write-off part of the debt will take place. As the main creditors are found in Asia the repercussions — politically and economically — will reverberate more acutely through this part of the world.

Let us start by taking a look at the figures. Total debt run up by the federal government, households, states, corporations etc. amounts to approximately 400 percent of Gross Domestic Product (GDP) — a trivial sum of USD 60 trillion. Even during the great depression of the 1930s, it never went above 350 percent of GDP. Federal debt account for one-quarter of this percentage, amounting to around USD 13–14 trillion. This is not a figure that cannot be managed, but the main problem is that it continues to rise instead of being brought under control.

Under favorable conditions, net interest payments will increase from around USD 250 billion now to USD 800–900 billion in 2020. If economic growth falters, the figure will be even higher because of lower tax revenue and higher social expenditure. Almost 25 percent of the federal budget must be used for net interest payments (9 percent currently) and this item will account for something like 80 percent of discretionary spending.

The task ahead is even more daunting when one considers a basic calculation of fiscal tightening required to stabilise the debt/GDP ratio, or the even more challenging task of bringing it down. Let us assume that the U.S. wants to stabilise its debt/GDP ratio in 2015. Denmark's National Bank has calculated that a fiscal tightening of 2.3 percent of GDP per year is necessary — accumulated 9.2 percent. If the more ambitious target of bringing the ratio down to 60 percent in 2020 is adopted, the annual fiscal tightening is 2.8 percent and accumulated 22.4 percent. The Euro-zone is much better placed with only 0.9 percent fiscal tightening required to stabilise the debt ratio and 1.4 percent to reduce the debt ratio to 60 percent in 2020 (both per year).

---

* First appeared in *Opinion Asia*, 10 July 2010.

Sometime in a not too distant future U.S. policymakers will come to the conclusion that the debt burden is too heavy, a millstone around the neck of the U.S. economy. Debt servicing will ask for too much money, monetary policy will be boxed in, and an expansionary economic policy cannot be pursued because of the financial resources needed to service the debt. Foreign creditors will smell that the mood is shifting and the political system's willingness to tax its citizens to service the debt waning.

It is often heard that the U.S. can disregard the debt burden because of the clout of the U.S. economy, giving foreign creditors no other choice but to hold on to U.S. treasury bonds and hope for the best. This is true, but only to a certain extent. The global share of the U.S. economy is constantly falling making the superpower less super and less relevant for other countries.

The main point is, however, that the U.S. cannot and will not accept the constraints on economic policy imposed by the burden — not of the debt — but of servicing the debt (payments on interest and principal). This will constitute a barrier for lowering unemployment, an issue likely to occupy the number one slot in any domestic political battle. Therefore, rumblings will come out of the U.S. auguring semi-protectionist measures in one form or another, and other unilateral steps indicating that the U.S. — a cornerstone of the global economic system — is not any longer willing to play by the rules laid down by itself. In choosing between honouring its commitments and respecting the rules of the game, or stimulating the U.S. economy, the second option will prevail.

Creditors will be left with two unenviable alternatives. One is to hold on to their assets and claim that they must be redeemed in full come what may. Another alternative is to write off a part of the U.S. debt thereby alleviating the burden on U.S. economic policy sufficiently to open the door to a more expansionary policy, while at the same time maintaining the U.S. as one of the main guarantors of the global economic system. In this scenario, creditors may loose some of their investment, but stronger American growth will compensate, compared to holding on and seeing the U.S. take unilateral steps, casting doubt over the whole panoply of rules governing the global economy.

You never know how people and countries will react, but for the global economy and for the creditors, the second alternative is by far the least risky and also the least costly one. The snag for Asia is that Japan is one of the victims, holding US$800 billion of treasury bonds and facing an even worse problem than the U.S. If an agreement to write off a part of the U.S. debt is handled clumsily, Japan may end in an economic and political crisis never seen before.

It may take the U.S. as debtor and its creditors in Asia a while to understand that these are the two alternatives they can choose from. But eventually, they will come to this realisation and agree to write off a part of U.S. debt.

The intriguing question is whether this *quid pro quo* can be confined to economics or whether the Asian creditors will ask for a political price acceptable to the U.S. Geopolitics cannot and will not continue unchanged when the U.S. negotiates with creditors who bailed it out.

U.S. and China May Move to Cap Military Spending*

Reading the mass media, it looks as if the U.S. and China are on a collision course. The Google episode and the sale of U.S. weapons to Taiwan convey the impression of two superpowers staring each other down. The two powers may, however, soon be forced into each other's arms by the dismal outlook for U.S. public finance and potential social unrest in China.

History offers a number of examples where a superpower sees its strategic options limited by financial constraints. Unless strategy is brought into line with financial strength, a superpower's posture will not be taken seriously and decline accelerates. This happened to the British Empire in the beginning of the twentieth century. The U.S. is fast moving towards such a policy dilemma. Equally, the door is opening for rising powers to move into the vacuum and gradually assume leadership.

This time, however, something else might happen because the option of an understanding between China and the U.S. to cap military spending could be on the cards. The idea sounds far fetched and wholly unrealistic, but the figures tell another story.

Measured as share of Gross Domestic Product (GDP) both countries are running military expenditures a little bit above 4 percent, but total outlays are definitely higher as some programs are "hidden" under quasi-civilian items. Military expenditures of this size can probably be sustained if national security warrants it, but remain highly unwelcome.

The U.S. is facing a deficit on the federal budget for the foreseeable future. Essential domestic policies imply steeply rising expenditure. Over the next decade, according to the Congressional Budget Office (CBO) Medicaid and Medicare on the federal budget will rise every year up to 6 or 7 percent and social security maybe half that amount — currently these three items account for no less than 40 percent of total expenditure. A forecast for the public debt reveals a significant increase bringing it above total Gross Domestic Product (GDP) from the current figure of approximately 70 percent. Net interest payments accounted for 8 percent (USD 234 billion) of the

* First appeared in *Opinion Asia*, 9 February 2010.

federal budget in 2009. A prudent estimate points to 20 percent — a sum of more than USD 700 billion — in 2019.

To prevent this from happening, taxes must be raised or expenditure cut. Higher taxes to raise revenue can probably be ruled out, especially in an election year. That leaves the expenditure side to stop net interest payments rising from USD 234 billion to 700 billion — i.e. asking for cuts of USD 466 billion. The snag is, however, that 60 percent of the federal budget is mandatory, so expenditure flows from existing laws cannot be cut unless new laws are passed, almost impossible to do and if tried, will be a time consuming process. Consequently discretionary spending must be cut, but this part of the federal budget accounts for only USD 1.333 billion of which almost half goes to the military. To squeeze USD 466 billion out of 1.333 billion is in itself a daunting task, but to do it if cuts in military spending are ruled out, makes it an impossible task. The conclusion seems inescapable that sooner or later, and probably sooner rather than later the size of the military budget (accounting for half of all discretionary spending) will be questioned. The money simply cannot be found elsewhere. Indeed, House Speaker Nancy Pelosi, has already stated that Obama's proposed freeze on selected discretionary spending should also apply to military spending, which was exempted.

Over a time span of several decades China may have the financial muscle to build a military comparable with what the U.S. has, with economic growth locked into a pattern of 10 percent or thereabouts and generally healthy public finances. China, however, faces structural problems in its economy.

The need for diverting an increasing share of growth towards social expenditure looms large every day. China's future pension burden plus its endeavors to develop the Western parts of the county top its list of priorities. Inequality has passed the danger threshold defined by the OECD, with China's Gini-coefficient at 0.47, above the 0.40 limit. If it is allowed to continue upwards, it moves into an alarm bracket, threatening the social and political stability that legitimises the monopoly of power arrogated to the Chinese Communist Party. Question marks over the purpose of large military spending may nullify the existing image of China as a nation not seeking influence through military power — an impression carefully created by China's leadership over many years. In short, a military build up can be achieved, but with a political price — domestically and abroad — that may outweigh potential benefits.

Modern strategic thought right sizes conventional military threats with a greater focus on threats related to social stability, political instability, and human security. A nation's ability to "defend" itself depends upon its social cohesion; diverting funds allocated to serve this objective endangers its stability and the political system's legitimacy, consequently undermining its security.

The break down of the American style of capitalism over the last couple of years may have cost the U.S. much more in global leadership than a military posture can compensate for. Not only has the model lost its lure, but the financial resources to further American influence are simply not available anymore. U.S. investments abroad and/or financial assistance are much more effective than carrier groups in spreading and securing influence. China is actually doing exactly this through a buying spree, especially in Africa accompanied by a policy message that it is "different" in the sense that it does not want to interfere in domestic matters, and leaves it to the host country to run its own affairs.

Logically, such considerations might lead the two countries to limit or even reduce military expenditure. As of now, the U.S. is the only military super power and China is the only challenger in the medium or long-term. They can act as the U.S. and the Soviet Union did during the cold war knowing that few if any other nations threaten them militarily.

An initiative to limit followed by a reduction of military expenditure between the U.S. and China would be a break through especially if traced by other powers. It will also save the American economy sailing into uncharted waters from the risk of capsizing under the burden of rising debt.

Mutual suspicion remains the main barrier for such an agreement. The U.S. fears that China hides military expenditure under other headings in its budget. China might think the U.S. is preventing its rise. Hard reality may break down such barriers. If not, the U.S. may inadvertently be drawn into the same trap it set for the Soviet Union in the 1980s: arms expenditure as a drag anchor steering the Soviet economy towards the rocks. China will have little benefit of a lame U.S. making the global scene even more complicated and dangerous than it is now.

China to the Rescue: Growing Out of the Financial Crisis*

While there is an emerging consensus on what ails the world economy there is no agreement on the treatment. Instead of a global economic policy a variety of national ones are being cooked up to satisfy national tastes that often contradict each other. The time has come — it is actually overdue — to recognize that stimulating global demand, bringing it into line with global supply, is the only cure.

The diagnosis reveals that global demand is too low, resulting in excess production capacity, exercising downward pressure on investment, wages, and property prices. The prescription calls for a rebalancing of demand and supply. Excess supply through over investment in the "fat" years, combined with an inventory built up, aggravate the policy dilemma. Experience tells us that cutting excess supply is an agonizing process that easily undermines confidence in a recovery, harming long-term growth prospects.

Individual countries may try to remedy excess production capacity by exporting more goods, but this shifts the calamity from one country to another doing no good for the global economy. If policy makers are allowed to walk down this path, protectionism will throw a spanner in the works of recovery as countries race to retaliate against each other.

But first we have to do away with the illusion that global growth will return to five percent. Growth will likely land one, maybe two, percentage points lower and stay there for a while, as the world waits to see how a rebalanced and restructured global economy will fare.

Taken together the U.S., Europe, and Japan account for more than half and may be even two-thirds of the global economy depending upon the calculating method. Europe is trying hard to reform its economy, but results are still disappointing. Japan is facing a low-trend growth, if growth at all, due to demographics and the inability to restructure.

And we are unlikely to see private consumption drive U.S. economic growth as it has done for many years. The paradigm has changed. The halving of the oil price from

*First appeared in *YaleGlobal online*, 28 July 2009.

summer 2008 to summer 2009 should have led to higher private consumption, but it didn't. A number of factors — the stock market, bankruptcies, and bailing out of GM to mention a few — depressed the willingness to spend and it is not clear to which extent better data will renew consumer confidence.

Personal saving as a percentage of disposable income has rocketed from zero in April 2008 to nearly seven percent in May 2009; the highest figure in more than six years. Demographics too are turning against the U.S. Economics tells us that private consumption for an individual peaks around 45–50 years of age and the baby boomers have passed that mark. There is no basis, then, to expect private consumption in the U.S. to rise or even correspond to the level around and prior to 2007. And without private consumption a recovery is unthinkable.

This leads to the conclusion that increasing demand can only be found outside the traditional heavyweights. The newcomers are China, India, and Southeast Asia plus a number of other countries around the globe. But as only China — and partly India — is playing in the big league, examining that country should prove instructive.

And it looks pretty good.

But the first step is to repudiate the thesis that China's domestic demand is still weak, signaled by the persistent balance of payments surplus. If domestic demand were rising as share of GDP, imports would pull the balance of payments towards a smaller surplus, runs the argument. But it is falling. The World Bank predicts China's surplus will fall to 8.3 percent of GDP in 2010 and 7.2 percent in 2011 from the 11 percent in 2007. The argument also overlooks the dramatic fall in commodity, food and energy prices: if the economy were unchanged, imports would have gone down, boosting the surplus further (they account for 28.8 percent of total import). Persistent domestic demand, holding up much better than exports and by doing so limiting the fall in imports, seems to be the best explanation for a falling, not rising surplus. Of course, the reported stock-piling of commodities by China's large state-owned corporations could have played a role too.

Secondly, the composition of China's imports suggests domestic consumption is changing. Parsing the data, when one separates imports used to produce exports primarily for the U.S. from imports destined for domestic demand an interesting dynamic emerges. Imports for production of exports fell much sharper than imports for domestic demand. The fact that this trend has persisted over almost two years — since mid-2007 — implies China's economy is being restructured.

Thirdly, recent figures suggest that real household spending is nine percent higher than a year ago, resulting in a hike in private consumption's share of total demand. Retail sales are rising even more —15 percent year on year — though this includes government purchases. On this basis it is plausible to assume that household spending together with government programs should prevent a fall in China's GDP growth below the six-to-eight percent bracket.

The room to maneuver for stimulatory measures is still available for China. But this is not the case for the U.S. and Japan, where public budget deficits have reached the breaking point with further measures likely to undermine whatever confidence in the economies are left. The U.S. is running a deficit estimated at 13.2 percent of GDP and Japan looks forward to as much as 11 percent according to the pessimists.

In the end, the world cannot expect the U.S. to lead the way out of recession and rebalance the global economy. On July 10, Larry Summers, Director of the U.S. President's National Economic Council said to Financial Times, "I don't think the worst is over" and added "The global imbalances have to add up to zero and so, if the U.S. is going to be less the consumer importer of last resort, then other countries are going to need to be in different positions as well." To rebalance the world economy we need to look to growth from countries like China instead of the U.S.

Moreover, as the rising savings rate in the U.S. is likely to slow down the recovery, it will be easier to reduce balance of payments imbalances that have harassed the world for so long. Indeed U.S. exports rose and imports fell in May resulting in the lowest trade deficit for nearly nine years. If this trend persists, and basic economic figures suggest it will, U.S. borrowing will fall, inducing global capital to flow into productive investment rather than U.S. treasury bonds. (Of course, mounting health-care cost, additional stimulus and greater welfare benefits could alter the situation.)

A reallocation of capital to healthier economies would make the goods and services market work in tandem with the capital market. This would not only benefit the global economy, harmed by the financial crisis, but also help weak economies overcome their imbalances. Most important of all: it would achieve a rebalancing without cutting global demand thus avoiding a global slump. But the U.S. must pay a price. China would begin to lead the global economy replacing the U.S. — a bitter pill, indeed.

How the U.S. and Asia Can Help Each Other*

For half a century the U.S. has guaranteed Asia's rise; the greatest ever socio-economic engineering experiment. It has become so self-evident that it is taken for granted as a plinth of U.S. foreign policy, but digesting the fall out from the economic crisis has resulted in an ambiguous, and even blurred picture. More starkly, any deviation from established foreign- and security policy may threaten Asia's continued rise.

Great powers fundamentally face a choice of three parameters when mapping out their policies: stabilise/destabilise the system, behave in a predictable/unpredictable manner and finally, adopt a policy to disrupt the balance, or alternatively choose non-disruption.

Long peaceful periods in history have all been characterised by stabilising, predictable and non-disruptive attitudes or policies. In between these periods, one or more powers have set in motion destabilising, unpredictable or disruptive policies — in some cases all three of them at the same time, to unsettle existing balances. Britain was a stabilising, predictable and non-disruptive power until 1914, while Germany was predictable in its growing endeavour to disrupt the system and gradually applied destabilising policies to that effect.

Before World War II Nazi-Germany, Fascist Italy and Imperial Japan became predictable as disruptive powers ultimately destabilising a geopolitical system already unbalanced by the incapacity of the established powers — Britain and France — and the unwillingness of the rising power, the U.S., to protect and safeguard the system.

A unique congruity of powers, influences, and policies rotating around the aforementioned three nations has stabilised Asia since 1978/1979, when Deng Xiaoping's reforms started to turn the hitherto established picture upside down.

A variety of signals augur, however, a less predictable constellation of parameters around the U.S. posture not as an Asian power, but a power in Asia with hard won rights and obligations. There are three elements explaining this changing picture.

---

*First appeared in *Opinion Asia,* 10 June 2009.

First, the terrorist attacks on the U.S. in 2001 shifted the image of who actually is the enemy and what kind of threats the U.S. and American society faces. The consequence is a restructuring of U.S. military giving less weight to conventional forces in favour of a force structure capable of fighting terrorism and to bring failed states under control. This raises the prospect for Asia of a less powerful U.S. military presence, which has been one of the main stabilising factors for decades.

Second, the economic crisis haunting the U.S. not only undermines its financial capability to support its foreign and security policies, but also puts a question mark on the American economic model and it correlated self-confidence. U.S. politicians are forced into placing higher priority to U.S. domestic problems and less to 'looking after' the rest of the world. It is costly to shoulder global leadership and the U.S. not longer possesses the unlimited financial power that served as platform for many foreign and security policies.

Third, the Non-Proliferation Treaty regime prevented the proliferation of nuclear weapons. But it has broken down with the risk that sooner or later, Asian powers might embark on the production of nuclear weapons. Several Asian countries are quite capable of doing so in short notice, but have held back because they were under the American umbrella that does not look particularly protective anymore. In tandem, a number of Asian countries plan to acquire nuclear power stations giving them technological know-how.

Taken together these three changes erode what used to represent terra firma for U.S. willingness to project power be it militarily, economically, or politically. It is highly unlikely that the U.S. will become a disruptive power, but more unpredictable policies cannot be ruled out. For the first time ever, the U.S. faces the question of what a stronger Asia means for the U.S. — how to manage rising powers that might, not necessarily will, challenge the U.S.. The development of fundamental weaknesses in the U.S. economy enhances its predicament. Policy options are getting more complicated as separate developments unfold among the larger Asian countries.

Japan is sliding gradually towards more unpredictability under influence from nationalistic groups, which may pull the country towards a destabilising and maybe even disruptive attitude. Russia as a power in Asia is likewise becoming more unpredictable as it seeks to carve a role under new circumstances with negative repercussions for stability.

The two rising Asian powers — China and India — are fast shifting into stabilizing, predictable and non-disruptive powers. They want to ensure stability in Asia as the first and most important condition for tackling what in their eyes remains political problem number one: domestic social stability. The last thing both want is to be disturbed in this endeavour by outside events demanding attention through financial and even military means. Both powers are not ready to step into the leadership role.

The logical conclusion is that the U.S. and Asia needs each other. Asia's rising powers need time to accumulate strength, experience, and political will to assume leadership. To prevent a vacuum, the U.S. must continue to remain a stabilising and predictable power in Asia for the foreseeable future. The U.S. needs help now to get over the severe economic downturn and while Asia cannot step in to replace falling U.S. domestic demand, a safety net can be stretched giving the U.S. economy time to find a way to recover.

This is where the circle was ostensibly squared when U.S. Treasury Secretary Timothy Geithner was in Beijing last week. His Chinese hosts were as eager as he was to get the U.S. economy going again. China is unquestionably ready and willing to 'lend' a hand — in their own interest as outlined above. It will however, expect the U.S. to realise that ultimately it is up to the U.S. to swallow the bitter pill and take measures to rebalance its economy. China will continue to "bail out" the U.S. on the condition that eventually the debt will be redeemed in real terms safeguarding its purchasing power; if not China will reappraise its willingness to act as the financier of the world's superpower, however agonising that may be for both parties.

The secret is that China wants a strong U.S. as a power in Asia — at least until Asian powers can guarantee stability, predictability and non-disruptive policies. China cannot work with a weak U.S., which would open the door for other unpredictable powers to wedge themselves into the Asian landscape.

Postscript to *The Global Economy in Transition: Debt and Resource Scarcities*

"This time is different" is the title of a book some years ago analysing 800 of financial crises and the folly bringing them about showing that each bubble at its time was judged to be sustainable because underlying elements had changed — this resulted every time in a crash because they had not; economic fundamentals were neglected.

My feeling, for what it is worth, is that this time *is* different; not with regard to the financial crisis, but for the way our societies develop, the role of social behaviour (individual versus groups), and whether human beings are likely to act according to economic incentives solely (homo oeconomicus or quality of life). A large mass of conventional wisdom, the whole edifice of economic theory, built over 250 years comes crashing down. It is not so much the question of Asia taking over as the next economic powerhouse — overwhelmingly likely — but what kind of societal structure or social fabric will follow from that shift. What is Asia going to do with its economic power? When the West started to move into pole position at the end of the 15th century it was because of commerce, technology, and military capabilities. It did change the world. It *was* different. When the West solidified its grip on world affairs with the industrial revolution, it gave rise to a totally new economic structure around capital formation (capitalism), colonialism, transport and technology. It *was* different. When the next big jump happened around 1950 around the audio-visual media, it opened up for human communication, and communication among machines unheard of. That changed human behaviour as we now see and feel. It *was* different.

So what are the main factors introducing — let us label it — a new age even if such a headline is worn out through prodigal use by politicians, academics, and commentators.

First of all there is a genuine risk that the role and importance of basic research — putting money into research with no other objective than deepening our knowledge and understanding of things — is on its way out. The financial crisis has led to sharp reduction of funds flowing into this sector because policy-makers find it easy to kill such project encountering resistance only from a few people doing basic research, but commanding very little political influence. It is hard to justify to voters whose welfare appropriations are cut. The repercussion on society will be felt in the long run when people to their astonishment will discover that applied research will not continue to yield breakthroughs unless supported by basic research.

Our societies are becoming poorer in the sense of having lost the drive to find out "who we are, where we come from, and how the big things controlling life" works.

We have turned our societies into a straitjacket of financial monitoring of all activities (cost-benefit), synchronization of our activities and accepting of uniform design flowing from computers. Buildings, cars, television sets, you name it, look completely alike. That being the case, why should we expect our mindset to be individualized — and it isn't. In short: the world as we know it today has become the managers of dream society where the question is how to manage things efficiently and not how to do them to achieve a purpose and even less what to do. The large input from management schools all over the world leads inevitably to a uniform way of thinking. They all learn the same approach, the same models, the same instruments, and how to apply the same method. The question becomes about margins determining who is winning by being better by a whisker to do the same things. There is no room left to do things in another way, break out of the pattern, and find new openings, or in more simple words try something new. If there are, they will be killed by the time gap between launching such ideas and the moment for delivering results. Creativity, imagination, and the individual's will, inclination and desire to do something else is waning and if left in some individuals, killed by managers.

Secondly, superficiality seems to be the result of the Internet and easy access to integration through various vehicles. People are getting used to finding what they want in a few seconds by a few clicks and are losing the ability to think for a longer time about a selected topic and to dig deeper. People act under a pressure of impressions and information choosing here and now, combining information available and suitable for what they work with right now instead of starting by sketching out what kind of information and knowledge they might need to solve a problem. The fundamental way of working has been turned upside down. There is nothing wrong with this swing, but as it looks now, it is crowding out the wish and ability to thinking deeply which has deep consequences for science and systematic approach. The audio-visual world demands our attention all the time leaving little time for cognitive thinking that requires us to switch off from outside intervention. No one really knows that the effect of this will be in the long run.

Intellectual discipline and rigidity (boring but imperative) exercised not only by scientist, but also other societal groups not the least politicians have been relaxed, markedly so. The stringency of thought, the quest for logic reasoning leading to a conclusion, and the tacit agreement to have supporting evidence ready are not any longer present in the daily mass communication. Gradually, we tend to be autodidacts accepting what we read and find on the net without scrutiny, critique and without looking for alternative views. Scientific evidence can be brushed away with "I think otherwise" without any evidence to tell why. There are certain things in life that are objective and cannot be contested — or there used to be. The world has become fluid — anything, everything is respectable and acceptable. This is maybe one of the biggest swing mankind has performed over centuries undermining all the benefits brought to us by the Age of Reasoning.

Thirdly, the segmentation of social sciences in various schools or disciplines has timed out. They are called social sciences exactly because they look at human behaviour and it is indeed strange to see what they have managed to do in isolating one discipline from others. The economists — I am myself Master in Science of Economics — has led the way into this still narrower blind alley forgetting and excluding what other social sciences can tell about human behaviour. The strange thing is that every time the world runs into a financial crisis or economic recession/depression, everybody seems to be taken by surprise, even if the omens were perfectly readable but dismissed, by overlooking human behaviour, preferring complicated and in many ways farfetched economic models.

What we will see in coming years or decades is much more interdisciplinary and intersectoral work collecting and assembling knowledge from various disciplines to form a holistic picture for the behaviour of the individual and the group.

It goes without saying that reconciling the need for deeper thinking and interdisciplinary and intersectoral approach at the same time is indeed an awesome task.

A lot more thinking about how human beings react and what shapes human behaviour alone or with other human beings are called for.